To. Bob.
Merry Christmas
1993
Love Marg. x x x

To. Bob.
Merry Christmas
1993
Love Marg. x x x

PART ONE

Hurricane at War

PART TWO

Messerschmitt Bf 109 AT WAR

PART ONE

Hurricane at War

CHAZ BOWYER

*To the permanent memory of Flight
Lieutenant Geoffrey 'Sammy' Allard*, DFC, DFM
*— and all other 'Trenchard Brats' who gave
their lives defending their birthright.*

© Chaz Bowyer 1974 & © Armand van Ishoven, 1977

This edition combines two books first
published in 1974 and 1977 by Ian Allan
Ltd under the titles "Hurricane at War" and
"Messerschmitt Bf 109 At War"

ISBN 1 85648 148 4

This edition published 1993 by The Promotional Reprint
Company Limited for Bookmart Limited, Desford Road, Enderby,
Leicester, UK, and exclusively for Coles in Canada.

Printed and bound in China

Contents

Foreword
BY GROUP CAPTAIN T. P. GLEAVE, CBE

Some writers with good reason have drawn an analogy between Sopwith's Camel of World War I and Sydney Camm's Hawker Hurricane of World War II. Each of these fighters was the mainstay of the Royal Air Force in its day, and both achieved great success and gained the affection of those who flew them. And incidentally each had a more glamorous sister to vie with it for the favours of 'suitors' writing subsequent aviation history—the dainty S.E.5a vis-à-vis the snub-nosed pugnacious Camel, and Mitchell's graceful Supermarine Spitfire vis-à-vis the rugged broad-shouldered Hurricane. There that particular analogy ends, because nothing the Camel and S.E.5a achieved in World War I can equal the lethal partnership formed by the Hurricane and Spitfire in the Battle of Britain in World War II when fighting in unison they did so with such devastating effect, and with such a decisive result.

After the Battle of Britain these two famous fighters more or less parted company each going its own way and choosing different paths. As the war progressed the performance of the Spitfire rose as each Mark was succeeded by another, with extensive redesign in the later stages, and in the roles it filled of fighter, fighter-bomber and air reconnaissance it had several very worthy contenders for equal merit in the enemy as well as in the Allied air forces. On the other hand the Hurricane, retaining its basic design to the end, fulfilled an ever-increasing number and variety of roles in virtually every conceivable department of air warfare and in almost every theatre of war, and some writers claim that in this versatility it proved itself unique, that it has no analogy, and no contender for equal merit. I believe this to be true. Perhaps when you have read Chaz

Bowyer's fascinating pictorial account of the *Hurricane at War*, interlaced as it is with the experiences of some of those who flew this great fighter on widely differing tasks in many lands, you will think so, too. You will certainly agree that the Hurricane was true to its name—to the enemy's great discomfort it 'raised the dust' wherever and whenever it appeared!

7

Introduction

The Hawker Hurricane, on its initial introduction to the Royal Air Force, gained instant fame as the first-ever fighter in RAF operational use to exceed 300mph in level flight; and will always be remembered for its major part in the defeat of the Nazi Luftwaffe over England in 1940, during the desperate struggle now known as the Battle of Britain. If these achievements were not sufficient to seal its superb reputation, the post-1940 world-wide service of the Hurricane would be ample to justify the inclusion of its name in any short list of the world's greatest fighter aircraft.

The background to the Hurricane's origin almost epitomises the pre-1939 ultra conservative attitude taken by officialdom to the air defence of Britain. It also exemplifies the foresight and determination of individual British manufacturers to produce the aircraft considered essential to that defence, despite lack of initial official backing or encouragement. In August 1933 Sydney Camm, Hawker's chief designer, had completed a four-gun biplane fighter to the official specification F 7/30, but (like many contemporary manufacturers) was personally convinced that the ultimate in biplane design was almost reached. Accordingly, privately, he commenced design of a fighter in monoplane configuration in October of that same year. On December 5th, 1933, a three-view drawing was completed and discussed in detail with Captain Liptrot, then in charge of the Air Ministry Performance Section. In the following month the design was altered to incorporate a new engine, the Rolls-Royce PV12—later immortalised by the name Merlin—and in March 1934 stressing calculations of the new monoplane were begun. In May drawings were started in the Hawker Drawing Office, whilst in June a one-tenth scale model of the proposed fighter was built especially for test-ing in the National Physics Laboratory's compressed air tunnel. Finally, on September 4th, 1934, the design was submitted to the Air Ministry. Though still awaiting official reaction, Hawkers went ahead with progressing the aircraft, and first drawings were issued to their experimental shop on October 17th, 1934. A conference, which included Air Ministry representatives, was held on the wooden mock-up at Kingston on January 10th, 1935, and on February 21st, Hawkers received an Air Ministry contract for the construction of one 'high speed monoplane', serial number K5083, to be built to the design submitted in the previous September, and to meet the requirements of Air Ministry Specification F.36/34. On November 6th, 1935, with Hawkers' chief test pilot, George Bulman, at the controls, K5083, the first prototype, made its first brief flight from Brooklands aerodrome. Further flight testing was carried out in February 1936 at RAF Martlesham Heath, and on June 3rd the Air Ministry finally placed a contract with Hawkers for 600 of the new fighters. On June 27th the Ministry also sanctioned officially the name *Hurricane* for the new monoplane. The first production Hurricane, L1547, made its first flight on October 12th, 1937, and within 15 months of that occasion 111 Squadron RAF began receiving its initial equipment of Hurricanes—the first RAF unit to do so. By September 3rd, 1939, the RAF had a total of 18 squadrons equipped with Hurricanes—exactly twice as many as Spitfire units.

It was the Hurricane which bore the brunt of the first eight months of war in France and, indeed, the few Hurricane squadrons there gave the all-conquering Luftwaffe its first bitter taste of RAF opposition. Following the collapse of France came the Battle of Britain—a period now generally recognised as encompassing operations throughout July to October 1940—and during which a total of 1,715 Hurricanes were flown in combat, more than the total of *all* other RAF fighters involved in the conflict. These claimed almost 80 per cent of RAF victories during that fateful summer and autumn. On July 1st the RAF had 29 Hurricane units and 19 Spitfire squadrons; while the main three Fighter Command Groups, 10, 11 and 12, showed an order of battle on July 7th which included 22 Hurricane units and only 13 equipped with Spitfires. Two months later, at the peak of the battle, a total of 30 Hurricane units were complemented by 18 Spitfire and 10 'other fighters' squadrons. Such broad statistics illustrate readily the debt owed to the Hurricanes and their crews during that epic defence. In the following years, 1941–1945, Hurricanes continued to give splendid service in every possible theatre of operations throughout the world, and in virtually every role possible for a single-engined fighter. Abyssinia, Egypt, Libya, Greece, Crete, Malta, Aden, Tunisia, Palestine, Syria, Russia, Italy, Sicily, Iceland, North Atlantic, India, Burma, Java, Sumatra—all were proud battle honours for the ubiquitous Hurricane.

It should be apparent from the foregoing brief summary that no author could properly claim a single book as being in any way adequate to offer a fully complete historical survey of the Hurricane and its many, many facets and achievements. Certainly, that is not claimed for this book. Rather I have attempted, by a collection of verbatim, private accounts and specifically selected illustrations, to at least provide the authentic 'atmosphere' of Hurricane operations in various major and minor contexts. Although such a treatment has meant necessarily compressing some of the Hurricane's most important contributions to the war into merely one man's experience, collectively they are offered as a genuine tribute to an extraordinary fighter, and no less a recognition of the courage and prowess of the men who served with Hurricanes in war.

In seeking suitable illustrations for these narratives, I was helped enormously by the individual contributors themselves. Long-stored photo albums were unearthed and dusted off to provide me with many of the privately-taken photographs used in this book. A simple thank you to such generosity seems inadequate, but is offered sincerely to each. Of the other illustrations, I am indebted yet again to the unselfish and willing help of many close friends and acquaintances. Ann Tilbury of *Flight International* provided her normal, unstinting assistance, not to mention charm and occasional cups of tea. Ted Hine of the Imperial War Museum could hardly have been more helpful. Peter Robertson and the Photographic Archives staff of the Canadian Public Archives, Ottawa, provided not only excellent photos but superb co-operation to a stranger. Equally generous in so many ways with aid and expert advice were Chris Ashworth, Norman L. R. Franks, R. Elias, 'Jeff' Jefford, Alfred Price, Chris Shores, Les Southern, Geoff Thomas, Richard Leask Ward. To all of them I owe a sincere debt of thanks. I am also very much indebted to Mr. M. Ross for his permission to quote the logbook of his brother, the late Flight Lieutenant J. K. Ross, DFC; to Miss Kerry Hood of Victor Gollancz for permission to use an extract from the late Wing Commander Ian Gleed's book, *Arise To Conquer*; and by no means least am I indebted to Group Captain Tom Gleave for so generously volunteering to write the Foreword to this book.

Chaz Bowyer
Norwich, 1974

The prototype Hurricane, K5083, known originally as the 'F.36/34 Single-Seater Fighter - High Speed Monoplane', in pristine silver sheen, after testing trials at RAF Martlesham Heath, February 1936, with armament and radio installed, and large production-style radiator bath.

First of the Many

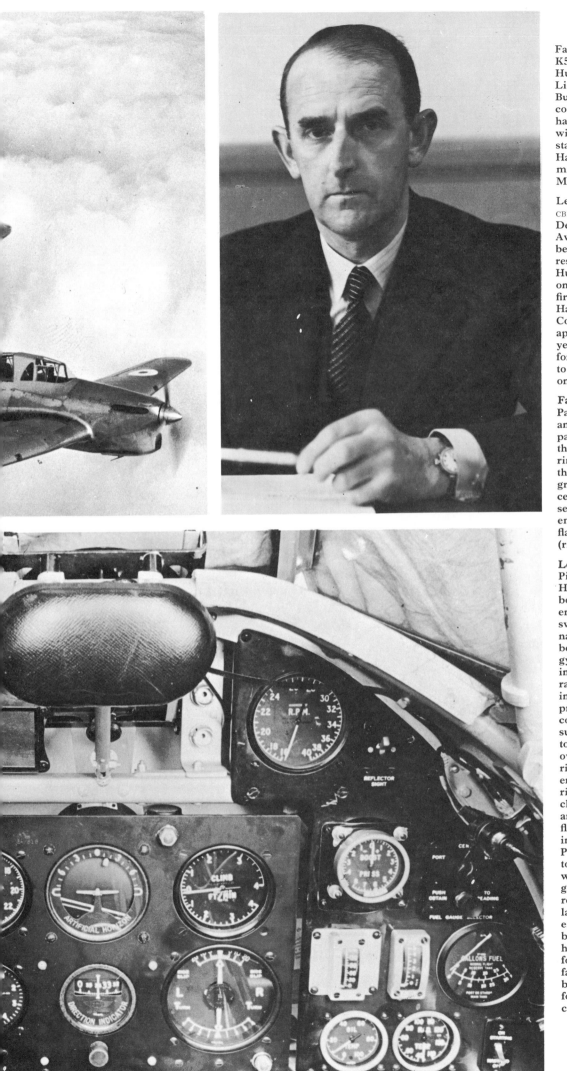

Far left: Two's company. K5083, the first-ever Hurricane, with Flight Lieutenant P. W. S. 'George' Bulman, MC, AFC at the controls (in casual trilby hat. . .), keeps company with another prototype and stable-mate, K5115, the first Hawker Henley. The latter made its initial flight on March 24th, 1937.

Left: Sir Sydney Camm, CBE, FRAeS, Director of Design, Hawker Siddeley Aviation Limited (as he became)—the man responsible for design of the Hurricane. Born in Windsor on August 5th, 1893, Camm first joined the H. G. Hawker Engineering Company in 1923, was appointed chief designer two years later, knighted in 1953 for his outstanding services to British aviation, and died on March 12th, 1966.

Far left: The Office. Part-view of the cockpit of an early Hurricane I. Of particular interest here are the crash pad fixed to the ring gunsight, gun button in the control column spade grip, compass (below the centre instrument panel), seat raise/lower handle, and emergency hand pump for flaps and undercarriage (right).

Left: Dashboard. Pilot's panorama in a Hurricane I. Starting from bottom left, anti-clockwise: engine starter; ignition switches; three switches for navigation lights and gun bearings heating; altimeter; gyro compass; turn & bank indicator; oil temperature; radiator temperature; fuel indicator; oil and petrol pressure (to left, in white cover); above latter, super-charger pressure gauge; to right, petrol tanks change-over switches; top right, right, gunsight illumination; engine revs counter; top right of central panel, rate of climb indicator; centre top, artificial horizon (for 'blind flying'); centre left, airspeed indicator; above, (marked P & S) undercarriage dial; top left, undercarriage warning buzzer; below, two gauges for oxygen supply and relevant pressure; below latter, clock; to left of clock, emergency boost. Gunsight bracket (top centre) is empty here but the sorbo crash pad for protection of the pilot's face is evident. The large bracket at left of photo was for installation of the camera film indicator.

Below: Exploiting the design's superb manoeuvrability here is L1648, one of the first 600-aircraft batch to be contracted. In 1940 this particular machine served with 85 Squadron.

Right: Later production version, displaying to advantage the wide track undercarriage of the design. Other improvements evident here include ejector-type exhaust stubs, anti-spin fillet added under tail section, and bullet-proof front windscreen. The first Hurricane to be fitted with three-bladed propeller was L1562.

Below right: L1547, the first production Hurricane, which made its first flight on October 12th, 1937, seen here on Brooklands airfield. This machine was eventually lost on October 10th, 1940, when serving with 312 (Czech) Squadron at Speke. Its pilot, Sergeant O. Hanzlicek, baled out but was killed, and the Hurricane crashed into the River Mersey.

Dawn Tableau. An 87 Squadron Hurricane, PD-P, and its steel-helmeted crew provide a watchful scene at Debden during the August 1939 'practice war'—within a month the real thing had started.

Into Service
ROY DUTTON

To the pre-war RAF pilots who were first to change their biplane fighters for the immensely more powerful monoplane Hurricanes, the new 'bus' was a mixture of excitement and new-fangled innovations. Roy Dutton was one of the privileged few to gain experience in Hurricanes at that time, being a member of 111 Squadron, the first RAF unit to be equipped. It stood him in good stead during the years 1939 and 1940, when he amassed a total of 911 sorties, fighting through the campaign in France and the Battle of Britain and being credited with at least 19 air victories. He eventually retired as Air Commodore CBE, DSO, DFC.

The first Hurricane received by 111 Squadron arrived in January 1938 and, with a total of some 300 hours flying experience, my first flight in the Hurricane (L1553) was on January 18th and lasted 20 minutes, involving three circuits and landings. I recall that this was a markedly strange experience, the Hurricane being by comparison to the ladylike Gauntlet, a large, powerful, high performance, low-wing monoplane with retractable undercarriage and landing flaps. It may horrify the modern pilot, but for the first flight each pilot was under orders to accomplish three take-offs and landings without retracting the undercarriage, and to keep the cockpit canopy open fully. This was exciting rather than frightening, but in consequence the whole aeroplane shook like the proverbial leaf. The feel was heavy; the draught seemed in keeping with the type-name of the machine, and the noise, speed and sense of power exhilarating, as was the wide open view.

After Squadron Leader John Gillan, the commanding officer, Flying Officer Peter Powell, my Flight commander in A Flight, and Flight Lieutenant Hugh Kennedy, B Flight commander, I think I was about the next one to fly a Hurricane. My memory may play me false, I make no claim, and it is of no matter. But at this time I think we only had three Hurricanes delivered—L1550, L1552 and L1553. L1555, in which John Gillan later made the record, 'down-wind' flight from Edinburgh to Northolt, was yet to come (and to be named 'State Express 555' thereafter), and there

Hurricane 'pioneers'. 111 Squadron's Hurricanes lined up at Northolt just prior to the unit's visit to the Paris Fête de l'Air, which took place on July 9th, 1938. Aircraft identifiable (from front) are L1559, L1560, L1548 and L1552 (total 12 aircraft). In foreground 111's commander, Squadron Leader John Gillan, briefs his pilots. Identification of pilots includes: 1. Plt Off R. G. Dutton, A Flt; 2. Either Sgt W. L. Dymond, A Flt (later awarded DFM and killed in action, September 2nd, 1940), OR Sgt J. T. Craig (later awarded DFM, killed in action after Battle of Britain. 3. Plt Off B. A. Mortimer, B Flt; 4. Plt Off S. D. P. Connors (awarded DFC and killed in action August 18th, 1940); 5. Sqn Ldr J. W. Gillan (OC); 6. Plt Off D. C. Bruce, A Flt; 7. Sgt Gunn, A Flt; 8. Plt Off

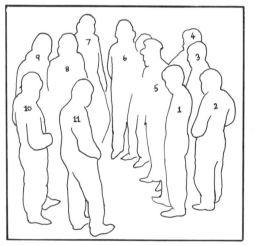

W. B. Skinner, B Flt & squadron adjutant; 9. Plt Off Heath, A Flt; 10. Fg Off R. P. R. Powell, A Flt Cdr; 11. Fg Off C. S. Darwood (killed in action, May 1940 at Seclin, France.)

was a queue for every pilot to launch himself—all circuits and bumps being critically observed. I recall that I had no difficulty in somehow making satisfactory arrivals and I was therefore let loose on the following two days which, from my log book, I see was the sum total of my Hurricane flying that month. On the latter two trips of 45 and 30 minutes respectively, we were allowed to retract the undercarriage and close the hood which improved the ride considerably, though I recall that, still not being acclimatised to the new beast, there was an impression of engine vibration and noise. The marked increase in speed in comparison with the Gauntlet also remains in my memory. On those initial trips we were, as I recall, forbidden to try any aerobatics. However, no doubt in keeping with our commanding officer's opinion of his brood being an undisciplined lot, not many of us abided by the injunction and I remember that my first loop

seemed to take up a lot of sky. (I see in my log book that I received the CO's written authority to carry out aerobatics on April 21st, 1938!)

111 Squadron, being the nucleus of the Air Fighting Development Establishment and the first to be equipped with the Hurricane, *ipso facto* proceeded to undertake the Service trials. In consequence, we, as a squadron, had the advantage of accruing some not inconsiderable experience on the type by the time war broke out. For myself, I had in September 1939 almost 400 Hurricane hours, 41 hours being at night. The Rolls-Royce Merlin in those early Hurricanes although reliable did have teething troubles, as did the aeroplanes, and a pretty close liaison with Ronnie Harker of Rolls-Royce, Hucknall and George Bulman and Phillip Lucas of Hawkers, Weybridge was maintained.

The first Mark had the two-bladed wooden propeller, fabric wings and re-

High-speed Hurri. L1555 of 111 Squadron being returned to its hangar at Northolt, 1938. It was in this machine that the squadron commander, John Gillan, flew his famous London–Edinburgh–London two-way flight on February 10th, 1938, achieving an average ground speed of 408.75mph—and, incidentally, acquiring for himself the nickname 'Down-wind' thereafter.

tractable tailwheel. At high speeds the wing gun bay panels sometimes partially blew out and the wing fabric distended like sausages between the ribs. On one occasion when in a near-vertical formation dive, I remember being violently rotated and had some difficulty in recovering—my port undercarriage leg had extended. I remember this well because the high air speed made it jam halfway down for good and that was that. Result—the first belly landing in a Hurricane, a bit of a bone-shaker because of the frozen ground at Northolt at the time and the alarming slide with the nose tipped right down due to the position of the ventral-mounted radiator. I remember as I slipped over Western Avenue on the airfield boundary, switching off the ignition in the hope that the propeller would stop horizontal. It didn't it stopped vertical and snapped like a carrot. Such pain as I suffered could, I reflected, have been entirely prevented had I been wearing a cricket 'box', for it

seemed that the entire force of deceleration impinged on the especially tender area of the male anatomy . . . !

With a total of all-but 750 hours on the Hurricane, I only suffered engine failure on three occasions and partial failure once. In April 1938, after taking off from Northolt, and having just tucked my wheels up and heading north toward Ruislip, there was a shattering silence. I doubt that I could have been but a couple of hundred feet up or so and frantically started to hand-pump some flap down before pitching hopefully into the limited bit of mead-owland below and to port. In the somewhat frenzied seconds available I entirely forgot to switch off the ignition, also to turn off the fuel. As things turned out this was fortunate for at about 50 feet up, and in the act of aiming to clear trees and cattle, the engine spluttered into uncertain life and I managed to nurse myself round to through about 200 degrees and flop over the north-west boundary of the airfield, wheels locked

Second RAF squadron to receive Hurricanes was No 3, seen here at Kenley aerodrome preparing for their part in the 1938 Empire Air Day display. Nearest three aircraft in front row are L1576, L1572 and L1569. All aircraft are fitted with the Watts two-blade fixed pitch propellers and kidney-type exhausts.

down. How I ever got the wheels locked down I never knew. I never had to pump so hard in my life. The engine then died for good and I could hardly believe that the undercarriage didn't fold up. I don't think we ever found out what caused the failure, but the odd engine cut, although not too common an occurrence, did happen and on taking up this particular machine (L1550) later in the day, it cut again but fortunately before I had lifted off and I managed to swing to port sufficient to obtain enough living space and pull up undamaged.

It was not until about early spring 1940 that improvements such as the three-bladed metal two-pitch propellers began to appear—at any rate, in 111 Squadron—and the limitations in performance of the early Marks showed up in odd ways. (The constant speed Rotol propellers did not appear until 1940.) Not surprisingly take-off time was poor by comparison and the effect of a muddy airfield—in this case, Wick, Caithness on March 21st 1940—caused me another engine failure incident. The big wooden propeller had scooped up the mud and effectively sealed the radiator honeycomb, thus causing overheating and partial seizure very shortly after crossing the coast. Thanks to a gale-force wind on

Above: In April 1938, 56 Squadron became the third unit to begin re-equipment with Hurricanes, based then at North Weald. One of its initial issue aircraft, L1609, is seen here on August 17th, 1939 being refuelled from a triple-hose bowser during that year's air exercises.

Left: Ready to go. Sergeant Brown, B Flight, 111 Squadron, about to climb into his Hurricane. An interesting view of the 1938–39 RAF fighter pilot's clothing.

21

the tail and a modicum of luck, a safe, dead-stick, wheels-down landing was accomplished.

Gauntlet flying ceased in mid-March 1938 and Hurricane trips, until then interspersed, were of short duration—most being of 30 minutes and very few more than an hour. Thus my first night flight in the Hurricane took place on March 15th after 26 hours on the type. I cannot recall whether it was moonlight or not, but the most noticeable thing was the considerable glare from the stub exhausts which seriously affected night vision, and 'blinkers' (anti-glare shields) fitted to the engine cowl were devised and became an early modification. Even with these, flying on dark nights in true blackout conditions and until cruise power could be used, reference to the newfangled Sperry blind flying panel was often necessary after leaving the flare path. It paid to make full use of the Link Trainer when it was introduced and become master of the situation. Fortuitously, I became the squadron blind flying instructor and did the full Link Trainer course at North Weald. Talking of night flying, in early December 1938, my Flight commander, the late Peter Powell, and I were ordered to Sutton Bridge during a moonless period to assess the effects of firing the eight .303 Brownings over the ranges there, and the sparsely populated countryside provided a true replica of the wartime blackout flying to come. I led off, with Peter a second or so behind, and the exhaust glare (as I expected) was such that I had to clamp on to instruments at once. Peter said that it was only my tail and purple formation-keeping lights that kept him safely orientated. The tracers from the guns and the

Luncheon Alfresco. Ground crew of a 79 Squadron Hurricane utilise the tailplane for a hurried snack between alerts in the air defence exercises of August 1939, at Biggin Hill. 79 had received its first Hurricanes in the previous November.

muzzle flash were no problem, only a fascinating experience. Maybe the 20mm cannon yet to come had the bigger punch, but the optimumly-ranged concentration of fire power was reassuring. Indeed, with the De Wilde mixture in the belts, the eight guns closely grouped in two batteries of four guns later proved their efficiency, especially in a dogfight, if not perhaps so lethal against, say a Junkers 88, which seemed to have a considerable capacity to absorb .303 rounds aimed from the rear.

Other than the basic exercises demanded by the flying training syllabus and that involved in developing tactics for attack against bomber targets (undertaken with such new types as the Wellington, Harrow, Hampden, Whitley and Battles), much demonstration air drill and formation aerobatics were undertaken and the few Hurricanes available were in demand at the Empire Air Day displays of 1938 and 1939. Special demonstrations were laid on at Northolt too, for example, VIP foreigners—including the Germans on one occasion! A highlight was the French Fête de l'Air at Villacoublay in July 1938 when, as official guests of the French Government and Air Force, a formation of nine Hurricanes provided a display at the cost of a splendid five days in Paris.

When the war came on September 3rd, 1939, we had already been on a sort of semi-alert since the Munich crisis in 1938, and the Hurricane was by that time fully operational. In 1938 however, if the situation in 111 Squadron was indicative of the situation in other squadrons in Fighter Command, we had a rather limited re-arming capability. The fewer Hurricanes in service in 1938 were, moreover, likely to have been a less potent operational force.

Bottom: By the outbreak of war in September 1939, the RAF was not the only air force to have Hurricanes. On September 3rd the Royal Canadian Air Force had a total of 270 aircraft on charge—19 of these were Hurricanes. The first six were in use by February 1939, and one of the earliest, serialled 313, is pictured here flying over Vancouver on April 3rd, 1939. It belonged to 1 Squadron, RCAF.

Wheels up. 32 Squadron takes off from Biggin Hill, early 1939. The unit's pre-1939 letter, KT, are much in evidence.

Blitzkrieg
ROLAND BEAMONT

Scramble. 87 Squadron's pilots demonstrate a 'panic' take-off, France, March 1940. Nearest Hurricane, 'D', is L1774. 87 had by this time been in France for six months, one of its members, Flight Lieutenant R. 'Bobby' Voase-Jeff, having destroyed the first Heinkel III to be brought down in France, on November, 2nd, 1939.

Royal inspection.
HM King George VI
visiting Lille-Seclin
aerodrome on December 6th,
1939. In foreground are
Hurricanes of 85 Squadron
(with white hexagon unit
markings on fins) and three
from 87 Squadron. Facing
these are two Gloster
Gladiators and a Bristol
Blenheim IV.

Being posted to France in October 1939, I could not claim to have an expert opinion on Hurricane operations at that time as I had come straight out from the 11 Group Fighter Pool at St Athan with the impressive total of 130 flying hours, of which 15 were on Hurricanes. But after six months and the 10 days from May 10th, 1940, I could claim to be almost a veteran. 87 Squadron was based on Lille Vendeville aerodrome which consisted of an almost circular field of mud, one large old hangar, a group of wooden huts and an extraordinary monument to Gallic ingenuity in the shape of a towering wrought-iron platform mounted about 20 feet above an enormous iron tank which together did duty as the station latrine. In hot weather this produced an aroma needing experience to be believed, and in the winds, rain, ice and snow—of which we had plenty—its successful use was an exercise in extreme fortitude and dexterity; as so frequently was Hurricane flying in France at that time. The wooden-hutted billets were far from draught-proof and kept little of the fearsome winter of 1939 outside, so that it was

often a relief to climb into the cockpits of our Hurricanes and shut the canopies to keep the wind off.

Flying during the early part of 1940 was restricted due to the tendency for all the airfields in northern France to become water-logged acres of black mud, and on one occasion we had to fly the whole squadron from Lille down to Le Touquet by taking off from the perimeter road as the airfield was in a totally impossible state. To a newcomer the Hurricane was an immensely powerful but not very demanding aeroplane. Its wide track undercarriage, stable and responsive flying characteristics and reliable engine and hydraulic system resulted in a general atmosphere of confidence in the squadron, so that the newcomer had no reason to become apprehensive. Getting lost over the flat, agricultural plain of northern France in the generally unpleasant prevailing weather was perhaps the only recurrent difficulty. But most of the flying consisted of formation practice and occasional patrols against reported enemy reconnaissance activity, and so one flew in sublime con-

Top left: Wing Commander Roland Prosper Beamont, DSO, OBE, DFC, **who flew with 87 Squadron throughout the battles of France and Britain, 1940.**

Centre: Internee. L1628 of 87 Squadron in which Squadron Leader W. E. Coope force-landed in neutral (then) Belgium on November 4th, 1939. He landed along a main road but was forced to swerve hard to starboard to avoid hitting a petrified civilian cyclist, thus ripping off his right wheel. This was the first of several Hurricanes to be 'interned' in Belgium prior to the German Blitzkrieg **onslaught of May 1940.**

Above: Seen here in France, early 1940, P2617 was first issued to the RAF in January 1940, saw service with No 1 (Canadian) Squadron later that year, and in August 1941 was reported on strength of 9 FTS.

fidence that one's formation leader knew precisely where he was. In the event I suspect that this was seldom the case, and we were very well lost on one occasion when operating from Senan, near Metz, over the Maginot Line in March 1940, and after two hours flying around apparently rather aimlessly we eventually landed at an airfield which turned out to be Metz itself. This airfield was situated at the base of a hill on which Metz stood with a towering steeple near the summit, and when, after my aircraft had been refuelled, I took off to return the short distance to base solo, my engine faltered and cut for a moment during the critical climb-out up the side of the hill over the roofs of Metz. For a brief moment it seemed inevitable that I would have to put down straight ahead amongst the houses, but while bracing for this unpleasant possibility the engine picked up again and the Hurricane climbed laboriously at virtually street level up the high street of Metz into the clear.

At about this time I had my first encounter with the enemy. This occurred one day in February 1940, when based at Le Touquet with 87 after our main airfield at Lille had become inoperable due to continuous rain and slush. We had found Le Touquet a hospitable spot and a champagne party was developing on the morning in question, more or less as a continuation of the previous night's activity, when the Readiness Section was scrambled. This consisted of the Australian Johnny Cock and myself (with about 170 hours total flying time) with fixed pitch Hurricane Is. As we strapped in hurriedly I noted with disapproval that the weather was far from convenient with solid low cloud and drizzle, and I hoped that our unreliable TR9 radios would be of use when wanted. In the event mine was not, but once committed over the cloud sheet in the Somme estuary area we were told to turn north-east and climb fast. Shortly afterwards we were surprised to see the unmistakable shape of a Heinkel III about 2,000 feet above and climbing hard.

He began to fire tracer at us at long range and we were just beginning to close in when the sky turned purple, vision became confused and I had time only to suspect oxygen starvation and push the nose down with controls centralised before virtually losing consciousness. Coming to just above the cloud sheet and feeling

H39, the only Rotol Hurricane to serve with the Belgian Air Force. The pilot here, Van den Hove D'Erstenrÿk (later killed in the Battle of Britain), wrecked the aircraft in March 1940 when force-landing with propeller trouble at Liege-Bierset.

Above right: Posing for the press. Pilots of 73 Squadron go through the motions of a briefing for the benefit of visiting journalists, late 1939. Third pilot from right is Flying Officer Edgar James 'Cobber' Kain, a New Zealander who became the RAF's first five-victory 'ace' of World War II, and was credited with at least 17 victories before his death in an accident on June 7th, 1940.

Right: Back from patrol. Hurricane landing at Vassincourt, France, 1939. Long identified as a machine of 1 Squadron (Fg Off P. P. Hanks), there is now evidence that in fact this was S-Sugar of 73 Squadron, piloted by Sergeant (later Wing Commander) P. V. Ayerst. The full-depth rudder stripes in red/white/blue were applied to avoid misidentification in the air by other 'friendly' aircraft—particularly French fighters.

decidedly out of contact with what was going on, I opened the canopy for fresh air, felt a jerk and eventually discovered that my oxygen hose was missing, having apparently been disconnected at the bayonet joint where I had failed to check it in the hurry to take off. Then, when calling for a homing over the unbroken cloud sheet, the aforesaid TR9 produced no recognisable assistance and left me to sort out the situation. I decided that a let-down over the sea was the only safe course and carried this out on a south-westerly heading, finally breaking cloud at very low level over a smooth grey sea, and made my way back north along the sand dunes of the French coast to Le Tourquet, where Johnny Cock was already back having thought that he had shot the Heinkel down, or at least seen it disappear diving steeply into the cloud cover.

When all-out war started on May 10th, 1940, the Hurricanes of the Air Component were soon heavily engaged and began to be reinforced from the UK, but they continued to sail into battle in the immaculate squadron formations of those days and sometimes got clobbered badly in the process. In my second combat, 87 Squadron in three Vics of three, intercepted a formation of Dorniers with Messerschmitt 110 escorts, near Maastricht, and the battle immediately broke up into a mêlée of individual combats. We had been sitting in the ditch by our Hurricanes which served as our Flight dispersal at Lille Marque, and sounds of gun fire and bombs had indicated activity in the direction of Lille, and very high and barely in sight in the afternoon glare was a small white parachute. This turned out to be a pilot of 85 Squadron from Seclin, but we did not see the end of his descent as the operations telephone suddenly shrilled and we were off to patrol Maastricht at 18,000 feet.

The field was too small for the whole squadron to be parked on one side and theoretically one Flight took off after the other, but in this event 12 Hurricanes thundered at each other from opposite ends of the field as they gathered speed

Above right: Neutrals. Belgian-built Hurricanes of the 2nd Escadrille in parade line on the ill-fated Schaffen-Diest airfield, just prior to Germany's lightning invasion of the Low Countries in the spring of 1940. On May 10th this was the sight which greeted Luftwaffe bombers and fighters when they approached from the direction of the woods in the far background. In a matter of minutes the Hurricanes were burning wrecks.

Above far right: Welcome back. Sergeant 'Sammy' Allard is greeted by fellow members of 85 Squadron at Seclin, May 1940, on return from a patrol in which he had destroyed at least two enemy aircraft. In less than two weeks of continuous fighting, Geoffrey Allard accounted for at least 10 German aircraft. He fought through the Battle of Britain, was commissioned, awarded two DFMS and a DFC, and was credited with 21 victories before his death on March 13th, 1941.

Below right: Stern attack. A Vic of 73 Squadron's Hurricanes demonstrating a line astern attack on a Fairey Battle. At this stage of the air war most RAF fighter units were still adhering to the inflexible pre-1939 combat tactics, but the stern test of actual air fighting soon proved such rigid manoeuvres to be useless—and, too often, fatal.

ponderously behind their huge fixed pitch propellers—a hump in the middle of the field ensuring that no one could judge if someone from the other Flight was on a collision course until both were converging on the hump at a combined speed of about 150mph. But there were no collisions and after a fleeting impression of other aircraft flashing by on either side we were clear and closing into formation in a long climbing turn towards the east. As we joined formation an indistinct radio message indicated activity in the Brussels area, and then directly ahead and a little above was a formation of big aircraft crossing from left to right. 87 continued at full power until I began to recognise the aircraft ahead as a squadron of Dornier 17 bombers.

There was no moment of hesitation. With the gunsight ON and gun button to FIRE, then ruddering the gunsight on to the nearest bomber in a 30 degrees deflection astern attack and opening fire with a long burst. I was still alongside Voase-Jeff's Hurricane and he told me later that I had opened fire 'miles out of range' as he wasn't in range himself and I was behind him! But all that mattered at that point was to get in at the enemy, and then the immediate sky became full of small twin-engined aeroplanes which I recognised as Me 110s. There was no time for tactics or formation drill and I broke into a hard port turn instinctively and saw a 110 go by close behind. A further maximum power turn to port brought me out of the immediate mêlée and then I saw a Hurricane diving away with a 110 close behind him streaming gunfire smoke. He was well out of range of my guns so I started to give chase, when ahead and crossing from right to left appeared a Dornier, its own nose down for home with twin trails of smoke from its full-throttle engines.

I was not able to close the range quickly and we were flying due east and down to 10,000 feet when I realised then I was not gaining much ground. At long range, with one ring vertical deflection, I fired a long burst from the eight Brownings and immediately saw the Dornier's port engine stop with smoke and a sharp yaw. Now I had him and a short burst from close range dead astern put him into a vertical dive into the low cloud at 2,000 feet. Being

almost certainly well into enemy territory by now and alone, and above a revealing white cloud sheet, I began to feel somewhat insecure and so dived through the cloud and turned on to a north-westerly heading over the rolling forests of the Ardennes. Presently the trees gave way to ploughed land and while looking for landmarks I was suddenly bracketed by shell bursts, whether friendly or otherwise I could not determine. This also seemed unhealthy so I dived to low level over the fields to provide a less sitting target and was then slightly shaken to experience tracer fire from behind. A hasty sideslip and quick look over the left shoulder and there, not 200 yards away, was another Dornier with this front gunner having a quite effective go at me.

A full throttle tight left turn at treetop height soon reversed the position and although this German flew his bomber with skill and tenacity in trying to out-manoeuvre my Hurricane, in less than two turns we were coming round on to his tail, then with engine boost over-ride pulled, banking into position for a broad deflection shot. With the Dornier in a perfect position for this at under 200 yards range, and with his top rear gunner now also opening fire, I pressed the gun button.

The price of neutrality. Schaffen-Diest airfield scene after the Luftwaffe's attack on May 10th, 1940. The shattered remains of this Hurricane illustrate a modification built in to most Belgian-built machines—the reinforced crash pylon of the cockpit framework. Due to the soggy grass airfields in use in Belgium at that period, landing and taxying accidents were not infrequent.

Three rounds went off—then silence. Now here was a predicament. I had out-manoeuvred this worthy bomber pilot whose aeroplane was almost as fast as mine at this ground level combat. He had three gun positions with an unknown amount of ammunition remaining, while I had eight guns and no ammunition, and the moment I broke the circle from behind his tail he could jump me again unless I could think up something. Closing in under his tail, and trying to keep between the fields of fire of his upper and lower guns, I used all the Hurricane's manoeuvrability and full over-boost power to roll away to the right from the lefthand circle, and then pushed the nose down to 50 feet above the fields on a northerly heading. Looking round I saw this determined German come round after me to level out some way behind and fire a few more bursts from steadily increasing range. Then as the Hurricane drew away, he pulled up, rocking his wings, before turn-

ing away to the east. I felt he'd scored a moral victory, but I was at least still around to have another go at his friends.

My third combat was a classic example of the weakness of inflexibility. We were now operating full-time from the grass field at Lille Marque and had been ordered off at three-squadron strength to patrol the ground battle area at Valenciennes at 10,000 feet. We made a fine sight as 36 Hurricanes formed up in the late afternoon sun in three squadron boxes, line-astern, four sections of Vic-threes to a squadron. I was flying No. 2 in the right-hand section of 87 Squadron, leading the Wing, and it made one feel quite brave looking back at so many friendly fighters. And then without fuss or drama about 10 Messerschmitt 109s appeared above the left rear flank of our formation out of some high cloud. The Wing leader turned in towards them as fast as a big formation could be wheeled, but the 109s abandoned close drill and, pulling

87 Squadron we had modified our tactics to an initial turn in towards the enemy when sighted, followed by flexible exploitation of the subsequent situation—in other words, every man for himself. We still flew in three Vics of three, but in extended battle formation with wing men weaving for cross reference, and at no time did we practise close No 2 cover, or the basic 'Finger-Four' formation flown by the Germans and adopted by the RAF tardily at the end of the battle. One of the most effective tactics used by our side was the head-on 'into the brown' manoeuvre. One had experience of this on August 15th, 1940 over Portland when, still with 87 Squadron and now flying out of Exeter, Squadron Leader Lovell Grieg led us straight into the starboard front of a dense mass of Junkers 87s, with Me 110s escorting, which the RDF had reported as '120-plus'. We were quite prepared to believe them and our somewhat unco-ordinated plunge right through the middle of this armada seemed to put them off their bomb aiming more than somewhat, in addition to destroying a number of them.

In the spring and summer of 1940, although without the elegance and high altitude performance of the Spitfire, the Hurricane was a machine of its time, and many of us would not have changed it for any other mount. We knew it as a rugged, stable, forgiving aeroplane which was tolerant of our clumsiness and the worst that the weather could do. It absorbed legendary amounts of enemy fire and kept flying. We could hit the target well with its eight guns and when in trouble we felt that we could outfly the enemy's best. The Hurricane and the Spitfire made a great team, but I never regretted my posting to a Hurricane squadron in that fateful time.

their turn tight, dived one after the other on to the tail sections of the Wing. Their guns streamed smoke and one by one four Hurricanes fell away. None of us fired a shot—some never even saw it happen—and the enemy disengaged, while we continued to give a massive impression of combat strength over the battle area with four less Hurricanes than when we started. We had had more than three times the strength of the enemy on this occasion and had been soundly beaten tactically by a much smaller unit, led with flexibility and resolution.

The Battle of France was soon over but the authorities were slow to react to facts and change the rules, and change came about the hard way by squadrons learning from experience and adapting themselves. Nevertheless, there were still some squadrons going into action in the beginning of the Battle of Britain in 'standard Fighter Command attacks', and many in the inflexible three-sections Vic formation. In

33

Battle of Britain

Getting ready. 111 Squadron refuelling at Wick, early 1940. Nearest Hurricane, L2001, was an A Flight aircraft, which was eventually lost when Sergeant Pascoe was killed in a take-off crash at Hatfield, June 19th, 1940. The triple-hose petrol bowser could feed three aircraft at the same time—a 'bonus' for quick turn-round between patrols throughout the Battle of Britain.

Tribute
TOM GLEAVE

Readiness. Pilots of 32 Squadron relaxing between sorties at Hawkinge forward airfield, July 31st, 1940. In background, Hurricane P3522, GZ-V, with a parachute harness ready for quick donning on its tailplane.

Tom Gleave, commander of 253 Squadron, took off from Biggin Hill on August 31st, 1940 at the head of seven Hurricanes to tackle an approaching bomber formation, and after plunging into a huge gaggle of Junkers 88 bombers and damaging two, was on the receiving end of a crippling burst of cannon fire. His Hurricane, P3115, erupted in flames and its starboard wing ripped off. Grievously burned, Gleave managed to take to his parachute and came to earth just east of his own airfield. His injuries led to him becoming one of the first plastic surgery patients of the legendary Archibald McIndoe—the 'Guinea Pigs'—and subsequently he returned to active service and eventually retired as a Group Captain.

At the time of the Battle of Britain the Hurricane was one of the finest fighters in the world. She was not the fastest, being some 30mph slower than the Spitfire and 33mph or so slower than the Messer-

schmitt Bf 109E-3. And above 20,000 feet her performance fell away rapidly. But below that height she was incredibly manoeuvrable, much more than the Spitfire and outstandingly against the Me 109. By contemporary standards, visibility from her cockpit was excellent, and she provided a superb gun platform. Immensely strong, she could absorb enormous punishment. I once saw a Hurricane being literally chewed up by the guns and cannons of an Me 109 from the cockpit aft, yet when I landed back at base that same Hurricane was already down safely and parked on the tarmac, looking like a half-devoured herring! The Hurricane was also easy to maintain, her serviceability being little short of remarkable. Equally important, she was comparatively easy to repair because of her simple construction as opposed to that of the Spitfire and Me 109 which, with their stressed skins, were in some ways 'delicate', to say the least. The Hurricane had a wide, generous and robust

undercarriage capable of withstanding very rough treatment—a boon in operational service, training units and at night. On the other hand the Spitfire and Me 109 had delicate undercarriages for which a heavy price in each case was paid in training, and even in squadron service, and it appears that on this account neither aircraft instilled much confidence in inexperienced pilots at night, apart from the other hazards of night flying.

To fly the Hurricane was sheer pleasure. She had no vices, other than the stall, from which even her feathered friends were not immune. She answered every call made on her with a will, sharing with the Spitfire the joy of having the impeccably-mannered Rolls-Royce Merlin to attend to her every whim. She took off without any marked swinging tantrum from which other, less well-bred types suffered. She was unbelievably stable, and in cloud or at night, when rudder and elevator tabs were properly adjusted, she would settle down into a 'rut' of her own making whether going up or down. And at no time was this virtue more precious than when taking off on a pitch-dark night and climbing into a coal-black void. Nor above all when coming in to land in bad weather or at night. Then, with flaps and under-carriage down, tabs adjusted, and at half-throttle, she would float down serenely until the airfield, or at night, the faint glow of the Glim lights or goose-neck flares

came into view. A gentle levelling out would cause her to sink until the vibration of her rumbling wheels told the pilot to close the throttle.

In a dogfight the Hurricane could almost turn on her tail as her guns spat tracer, lead and incendiary at anything that dared try to join the circle. In pursuit she could cut the corners, and only when the superior climb or dive of the Me 109 took it out of danger had she to look for other 'game'. When making her own getaway, she took without complaint the quickest of flick-rolls and U-turns, and 'standing on the rudder bar' held no terrors for her or her pilot. Though she played a great part in fighter-versus-fighter events, she perhaps found her most profitable role in the Battle of Britain in attacking enemy bomber formations and their close escorts —close-knit mêlées ensuing in which her magnificent manoeuvrability and control paid handsome dividends. Meanwhile the Spitfires held at bay and fought the massive enemy fighter top covers above. In this way, with the graceful Spitfire holding the ring and the Hurricane, like the Amazon she was, clobbering everything that wore a swastika within it, those two great fighters were complementary to each other. It was a lethal partnership that has never been excelled and, perhaps, never will be. In it the wonderful Hurricane was at least an equal partner. A true 'fighting lady', if ever there was one.

Below left: Before the storm. B Flight pilots of 17 Squadron, Debden, July 1940. From left: Fg Off H. A.C. Bird-Wilson, Plt Off Leeming (killed in action, August 25th, 1940), Sgt D. A. Sewell, Sqn Ldr C. W. Williams (OC), killed in action, August 25th, 1940, Plt Off D. H. Wissler (killed in action, November 11th, 1940) and Plt Off J. K. Ross (killed in action after Battle of Britain).

Readiness. Squadron Leader E. A. McNab, commander of No 1 Canadian Squadron, seated in his Hurricane at Northolt on September 12th, 1940.

First Flight
GRAHAM LEGGETT

September 5th, 1940. E Flight dispersal, 5 OTU, Aston Down. With mounting excitement I walk out to the Hurricane and settle into the familiar cockpit. Familiar because although I am about to fly a Hurricane for the first time, as a student at Hawker Aircraft I helped assemble the first production machines. Ever since Cyril Wells and Ben Hogbin positioned the jigs and skilfully built the basic airframe, the Hurricane had been 'my' aeroplane. At Brooklands the pro-

totype was piling up the hours and, in no time it seemed, the first squadron, 111, was formed at Northolt. Knowing the nuts and bolts was to help me save a machine later, but for the moment I 'flew' deadly combat within the Erection Shop walls. Bill Clarke once prised me from the cockpit, muttering 'Hop out now and let Mr Sopwith (T.O.M.) have a go.' But now it is for real. 173 hours in Tiger Moths and Miles Masters are to be put to the test in a powerful machine of which no trainer version exists.

Cockpit check—thumbs up—switches on—press the starter button. A few turns of the two-bladed airscrew, blue-grey smoke puffs from the exhausts and the Merlin roars into life. Jinking to improve forward vision on differential brakes proves tricky and I suspect the pilot of an approaching Blenheim expressed an opinion

Scramble. 56 Squadron gets away from North Weald aerodrome.

before I gave him a spot on which to land. At take-off power the Hurricane needs a fair bit of right rudder, then, almost unexpectedly, she leaps eagerly off the grass and flies. Unconsciously moving the stick when reaching for the undercarriage lever, I immediately have to pick up the nose and port wing—God! these controls are sensitive! But what a beautiful aeroplane—instant obedience to the controls, superb view, and what power. So much in fact that one's leg aches holding her in a prolonged climb. Levelling out at 10,000 feet, I check position and fuel and apply aileron. Easing back the stick the nose follows the horizon effortlessly—in fact, she almost flies herself and the rudder seems superfluous. More bank, now rudder to steady the nose, back with the stick, and she's tearing round vertically in the opposite direction. For the next 15 minutes

I have the time of my life. Diving and climbing turns, rolling, stalling—the Hurricane flies like the thoroughbred bird she truly is. There's much to learn, but already I know the Hurricane's secret—superb manoeuvrability, the quality above all others that is to make her a legend.

Now it's time to try a landing, without the help of an instructor. R/T reception on the novel TR9 is poor, though I'm later to be astonished by the efficiency of VHF. Once in the circuit things happen rather quickly, but the Hurricane's lack of vices and ready response at low speed brought her cleanly to touch-down and she sat down quite daintily. A couple more circuits and I'm taxying in, feeling pretty pleased with myself, and more than pleased with this wonderful aeroplane that has become the focal point of my young being.

About to taxy. Hurricane P3522, GZ-V of 32 Squadron prepares to take off from Hawkinge, July 31st, 1940.

Widge
IAN GLEED

Ian 'Widge' Gleed, a pre-1939 pilot who flew Gloster Gauntlets with 46 Squadron, first saw action with 87 Squadron in France during the May 1940 German *Blitzkrieg* offensive. He remained with 87 for nearly two years of operational flying, rising to command of the squadron and gaining nearly 20 victories—all on Hurricanes. Promoted to Wing Commander, he subsequently commanded a fighter Wing in North Africa and was killed in action on April 16th, 1943, having received a DSO, DFC and two foreign gallantry awards for his prowess and inspired leadership. The following account, in his own words, describes intimately his thoughts and actions during just one massive combat of the Battle of Britain struggle, specifically August 25th, 1940.

I glance back at the 'drome. Twelve dots are climbing behind us. Lucky devils, 213 Squadron: they are after the bombers again. It's a glorious day. The sun beats down on us. The sea looks most inviting. Hope I don't have to bathe just yet. At last we are slowly catching B Flight up. I glance at the instrument panel. Everything looks normal; radiator temperature on the high side, nothing to worry about, as it's a hell of a hot day. It seems hard to realise that over the sea masses of Jerry aircraft are flying, aiming to drop their bombs on the peaceful-looking countryside that lies beneath. Up, up. My two wing men are crouching forward in their cockpits, their hoods open. I slide mine open: it's too damned stuffy with it shut. My mouth feels hellishly dry; there is a strong sinking feeling in my breast. Thank God a doctor isn't listening to my heart. It's absolutely banging away. Turn on the oxygen a bit more. We are now at 20,000. It is cooler now, so I slam the hood shut. It's a hell of a long way to fall. Once more the

sun shines from the sea, its reflection off the surface makes it nearly impossible to look in that direction. Yet that direction is where the Hun is coming from. At last, 22,000 feet. We all throttle back and close up. I climb to 26,000, level out. On the R/T rather faintly comes, 'bandits now south-west of Portland Bill.' We are in perfect position to intercept them.

Below us, like a model, lies Portland Harbour. A sunken ship standing in shallow waters, half submerged, looks like a microscopic model. Back with the hood. I strain my eyes peering at the blue sky. Nothing yet. Far below us another squadron is weaving; just below me B Flight is weaving violently. Dickie and 'Dinkie' criss-cross behind my tail. I peer forward, heading out to sea.

'Tally-ho.' 'Christ, there they are.' A weaving, darting mass of dots gradually drift toward us, looking like a cloud of midges on a summer evening. 'Hell! was I born to die today?' 'Line astern, line astern, go.'

Dickie and 'Dinkie' swing under my tail. The Jerries seem miles above us; lines of smaller dots show where the 109s are ready to pounce. Beneath them, about our height, circles of 110s turn, chasing each others' tails, moving as a mass slowly towards us. Far below, the bombers are in tight formation. Somehow they look like tin soldiers. 'Steady; don't attack too soon.' Johnny and B Flight have dived, heading for the bombers; they have swung into line astern and now swing into echelon. The 110s continue circling. They seem to make no attempt to dive. 'Here goes'. I dive at the nearest circle of 110s. 'Christ! look out.'

A glance behind shows 109s literally falling out of the sky, on top of us. Messerschmitts. I bank into a steep turn. Now we are in a defensive circle, the 109s overshoot us and climb steeply. Now's our chance. I straighten out and go for the closest 110. 'You silly b . . . . . .!' He turns away from me. I turn the firing button on to Fire; at exactly 250 yards I give him a quick burst. White puffs are flashing past the cockpit. Another burst. 'Got him!' A terrific burst of fire from his starboard engine, a black dot and a puff of white as the pilot's parachute opens. I bank into a steep left-hand turn and watch for a split second the burning 110 going vertically downwards. The parachustist is surrounded by 'planes, darting here and there. 'Thank God! got one of them. Now for another'. Below me another circle of nine 110s are firing at a solitary Hurricane which is turning inside them. I shove the nose down, sights on the last one, thumb the firing button. 'Oh, what a lovely deflection shot! Got him!' White smoke pours from one engine, more white vapour from his wings; his wings glint as he rolls on his back. Another burst. 'Hell, look out!' A large chunk of something flashes by my wings; as I glance behind I see tracer flash by my tail.

A 109 is just about on my tail; the stick comes back in my tummy, and everything goes away. Now an aileron turn downwards, down. 'That was a near one.' I miss a 110 by inches—down; at 400mph on the clock. The controls are solid. Nothing seems to be behind me. I wind gently on the trimming wheel, straighten out and start a steep climb. What seems miles above me the Jerries still whirl. I can't see any friendly 'planes at all. 'Hell! where am I?

About ten miles off the coast. Hurrah, they're going home.' I turn for the shore, weaving fiercely. Over to the west the bombers are haring back in twos and threes. Two Hurricanes appear to be chasing them. I can catch them easily. 'Here goes. There's one. Looks like an 88. That will do me nicely.' The escort fighters still seem a long way above me. I am gaining fast—about 400 yards now. 'Damn, the 'Hurricanes' have black crosses on them—109s; coming straight for me, head-on attack. Right, you bastards! I'll give you hell before you get me.' Sights on, I thumb the button. A stream of tracer tears over my head. 'Blast! missed him. Now come on number two.' He heads straight for me. I yank back on the stick, kick on rudder and turn down on to the 109. 'That shook you up, didn't it'. Sights on. Brmmmmmmmm, brrrrrrrrrr. mmmmmmmmm. A streak of black comes from his engine, a stream of tracers flashes past my nose. 'God, I must get out of this.' Another aileron turn. 'Down, down, down. Pull out now, or you'll be in the drink.' The coast is nearly out of sight. 'Oh God, don't let them get me.' I screw round in the cockpit. Nothing is in sight. I scream along just above the water. I glance at the rev counter. I'm so deaf that I'm not sure that the motor is going. It looks all right. I hurtle past many patches of oil. At last the cliffs loom up. I turn westwards. Several patches of fluorescence show where pilots are in the water. Motor-boats are chugging towards them. The sea is dead calm, glassy. 'I'm still alive.'

Scramble. A Vic of three Hurricanes from 312 (Czech) Squadron fly over V6935, Speke, 1940.

Battle over London

J. SAMPLE

On September 15th, 1940, the true climax of the Battle of Britain was reached. On that Sunday RAF Fighter Command achieved final and unequivocal superiority over the assaulting Luftwaffe formations over southern England. Appropriately, it is this date which annually commemorates the Battle throughout the British Commonwealth. The following first-hand account was by the late Squadron Leader J. Sample, DFC, on that date commander of 504 Squadron. The sergeant pilot mentioned, who landed by parachute in a Chelsea garden, was R. T. Holmes, whose victim crashed in the forecourt of Victoria rail station, London.

At lunchtime on Sunday, my squadron was somewhere south of the Thames estuary behind several other squadrons of Hurricanes and Spitfires. The German bombers were three or four miles away when we first spotted them. We were at 17,000 feet and they were at about 19,000 feet. Their fighter escort was scattered around. The bombers were coming in towards London from the south-east, and at first we could not tell how many there were. We opened our throttles and started to climb towards them, aiming for a point well ahead, where we expected to contact them at their own height. As we converged on them I saw there were about 20 of them, and it looked as though it were going to be a nice party, for the other squadrons of Hurricanes and Spitfires also turned to join in. By the time we reached a position near the bombers we were over London—central London I should say. We had gained a little height on them too, so when I gave the order to attack we were able to dive on them from their right.

Each of us selected his own target. Our first attack broke them up pretty nicely. The Dornier I attacked with a burst lasting several seconds began to turn left away from his friends. I gave him five seconds and he went away with white smoke streaming behind him. As I broke away and started to make a steep climbing turn I looked over the side. I recognised the river immediately below me through a hole in the clouds. I saw the bends in the river, and the bridges, and idly wondered where I was. I didn't recognise it immediately, and then I saw Kennington Oval. I saw the covered stands round the Oval, and I thought to myself; 'That is where they play cricket'. It's queer how, in the middle of a battle, one can see something on the ground and think of something entirely different from the immediate job in hand. I remember I had a flashing thought—a sort of mental picture—of a big man with a beard, but at that moment I did not think of the name of W. G. Grace. It was just a swift, passing thought as I climbed back to the fight.

I found myself very soon below another Dornier which had white smoke coming from it. It was being attacked by two Hurricanes and a Spitfire, and it was travelling north and turning slightly to the right. As I could not see anything else to attack at that moment, I went to join in. I climbed up above him and did a diving attack on him. Coming in to attack I noticed what appeared to be a red light shining in the rear gunner's cockpit, but when I got closer I realised I was looking right through the gunner's cockpit into the pilot's and observer's cockpit beyond. The

Top right: 'His starboard engine exploded'—a Heinkel III at the receiving end of an eight-gun burst of machine gun fire.

Centre right: 'He streamed smoke and fell straight down'—a Junkers 88 about to die.

Centre left: Vapour trails—a constant scene in the skies of England during the summer of 1940, recalling Stephen Spender's lines: ". . . and left the vivid air signed with their honour".

Far right: 'Tally-Ho'. A Heinkel III sits dead-centre of the gun ring.

Right: Climbing to battle. 85 Squadron's Hurricanes, led by Squadron Leader Peter Townsend, DFC, in tight formation above a cloud carpet in the late summer of 1940. Nearest aircraft is V6611.

red light was fire. I gave it a quick burst and as I passed him on the right I looked in through the big glass nose of the Dornier It was like a furnace inside. He began to go down, and we watched. In a few seconds the tail came off, and the bomber did a forward somersault and then went into a spin. After he had done two turns in his spin his wings broke off outboard of the engines, so that all that was left as the blazing aircraft fell was half a fuselage and the wing roots with the engines on the end of them. This dived straight down, just past the edge of a cloud, and then the cloud got in the way and I could see no more of him. The battle was over by then. I couldn't see anything else to shoot at, so I flew home. Our squadron's score was five certainties—including one by a sergeant pilot, who landed by parachute in a Chelsea garden.

An hour later we were in the air again, meeting more bombers and fighters coming in. We got three more—our squadron, I mean. I started to chase one Dornier which was flying through the tops of the clouds. Did you ever see that film *Hell's Angels*? You'll remember how the Zeppelin came so slowly out of the cloud. Well, this Dornier reminded me of that. I attacked him four times altogether. When he first appeared through the cloud—you know how clouds go up and down like foam on water—I fired at him from the left, swung over to the right, turned in towards another hollow in the cloud, where I expected him to reappear, and fired at him

again. After my fourth attack he dived down headlong into a clump of trees in front of a house, and I saw one or two cars parked in the gravel drive in front. I wondered whether there was anyone in the doorway watching the bomber crash. Then I climbed up again to look for some more trouble and found it in the shape of a Heinkel III which was being attacked by three Hurricanes and a couple of Spitfires. I had a few cracks at the thing before it made a perfect landing on an RAF aerodrome. The Heinkel's undercarriage collapsed and the pilot pulled up, after skidding 50 yards in a cloud of dust. I saw a tall man get out of the right-hand side of the aircraft, and when I turned back he was helping a small man across the aerodrome towards a hangar.

43

Combat Report-1
J. H. LACEY

James H. Lacey, 'Ginger' to all who knew him, was a sergeant pilot at the opening of the Battle of Britain, serving with 501 Squadron, AAF, with which unit he had already been 'blooded' in combat in France during the May 1940 *Blitzkrieg*. By the end of the Battle of Britain he had been credited with at least 16 victories in the air. On September 2nd Lacey was at the head of a section of Hurricanes patrolling over the Ashford Kent area just after 8am. He sighted some 50 Dornier 215 bombers, escorted by about another 50 Messerschmitt 109s. In his own words:

I was leading Yellow Section of A Flight, when No 501 Squadron attacked the Me 109s escorting about 30 Do 215s . . . three Me 109s had climbed above the Flight, and to prevent them diving on to the squadron from behind, I also climbed and attacked them. I was able to get in a good burst of about five seconds at a red-cowled 109, but the EA immediately turned, and I observed no damage. I followed it round in the turn, I was unable to bring my guns to bear, but after about 30 seconds of circling, the Me 109 pilot jumped out and did a delayed drop of about 5,000 feet, before opening his parachute. Most of the other Me 109s were engaged, so I dived out of the dog-fight and attacked No 5 in the last formation of Do 215s . . . Almost as soon as I opened fire, the Do 215 broke out of formation, and turned SE with smoke issuing from its starboard engine . . . I continued to fire until my ammunition was exhausted, when I broke away to the side, and then formated on it about quarter of a mile away, to the right, to observe results. The enemy aircraft lost height rapidly, until it reached 5,000 feet, which seemed to be its absolute ceiling on one engine, and then proceeded out to sea towards France, losing height very slowly . . . I then returned to base and landed.

Below: Return from combat. A 32 Squadron Hurricane lets down at Biggin Hill, August 15th, 1940; whilst two companions behind circle into finals.

Above: Ammunition exhausted, fuel low, a Hurricane of 17 Squadron piloted by Flight Lieutenant W. J. Harper, rolls towards its dispersal at Debden, July 1940, assisted by two of the faithful groundcrews.

Far left: Pilot Officer A. G. Lewis, DFC climbs out of his 85 Squadron Hurricane, VY-R, at Croydon, September 1940. A South African, Lewis fought in France with 504 and 85 Squadrons gaining nine victories. In September 1940 he joined 249 Squadron and added a further nine victories to his tally. He eventually commanded 261 Squadron in Iraq and Ceylon and ended the war with a credited score of 21 at least.

45

Group Captain (later Air Vice-Marshal) Stanley F. Vincent was commander of RAF Northolt during the high summer of 1940. A fighter pilot of repute during the 1914–18 air war, Vincent was 43 years old —possibly the oldest of the 'Few'—when, typically, he took off alone on September 15th seeking the Luftwaffe.

When at 19,000 feet near Biggin Hill I saw a large formation of enemy bombers, escorted by fighters, in the south-east, and when flying towards it saw a formation of 18 Do 215s approaching from the south, escorted by 20 Me 109s. The bombers were in Vics of three sections in line astern— fighters 2–3,000 feet above and in no apparent formation. There were no other British fighters in sight, so I made a head-on attack on the first section of bombers, opening at 600 yards and closing to 200 yards. I saw the De Wilde (incendiary) ammunition hit the EA. On breaking away I noticed that five of the bombers were continuing northwards together with apparently all the fighters, whilst 13 of the bombers had turned right round and were proceeding due south. I made further attacks on the retreating bombers, each attack from climbing beam, and I could see the De Wilde ammunition hitting in each attack. In one instance I could see De Wilde hit the main part of the fuselage and the wing group. One Dornier left the formation and lost height. With no ammunition left I could not finish it off. I last saw the bomber at 3,000 feet dropping slowly and still travelling south.

Far left: Re-arm, re-fuel, stand by. Pilots of 061 Squadron, AAF at Tangmere 1940 stretch their legs while waiting for the ground crews to replenish their aircraft. Pilot at left is Max Aitken. Note the flat-loader home-made trolley in front of Aitken, used for transporting ammunition.

Far left: Turn-round. The 'erks' (ground crews) clamber over the aircraft to prepare it for its next sortie. At the height of the battle turn-round time on some fighter squadrons reached an all-time 'low' of four minutes in practised hands.

Above: Pause for a few moment's relaxation. 601 Squadron pilots in the Readiness hut, Tangmere. Round the table, from left: Flight Lieutenant W. H. 'Willy' Rhodes-Moorhouse, DFC (killed in action, September 6th, 1940), Charles Lee Steer, Pilot Officer R. S. 'Dick' Demetriadi (killed in action, August 11th, 1940) and Flight Lieutenant Max Aitken (now Sir Max Aitken, Bart, DSO, DFC).

Left: War Trophy. 17 Squadron pilots displaying the fin of a Junkers 88, the destruction of which was shared between them, August 1940, From left: Sqn Ldr C. W. Williams, Plt Off J. K. Ross and Fg Off C. A. H. Bird-Wilson. The chalked figure '78' referred to the squadron's claimed total victories as at August 21st, 1940.

Hurricane VC

J.B. NICOLSON

Hurricane VC—Flt Lt James Brindley Nicolson of 249 Squadron who, for his first combat sortie on August 16th, was later awarded a Victoria Cross. In 1945, as Wing Commander, VC, DFC, Nicolson failed to return from a bombing sortie.

James Brindley Nicolson was unique as a fighter pilot in that he was the only man to gain the award of a Victoria Cross for fighter operations during the 1939–45 war. Originally joining the RAF in December 1936, he was trained as a pilot and joined 72 Squadron, with which unit he was still serving after the outbreak of war. In May 1940 he was posted to 249 Squadron, and on August 16th, 1940, was acting A Flight commander when he engaged in his first air combat. It was this combat which is described here, in his own words, and which led to the VC award. The severe burn injuries he received that day kept him away from operational flying for a year, and in October 1942, as a Wing Commander, he was posted to the Far East for a staff job at Alipore, Calcutta. On August 4th, 1943, Nicolson finally got his wish for active operations when he was appointed CO of 27 Squadron, flying Beaufighters and Mosquitos against the Japanese. His tour with 27 resulted in the award of a DFC. On May 2nd, 1945, Nicolson was a 'passenger' in a Liberator bomber of 355 Squadron raiding Japanese targets. The bomber crashed in the sea, with only two survivors—Nicolson was not one of these. The following account of his VC combat was published shortly after his award was announced. For propaganda purposes it omits the fact that Nicolson received a further injury during his parachute descent—a bullet in the buttock fired by an over-zealous Royal Artillery gunner . . .

That day was a glorious day. The sun was shining from a cloudless sky and there was hardly a breath of wind anywhere. Our squadron was going towards Southampton on patrol at 15,000 feet when I saw three Junkers 88 bombers about four miles away flying across our bows. I reported this to our squadron leader and he replied, 'Go after them with your section'. So I led my section of aircraft round towards the bombers. We chased hard after them, but when we were about a mile behind we saw the 88s fly straight into a squadron of Spitfires. I used to fly a Spitfire myself and I guessed it was curtains for the three Junkers. I was right and they were all shot down in quick time, with no pickings for us. I must confess I was very disappointed, for I had never fired at a German in my life and was longing to have a crack at them. So we swung round again and started to climb up to 18,000 feet over Southampton, to rejoin our squadron. I was still a long way from the squadron when suddenly, very close in rapid succession, I heard four big bangs. They were the loudest noises I had ever heard, and they had been made by four cannon shells from a Messer-

schmitt 110 hitting my machine.

The first shell tore through the hood over my cockpit and sent splinters into my left eye. One splinter, I discovered later, nearly severed my eyelid. I couldn't see through that eye for blood. The second cannon shell struck my spare petrol tank and set it on fire. The third shell crashed into the cockpit and tore off my right trouser leg. The fourth shell struck the back of my left shoe and made quite a mess of my left foot. But I didn't know anything about that, either, until later. Anyway, the effect of these four shells was to make me dive away to the right to avoid further shells. Then I started cursing myself for my carelessness. What a fool I had been, I thought, what a fool! I was just thinking of jumping out when suddenly a Messerschmitt 110 whizzed under me and got right in my gunsights. Fortunately, no damage had been done to my windscreens or sights and when I was chasing the Junkers I had switched everything on. So everything was set for a fight. I pressed the gun button, for the Messerschmitt was in nice range; I plugged him the first time and I could see my tracer

Section Leader. Flight Lieutenant Ian 'Widge' Gleed, DFC in Hurricane P2798, LK-A, *Figaro* leading a section of 87 Squadron's aircraft from Exeter to Bibury, September 1940. This Hurricane fought (with 87) through the battles of France and Britain, 1940, and Ian Gleed was almost its only pilot during that period, gaining nearly 20 victories in this machine.

Freedom Fighters. 310 Czech Squadron at Duxford, September 1st, 1940. The unit was formed initially on July 10th, 1940 and had its first combat on August 26th. The seated pilot in RAF uniform (centre) is an Englishman, Flight Lieutenant J. Jefferies, DFC, a Flight commander of the original unit. In background, Hurricane P3143, NN-D.

Right: Freedom fighters. No 303 Polish Squadron's aircraft at Northolt in September 1940. Each aircraft carried the Polish insignia 'Kosciuszko' just aft of the cockpit. 303 first formed on August 2nd, 1940; and a total of 154 Polish pilots fought in the Battle of Britain, 30 of these being killed in action.

Below right: Two Vics of well-worn Hurricanes of 245 Squadron from Aldergrove, Northern Ireland, late 1940. Nearest aircraft is P3762, DX-F.

bullets entering the German machine. He was going like mad, twisting and turning as he tried to get away from my fire. So I pushed the throttle wide open. Both of us must have been doing about 400mph as we went down together in a dive. First he turned left, then right, then left and right again. He did three turns to the right and finally a fourth turn to the left. I remember shouting out loud to him when I first saw him, 'I'll teach you some manners', and I shouted other things as well. I knew I was getting him nearly all the time I was firing.

By this time it was pretty hot inside my machine from the burst petrol tank. I couldn't see much flame, but I reckon it was there all right. I remember looking once at my left hand which was keeping the throttle open. It seemed to be in the fire itself and I could see the skin peeling off it. Yet I had little pain. Unconsciously too, I had drawn my feet up under my parachute on the seat, to escape the heat I suppose. Well, I gave the German all I had, and the last I saw of him was when he was going down, with his right wing lower than the left wing. I gave him a parting burst and as he had disappeared, started thinking about saving myself. I decided it was about time I left the aircraft and baled out, so I immediately jumped up from my seat. But first of all I hit my head against the framework of the hood, which was all that was left. I cursed myself for a fool, pulled the hood back (wasn't I relieved when it slid back beautifully and jumped up again. Once again I bounced back into my seat, for I had forgotten to undo the straps holding me in. One of them snapped and so I only had to undo one. Then I left the machine.

I suppose I was about 12–15,000 feet when I baled out. Immediately I started somersaulting downwards and after a few turns like that I found myself diving head

first for the ground. After a second or two of this, I decided to pull the rip-cord. The result was that I immediately straightened out and began to float down. Then an aircraft—a Messerschmitt I think—came tearing past me. I decided to pretend I was dead, and hung limply by the parachute straps. The Messerschmitt came back once, and I kept my eyes closed, but I didn't get the bullets I was half-expecting. I don't know if he fired at me; the main thing is that I wasn't hit.

While I was coming down like that, I had a good look at myself. I could see the bones of my left hand showing through the knuckles. Then for the first time I discovered I'd been wounded in the foot. Blood was oozing out of the lace holes of my left boot. My right hand was pretty badly burned too. So I hung down a bit longer and then decided to try my limbs, just to see if they would work—thank goodness, they did. I still had my oxygen mask over my face, but my hands were in too bad a state to take it off. I tried to, but I couldn't manage it. I found too that I had lost one trouser leg and the other was badly torn and my tunic was just like a lot of torn rags, so I wasn't looking very smart. Then, after a bit more of this dangling down business, I began to ache all over and my hands and leg began to hurt a lot.

When I got lower I saw I was in danger of coming down in the sea. I knew I didn't stand an earthly if I did, because I wouldn't have been able to swim a stroke with my hands like that. So I wriggled about a bit and managed to float inland. Then I saw a high tension cable below me and thought it would finish me if I hit that. So I wriggled a bit more and aimed at a nice open field. When I was about 100 feet from the ground I saw a cyclist and heard him ring his bell. I was surprised to hear the bicycle bell and realised that I had been coming down in absolute silence. I bellowed at the cyclist, but I don't suppose he heard me. Finally, I touched down in the field and fell over. Fortunately it was a still day. My parachute just floated down and stayed down without dragging me along, as they sometimes do. I had a piece of good news almost immediately. One of the people who came along and who had watched the combat, said they had seen the Messerschmitt 110 dive straight into the sea.

First Fights
GRAHAM LEGGETT

To go into battle is the most overwhelmingly exciting event any 19 year old can experience. To do so at the controls of a Hurricane has left indelible images upon the mind's eye of those who had that unique privilege. The heat of the Scramble, the chase across a field of balloons supporting a silvery Thames, the thrust above London's blanketing murk. The misty shapes of adjacent aircraft swirling through cloud and then, suddenly, the sheer beauty of a squadron of Hurricanes bursting through into the sunshine above. Through the earphones a controlling voice plotting 'bandits', AA puffs growing into a dark cloud against the blue. Higher yet, hoods

87 Squadron formation, September 1940. Pilots were Ian Gleed (aircraft 'A'), Ken Tait (E), Sgt F. Howell (Z) and Francois de Spirlet (T).

are snapped shut, radiator shutters adjusted, oxygen masks wheezing loudly. Faint wisps streaming from exhausts, thickening into white trails. Someone reports 'aircraft above' as loosely connected white trails pass overhead, curving as they work towards the sun. Stepped down in threes line astern, 12 Hurricanes swing round, gun buttons and sights are set, an urgent voice warns 'Snappers astern'. Tracer snaking past the cockpit, blunt yellow noses on slender bodies flashing past, iron crosses on straight, squared wings flitting so briefly through gunsights, blue bellies arcing into the void.

At this stage of the Battle of Britain (October), Luftwaffe tactics consisted of high-flying formations of Bf 109s attacking London with 550lb bombs. On October 25th, 46 Squadron was scrambled from breakfast in the Mess, only in time to see 20 of these fighter/bombers far above, heading home. But later in the day we met another 20 head-on, and at least had the pleasure of seeing them jettison their bombs as they turned tail and dived back to France. If only we had more height. Clearly the Hurricane was at its best around 15,000 feet, but without wishing to swap mounts, one had to envy the Spitfire's ability to tackle the 109s from higher altitude. Against massed bomber formations the Hurricane had proved herself a battle-winner; against current Luftwaffe tactics she would be more effective with extra power. Nevertheless Hurricane pilots gave as good as they got and, as was to happen repeatedly, the Germans, confidence ebbing, failed to press home their advantage.

As October 1940 drew to a close our squadron (46) was being jumped almost daily. On the 29th, in Hurricane V7610, I was scrambled to 15,000 feet over base (Stapleford Tawney). As 'Pip Squeak' aircraft, I provided our IFF radar blip and, therefore, missed some of the R/T transmissions. But I did hear our 'Arse-end Charlie' shout 'Snappers' and, even as we broke, saw one of our formation plunge away in flames. As I completed a 360 degrees vertical turn, a 109 came towards me from slightly below with a Hurricane reaching for its tail. The 109 pulled up in a steep climbing turn to port and I followed. Almost at once he was in my sights,

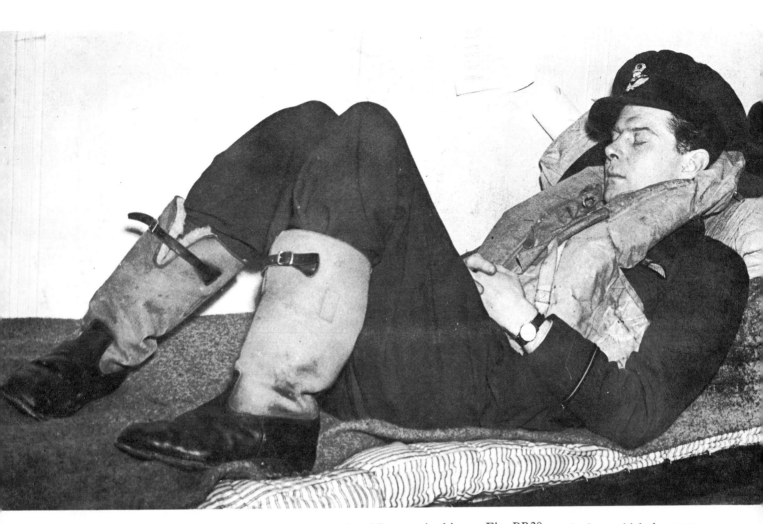

climbing steeply. Jabbing my thumb on the button I fired two long bursts from fully astern, breaking away sharply as another 109 attacked from above. It pulled up again and, with everyone else, disappeared. Just how the sky empties itself, when only moments before it had been full of aircraft, was very mysterious. Eventually I found another Hurricane and together we returned to base. At the subsequent postmortem I learned that 'my' 109's pilot had baled out just as I broke away.

Early in November 1940 we learned that Italian aircraft were operating in south-east England. November 11th was indeed a day to remember. In Hurricane V7604 I was in a formation of 12 patrolling a convoy off Harwich, below cloud. Soon we were vectored on to 40-plus bandits at 12,000 feet. Then, through a break in the cloud, we beheld a lovely sight! A dozen plump twin-engined bombers some 5,000 feet above. Already Hurricanes of 257 Squadron were tearing into them and as we clawed up underneath the bombers, jettisoned bombs plunged past our wing tips. Now the bombers were falling away as well and odd bits of wreckage fluttered down. One bomber dived away to star-

board and I recognised it as a Fiat BR20— the Regia Aeronautica had come to 'finish off' Britain! I turned in on a quarter attack and even as I pressed the gun button, a door flew open and the crew started diving out. The remaining Italians pressed on towards Orfordness—at last I had bombers to shoot at. After some clumsy attacks on various targets I singled out a BR20 on the extreme left for close attention. My first attack was good and he let his bombs go in the sea. Closing in again I fired a long, steady burst—and ran out of ammunition! My quarry was now diving inland and there was nothing else to do but escort him down. Over my shoulder I observed only two remaining bombers and what looked like a cloud of midges darting all over the sky. This turned out to be the fighter escort, some 40 Fiat CR42 biplanes, which had mislaid the bombers somewhere over the North Sea. Some of the Hurricanes had ammunition to knock down a few, and one hapless CR42 pilot lost his head to a Hurricane's airscrew. After a few minutes my BR20 nosed towards a large field and came to a standstill in a fir plantation.

A photo which, in a way, sums up the effort made by RAF fighter pilots during the desperate struggle in the air in 1940. Flying Officer W. P. Clyde of 601 Squadron AAF snatches a brief sleep between sorties. The high-key tension of constant fighting during the battle swiftly exhausted pilots, and sleep was taken anywhere, anytime it was possible.

53

Russian Episode
J. K. ROSS DIARY

Gloster-built Hurricane IIb, Z5252, piloted by a Russian General, prepares for take-off from Vaenga airstrip, near Murmansk. To assist performance, this machine was fitted with only eight machine guns.

Centre: Hurricanes of 134 Squadron preparing for a sortie over the fighting zone. In foreground, Z5236, GO-31, and behind, Z5159, GV-33. The sub-zero air temperatures, combined with inferior petrol (of Russian origin) combined to give much trouble with the Hurricanes' engines.

Below: Panoramic view of a Vaenga dispersal, with Hurricanes of 151 Wing heavily muffled against the searing cold, and equally well protected RAF personnel taking the opportunity for a sled tow.

It is not generally recognised just how massive was the aid, in terms of material and machines, given to the USSR by the Allies during 1941–45. This assistance was particularly evident in the context of the Hurricane. Altogether a total of nearly 3,000 Hurricanes were supplied to Russia —just under 20 per cent of all Hurricanes built. When Germany opened hostilities against Russia on June 22nd, 1941, the British Prime Minister, Winston Churchill, immediately pledged utmost support to the new ally, firstly in the form of large shipping convoys of vital war materials round the North Cape and into Russian ports at Murmansk, Arkhangel'sk and Petsamo. To protect these convoys, two new RAF squadrons, 81 and 134, were formed as 151 Wing RAF in August 1941. Equipped with Hurricane IIBs, these were shipped to Vaenga airfield, some 20 miles from Murmansk, and there provided operational example and instruction to the Red Air Force. One of the Flight commanders of 134 Squadron was the late J. K. Ross, a veteran of the Battle of Britain in which he had served with 17 Squadron, gained four certain victories and three probables, and was later awarded a DFC. His log book entries for the time he served in Russia, which were virtually a day-to-day diary account, are reproduced here verbatim—a unique document, and a tribute to a truly courageous man.

Formation of No. 151 Wing
On July 29th, one complete Flight of 17 Squadron detached and sent to Leconfield to form No 134 Squadron of 151 Wing. Flight consisted of—CO, S/Ldr A. G, Miller, Self, P/Os Cameron, Furneaux, Wollaston, Sheldon and Sgts Barnes. Clark, Campbell & Gould. Flight personnel were mostly from B Flight, 17

Squadron, with Turner as F/Sgt in charge. One complete Flight of 504(F) Sqdn under S/Ldr Rook formed the other squadron (No 81) to complete Wing under W/Cdr Isherwood. Wing to be equipped with Hurricane IIB aircraft. Main party of Wing left Leconfield to embark on August 13th, but the Carrier party (24 pilots) left for Glasgow on the 16th and joined HM Aircraft Carrier *Argus* on 18th. *Argus* left Glasgow on the morning of 19th and arrived at Scapa Flow the next day to pick up the escort.

Scapa Flow—Visited HMS *Prince of Wales* on Aug 22nd, and HMAC *Victorious* the next day. Remained at Scapa for a week or so before proceeding on our journey.

Journey from Scapa to Murmansk, USSR
Left Scapa on morning of Aug 30th and, escorted by cruiser *Shropshire* and three *Tribal* Class destroyers, set out for Iceland. Reached Iceland on 31st, but fog so thick that convoy did not attempt to refuel there, but pushed off towards Spitzbergen to rendezvous with HMAC *Victorious* and two cruisers and three destroyers.

Sept 1st
Thick fog and convoy proceeding at reduced speed.

Sept 2nd
As previous day; fog still thick. At midday position somewhere about 73N 8W.

Sept 3rd
Time for rendezvous with *Victorious* fixed at 20.00hrs. Fog still thick during morning but cleared towards evening. Received news that two Fulmars from *Victorious* had destroyed a Dornier 17 and also that the *Victorious* and convoy were being shadowed. Fog returned with evening and rendezvous not effected.

Hurricane IIb of 151 Wing housed in its 'shanty-type' wood hangar, Vaenga. Overhead a Russian SB3 bomber comes in to land.

Sept 4th

Weather clear up to about 10.00hrs, but patches of fog later in day. Joined with *Victorious*'s convoy early in the day. Several flaps when Fulmars or Martlets scrambled as convoy still being shadowed. Owing to shadowing, original course altered, and whole convoy (11 ships) headed NE towards Franz Josefland.

Sept 5th

Still proceeding NE and at 09.00 hrs reached position 78N 40.40 E, when we turned due E. At about 12.00hrs altered course to SE and headed towards Norgan Jembla (sic).

Sept 6th

Still heading S. towards Russian coast. Weather bad and sea very rough.

Sept 7th

Arrived at position 69.30N:33.10E and flew off *Argus* by Flights to proceed to Vayenga (sic) aerodrome. CO led first Flight but unfortunately F/Lt Berg and Sgt Campbell hit the ramp at end of flight deck, breaking two undercarriages. Both machines crash-landed on arrival. I led B Flight, 134, and arrived quite OK (0730, Hurricane Z3763).

RUSSIA

Sept 8th

No flying done as main party had not arrived from Archangel with necessary equipment. Started organising dispersal points and living accommodation. In evening were invited by the Russian General commanding local forces to a banquet to meet the 'brave Russian pilots' who had shot down '15 or more' of the 'enemy crafts' each. Evening quite successful, everyone toasting everyone else, but the whole Wing passed out completely after drinking vodka. I was so bad I completely missed the concert given in our honour.

Right: A Russian pilot tries his hand at running the engine of an 81 Squadron Hurricane at Vaenga.

Centre right: Hurricane talk. Squadron Leader A. G. Miller, OC 134 Squadron (in greatcoat, centre) chats with the noted Soviet fighter pilot, Captain Safanov (with 'chute) and other 'student' Russians. Behind Miller are two members of 134, who helped 'convert' the Russians on to Hurricanes, Pilot Officer Elkington (in fur jacket) and Flight Lieutenant J. K. Ross, DFC.

Right: 151 Wing personnel, mainly the non-flying officers. From left: Flt Lt Hubert Griffiths (Wing adjutant); Flt Lt V. A. Cottam (Senior interpreter); Flt Lt Murphy (Equipment); Flt Lt Willis (Cyphers); Flt Lt Gordon (Accounts); Sqn Ldr A. G. Miller (OC 134 Squadron); Plt Off Pratt (Cyphers); Wg Cdr H. N. G. Ramsbottom-Isherwood, DFC, AFC (151 Wing commander); Sqn Ldr A. H. Rook (OC 81 Squadron); Flt Lt Hodgson (Interpreter); Fg Off Goodman (Cyphers); Flt Lt Gittins (Engineering); Plt Off Nicholls (Cyphers); Flt Lt Fisher (Signals— kneeling). The pet 3½ months old reindeer was named 'Droochok' ('Little Friend'). Photo taken November 14th, 1941.

Sept 9th

Wing spent practically whole day in bed, thoroughly ill after previous night. Did not eat anything all day. No flying done.

Sept 10th

Still completing armament of aircraft and painting on letters. Dispersals getting fit to live in. Weather not very good.

Sept 11th

11.30. 134 Sqdn came to Readiness in morning. B Flight (Self, Cameron, Furneaux and Melann) led by a Russian Captain (Kuharenko) patrolled from Vayenga to the Finnish frontier and along the front. Considerable activity observed on front, mostly artillery fire. No enemy aircraft encountered. Russian pilot flying an I.20 aircraft. Self flying aircraft Y (Z3763) had engine cut three times over enemy territory due to inferior quality of Russian petrol (95 Octane) but managed to return OK.

Sept 12th

11.15. B Flight patrolled Zone 4 but saw nothing. 81 Sqdn fired at Me 110.

Sept 12th

14.00. Hurricane Z3763,Y. B Flight again patrolled Zone 4 and along front. No activity anywhere. Later in day 81 Sqdn again had luck and shot down two 109s

destroyed, two damaged.

Sept 14th

Z3763,Y. 14.00. One He 126 destroyed. B Flight dispersal becoming organised and more like home.

Sept 15th

Z3763,Y. 10.45. Squadron continuing front line patrols, but as yet no luck at all.

Sept 16th

No flying owing to weather. Vayenga definitely a dump.

Sept 17th

Z3763,Y. 11.55. Squadron beginning to escort Russian bombers on raids over the lines. This at least should reproduce results.

Sept 17th—23rd

Very little flying carried out owing to bad weather. Two heavy falls of snow on 22nd & 23rd. Visited Murmansk, but found it definitely a dump also.

Sept 24th

Z3763,Y. 11.55. Escorted four Russian bombers to bomb AA position, just west of the line. No E/A sighted. Only AA. B Flight only, self leading.

Sept 26th

Z3763,Y. 17.15. Captains Safanov and Kuharenko first solos. Self and Cameron patrolled round front line to try and sniff out a little trouble. No luck, not even AA.

Sept 27th

Z3763,Y. 07.20. B Flight patrolled front line during early morning looking for trouble. Found it by way of AA—very fierce and accurate. Flight patrolling at about 2,000ft scattered wildly but reformed soon after. Thought I was hit once as engine coughed and emitted black smoke. B Flight acted as high cover to A Flight, who escorted four Russian bombers to bomb front line. A Flight sighted 109, but we saw nothing. F/Lt Berg took off at approx. 15.00hrs on a scramble with two men on his tail. Aircraft spun in from 100 ft. Both men killed and Berg injured. In evening B Flight escorted five Russian bombers to bomb in Zone 1. No activity observed.

Sept 28th

Z3763,Y. 17.35. Escorted seven Russians to bomb in Zone 1. B Flight close escort, self leading. A Flight as top cover. Both Flights crossing over top of bombers. Bombing appeared quite good. Extensive AA but no EA activity.

Sept 29th

Z3763. 17.50. No activity from EA but very heavy AA during escort for three Russian bombers. One bomber shot down, crew baled out. Captains Safanov and Kuharenko local flying. Safanov made Hero of Soviet Union (Gold Star).

Oct 1st

No operational flying. Flew Russian Y-2 biplane for few minutes with Captain Kuharenko. Safanov and Kuharenko local flying and both getting to like Hurricane.

Oct 2nd

Z3763. 17.55. Went to investigate 'noise above cloud' but found nothing. Safanov and Kuharenko flew Hurricanes—aerobatics mostly. Safanov to instruct other Russian pilots.

Oct 3rd, 4th & 5th

Weather bad. No operational flying. Russians did not attempt to fly.

Oct 6th

Aerodrome attacked by 14 Ju 88s, escorted by 109s, while A Flight was practice flying. Cameron two damaged; Furneaux $\frac{1}{2}$ confirmed (with Rook); Barnes and Elkington one confirmed. F/Lt Rook one Me 109 confirmed. Several more damaged. B Flight aircraft took off during bombing. Aerodrome machine-gunned at same time. 134's score, $1\frac{1}{2}$ destroyed and three probables. Safanov taught Captains Palcoonikov and Pogarielli to fly Hurricanes. Pogarielli pranged aircraft and broke wing tip.

Oct 7th

Weather bad. No ops. Pogarielli local flying. Russians broke second Hurricane.

Oct 8th

Z3763. 11.40. Bomber escort. B Flight close cover to seven Russian bombers, A Flight high cover. Bombed aerodrome over Finnish frontier. Only one EA seen. Having landed only 15 minutes, ordered B Flight patrol Zones 2–4. Several Ju 88s about but none sighted—cloudy.

Oct 9th

Snowed hard all day, no flying.

Oct 10th & 11th

Snowed hard both days. Russians flew Hurricanes in between snow-storms.

Oct 12th

Z3763. 16.00. Weather cleared towards evening. B Flight patrolled Zone 1 to intercept four Me 110s reported to be attacking front line. No 110s seen. No AA.

Hurricane IIb, Z3768 of 134 Squadron, being overflown by a Vic of 151 Wing's other Hurricanes. The ground conditions, even in relatively 'warmer' conditions, were a severe test of the aircraft's ruggedness.

Oct 13*th*
Weather fairly good all day, but cloud fairly low. Squadron detailed to escort SBs to bomb Target No. 13 but this op cancelled owing to weather conditions. Several new Russian pilots went solo on Hurricane. B Flight, 134 Squadron still acting as OTU for Russians.

Oct 14*th*
Fog all day, no flying of any kind.

Oct 15*th*
Z3763. 16.35. B Flight did voluntary stand-by at 1530hrs owing to report of four Ju 88s having crossed line. At 1610 were told the flap was over—and immediately afterwards 88s bombed Murmansk. Took off immediately but of course we were too late. Definitely a case of bad control. Snowstorms.

Oct 16*th*
Z3763. 13.15. Bomber escort for seven Russians to bomb target at western end of Zone 1. A Flight close cover, and B Flight crossing over 2,000ft above (14,000 ft). Weather perfect over German lines.

Only one burst of AA. This is thought to have been a signal to enemy fighters of our presence. Fighters however did not appear. At about 1530hrs smoke trails seen near lines and shortly afterwards Ju 88s came over aerodrome and dropped seven bombs on same. Control of course knew nothing until bombs fell, so once again squadron took off amid falling bombs, but we were too late to catch 88s.

Oct 17*th*
Z3763. 0930. Squadron (self leading) detailed to escort three SB3 and four SB2s to bomb east of Petsamo. Flights flew in cross-over cover and raid successfully carried out. No AA or enemy fighters.
This was last day of operations for B Flight as Russians took over our aircraft next day to form No 1 Russian Hurricane Squadron, under Senior Lieutenant Yakovenko. Wing of three Russian Hurricane squadrons formed by October 19th, led by Captain Safanov, with Captain Kuharenko second in command. We sailed from Vayenga on November 28th.

61

Armament

Full Blast. The effect of eight Browning .303 machine guns spectacularly illustrated by this night shot.

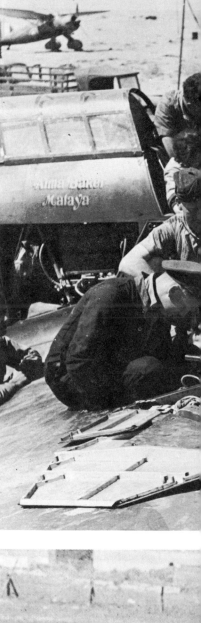

Right: Starboard wing gun installation of a Hurricane I, showing the four Browning .303 guns and their associated ammunition feed chutes.

Below: Ammunition was usually delivered from a Maintenance Unit already belted and in boxes, but armourers in front-line squadrons (when facilities existed) ran all belts through a Belt Positioning Machine (as here) to ensure positive alignment of each round with the rest of the belt, thus eliminating one possible cause of jamming in the guns.

Left: Armourers (nearest) and other ground tradesmen refurbishing Hurricane I, V7795, in the Western Desert, North Africa, 1942. This was one of two Hurricanes titled *Alma Baker Malaya*, being 'presented' (ie paid for) by C. Alma Baker OBE, a lady resident in Malaya. The Browning guns and their ammunition chutes can be plainly seen on the wing, prior to installation.

Centre: Armourers of an Auxiliary Air Force squadron (believed to be 601) lapping in the .303 ammunition belts. The tubes evident in the leading edge were blast tubes, inside which lay the gun barrels when installed.

Below: Desert doings. Conveying ammunition to Hurricane P3728 of 33 Squadron at Fuka satellite airfield, late 1940.

Above: Once serviced, harmonised and armed, the guns are tested for smooth operation in the station stop butt—in this case a rather elaborate brick edifice in the Middle East. The red flag hoisted above the butt indicated live firing in progress—just in case passers-by were deaf!

Centre: Stepped-up starboard echelon of 87 Squadron's Hurricane IIcs.

Above far right: Hurri-Bomber. BE417, AE-K of 402 Squadron (Canadian) at Warmwell, early 1942, being loaded with its complement of 250lb GP bombs. Note exhaust anti-glare panel and brick-red doped fabric patches over machine gun ports.

Below far right: Peel off. Hurricane IIcs of No 1 Squadron RAF 'flake off' for a ground strafe, circa September 1942, just prior to the unit's re-equipment with the Hurricane's successor and stable-mate, Hawker Typhoons.

Right: Heavier punch. A four 20mm cannon Hurricane IIc, BD867, QO-Y of 3 Squadron RAF displaying the barrels of its main armament. Note the cordite streaking under the wing.

Loaded for game. Hurricane IIb, with two 250lb GP bombs and 12 × .303 machine guns, ready for a low-level sweep over France, spring 1942.

Below: Muscle-power. Loading the port wing carrier of a 402 Squadron Hurricane IIb, 'Q', at Warmwell on February 9th, 1942. From left: LACs J. Holland and P. Laroche; Cpl L. Lott; LAC H. McGuiniss. The bomb is a 250lb GP (General Purpose), tail-fused.

Above: A late-series Mk IV, KZ706, fitted with the large 'Long Tom' RP rails for tests over Pendine Sands towards the end of the war. During initial trials with RP on Hurricanes, blast protection plates were fitted under the wings, but in the event were found to be superfluous.

Left: Rocket Battery. Hurricane IV, BP173, bearing eight three-inch rocket projectiles (each with a 60lb High Explosive head). Built originally as a IIb, this machine was modified by Hawkers to Mark IV specifically for RP trials and went to the A & AEE, Boscombe Down for such trials on July 29th, 1942.

Bottom left: Crutching down. Once hooked on to the carrier, the bomb was steadied by crutching down two pairs of pads above the bomb. Transit rings in the bomb noses here indicate tail fusing. The small housing inboard of the wing gun ports housed the G42 cine camera, wired electrically to the cockpit for either co-ordinated operation when guns were fired or triggered independently (camera only).

69

Hurri-bombers

J. W. BROOKS

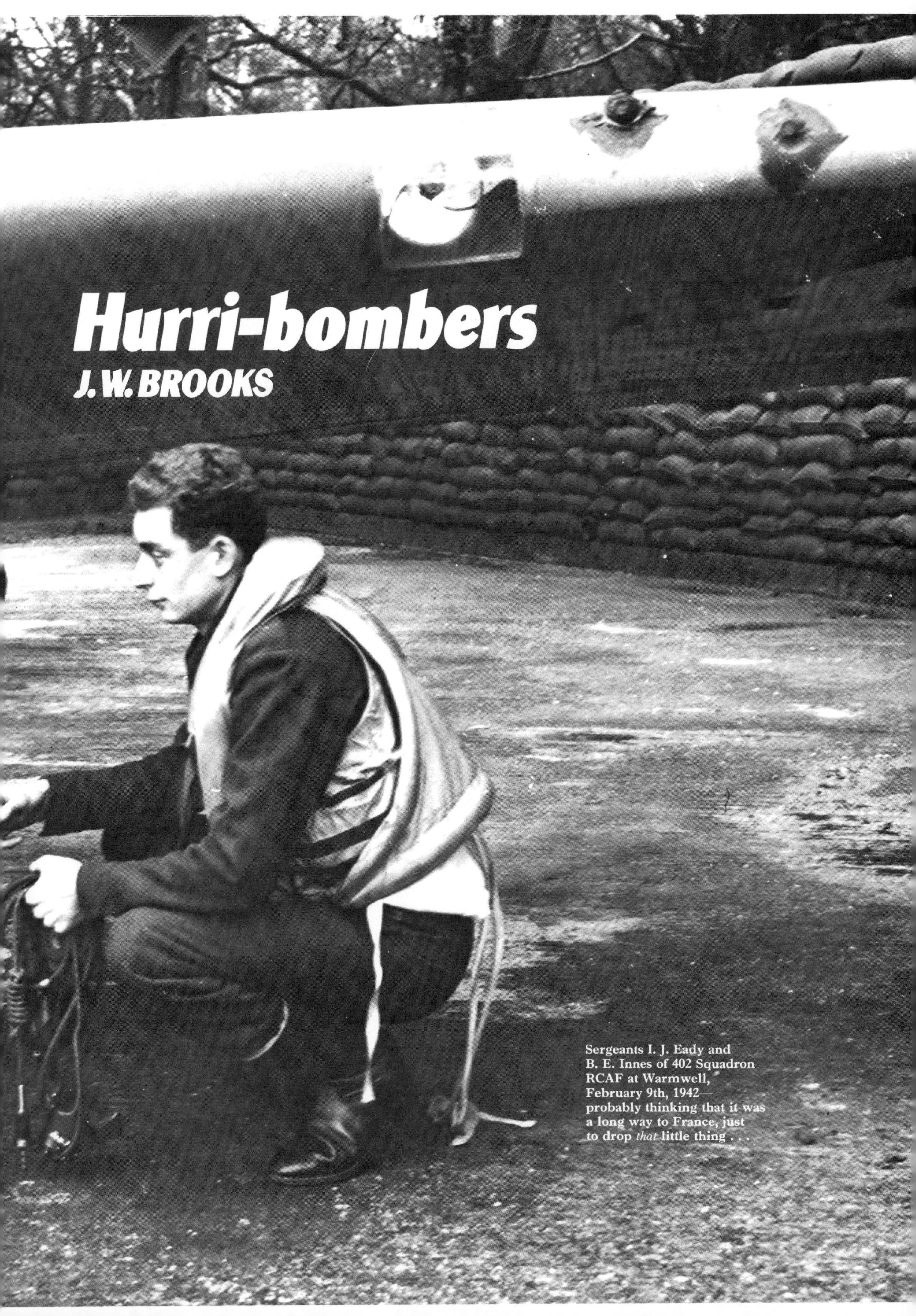

Sergeants I. J. Eady and
B. E. Innes of 402 Squadron
RCAF at Warmwell,
February 9th, 1942—
probably thinking that it was
a long way to France, just
to drop *that* little thing . . .

How does one describe the feelings of flying a Hurricane? Remain objective and understandable, yet avoid nostalgia on the one hand and pure technicalities on the other? To even attempt it for someone who has never been a pilot would be virtually impossible—rather like trying to explain colour to a person who was born blind. The Hurricane was the first real war plane I flew and therefore holds a place in my memories which no other aircraft has taken, not even the Spitfire. It was the aircraft in which I learned the 'art' of staying alive because it was practically viceless, besides being very kind to ham-fisted beginners like myself. It could take enormous punishment, not only from its pilot but also from the opposition—something the delicate, feminine Spitfire would never do. One Hurricane I saw had the tail plane and elevators almost completely destroyed in a collision with a Messerschmitt 109, yet it flew over 100 miles across the Channel back to base at Manston. The stick movement was somewhat restricted, but it got down OK. The odd bullet hole through the fabric of the rear fuselage or control surfaces was not considered to be of any consequence and was patched up with a small square of fabric and red dope. After any long spell of ops, some of our Hurricanes looked as though they had caught some spotty disease, although this was very quickly 'cured' with dabs of green and brown paint after the red dope had dried.

Our Hurricanes (and Spitfires, of course) were always coloured with drab browns, greys and greens—for camouflage it was said. Yet our German counterparts always seemed bright and gay in contrast, with yellows and reds on silvery backgrounds. One *Geschwader* based at St Omer, known (I think) as 'Hermann Goering's Own', had the noses of their 109s painted a bright yellow as far back as the cockpit, together with splendid insignia in equally bright colours along each side. There seemed to be no attempt at concealment and one could see them quite plainly a distance away, with the sun glinting on their silver wings. They looked for all the world like model aircraft. However, the Hurricane's drab colours were of some use, and on two occasions saved me from what could have been nasty situations. I liked my drab colours.

To actually fly the Hurricane was a delight. A pilot had to find out for himself, since there was no dual-controlled Hurricane built (until much later). You simply got in and flew it and very few pilots ever came to grief during the first flight, It was later, when one found how 'easy' it appeared, that over-confidence replaced prudence and accidents occurred. No aircraft will put up with silly abuse by its pilot, not even the Hurricane, yet I believe it was the most forgiving. Because it had a tail wheel, as against the usual nose wheel of today's aircraft, a pilot could not see straight ahead when the Hurricane was on the ground and he had to look at an angle each side past the large nose. This meant one had to swing from side to side during taxying to spot any obstructions, such as chocks and other equipment which always seemed to clutter up airfields. On take-off, to keep straight, a pilot had again to look at an angle (I always looked to the left side) until the tail came into flying position, when one could see straight ahead. The Spitfire, especially the late Marks, were even worse than the Hurricane in this respect. Being a propeller aircraft, due to torque there was a pronounced swing which had to be held with rudder. This, coupled with the fact that one could not see straight ahead, could make things a little difficult—especially in a crosswind. Nevertheless, the controls were effective down to very low speeds and, after a few hours' handling, one hardly noticed these things. The tail came up quite quickly as one opened the throttle and within no time at all one was airborne. Compared with modern aircraft the take-off run was minute. We flew from grass fields not much bigger than a couple of football pitches and in our ignorance thought little about it.

Once in the air with the wheels up, the Hurricane was a delight. You didn't so much fly it as 'wear' it. The lightest touch on the controls was all that was needed and even this was done quite unconsciously. You appeared to think the aircraft into a turn or out of it. At high speeds the controls did tend to stiffen up and this was common on all aircraft. Yet the Hurricane could still be manoeuvred quite adequately. It was better than the Spitfire in this respect and far superior to the Messerchmitt 109. On the other hand it was slower than both of those aircraft, although more manoeuvrable. It could literally 'turn on a sixpence'. This was probably the reason that the Hurricane was considered ideal for tackling bomber formations, while the faster, sleeker Spitfire took on the escorting fighters. Unfortunately this 'arrangement' did not always work out in practice and Hurricanes had their work cut out with the later Marks of 109s and even more so with Focke-Wulf 190s. For this reason the Hurricane was relegated to defensive or fighter-bomber roles. It was sent on offensive sweeps in 1941 but was usually employed as close escort to Blenheim and Boston light bombers. These operations (known to the RAF as 'Circus') were primarily adopted to bring up the German fighters for the loosely-scattered Spitfire squadrons to scrap with. The Hurricanes' job was to fend for the bombers if the 109s got through—which they invariably did. I don't think these sweeps did any damage to the German war effort—the bomb load carried was far too small—but what they did do was to boost the morale of the RAF and the British people.

It was on one of these sweeps that a real ding-dong scrap took place. We Hurricanes had 109s passing through our formation, between individual aircraft, going in the opposite direction. Their tactics were to scream down from high above and make head-on attacks. Then, after passing through, to pull up, turn round and make another attack from the rear. The Hurricane escort couldn't leave the bombers, so we were easy prey for this sort of tactic. On one occasion I was attacked from the rear in this fashion. The 109 pilot badly misjudged his speed and/or mine and overshot. He then did a rather foolish thing—he pulled up to see where I'd gone and presented himself right in front of me, about 100 yards away. I simply fired and he blew up—I was most astonished.

Somehow the very ruggedness of the Hurricane's design seemed to give the pilot a sense of security, albeit a false sense. It was only made of sheet aluminium, wood and fabric, and one's only protection was the engine in front and a sheet of armour plate behind the seat. This latter, unfortunately, was not much good against the heavy cannons that German fighters carried. The 30mm Mauser firing through the prop boss in the case of the 109 made a nice neat hole as clean as a whistle. The Merlin engine which powered both the Hurricane and the Spitfire had one serious defect, when compared with the Daimler-Benz engine of the 109. The Merlin fuel system was carburetter-controlled (the SU carb), whilst the DB had fuel injection. This enabled a German pilot to bunt ie push his stick forward if he was being chased, whereas the Merlin would cut out completely under those circumstances. We had to roll over on to our backs and pull back on the stick, which was time-consuming and one lost sight of the target. Later Marks of Spitfire were fitted with fuel injection, but the Hurricane never was. The Hurricane could only be glided upside down, whereas a 109 could actually fly that way.

In late 1941 the Hurricane became a fighter-bomber and its prime job was purely low-level attacks on Channel shipping and against static targets over France and the Low Countries. It was fitted with a faired bomb rack under each wing, carrying (normally) two 250lb bombs. During the Dieppe raid this was doubled to two 500lb bombs—which was also the effective bomb load of the Blenheim and Boston light bombers! It was about then that skip-bombing was 'discovered'—the Americans 'rediscovered' it about a year or so later, much to our amusement. At Manston (my base) one squadron had bombs and 10 machine guns (.303) and the sister squadron had just four 20mm Oerliken cannons for armament. During a shipping strike the cannons went in first to shut up the opposition and the 'bombers' used to be right in behind them. Those convoys of smallish ships used to hug the coast and were always escorted by flak ships. These were modified tugs simply bristling with guns of all sorts and could put up an awful lot of hot metal. During any attack it was necessary to fly straight at the target, just skimming the waves and releasing the bombs at the last minute. Then one had to fly straight through all the heavy flak, hoping for the best. It was now that the Hurricane was most vulnerable. Underneath the pilot was a large radiator which if it got as much as a single bullet in it usually meant 'curtains'! The engine either seized up solid or caught fire. This meant that a pilot had to get out. Unfortunately one was too low to bale out and if you did have the speed to pull up, you were a sitting duck. The casualties in such raids were very high.

Favourite targets during late 1941 and early 1942 were the German air bases in France. The Hurricane was ideal for such work since it could fly very low (a couple of feet) and be jinked at the same time to avoid the ground defences. On a personal note, when flying the Hurricane under combat conditions I used to screw up the throttle friction nut tightly and then use both hands on the control column spade grip. This allowed one to use all one's strength in manoeuvres—although thinking back, the poor Hurricane must have been terribly strained at times.

One other type of operation which 607 Squadron used to do from Manston in early 1941 was night intruder. This called for single Hurricanes to go out at night to various German airfields in France and the Low Countries and wait around for returning German bombers. The Luftwaffe bases were often lit up like Christmas trees, having an approach and landing system called (I believe) Lorenz visual. This comprised a line of white lights leading to the runway in use, with crossbars of other lights, usually coloured. The idea was that an approaching aircraft in bad visibility could line itself with the runway and descend as it crossed the coloured lights at a given height. There was also another squadron (No 1, RAF) at Manston with long-range Hurricanes painted black, whose sole task was night intrusion. Their most famous pilot was a Czech, Karel Kuttelwascher, who was reputed to have shot down many enemy aircraft over their own bases. The Hurricane was not easy to fly on instruments, particularly at night. It was preferable to have an horizon to go by and we always tried to operate when there was a moon on a nice clear night. We were all pretty 'green' at that time, with only a few hundred hours actual flying to our credit, but we all seemed to cope OK.

It was about that time (1941) that we started carrying the small rubber dinghies. It was put in a pack about four inches thick and was placed between the pilot and his parachute—dimensions being (as far as I remember) 18 inches by 12 inches by four inches. The inflation bottle was situated in the forward part of this pack, so that as a pilot moved his legs they rubbed against the inflating cock, a black, knurled ring. This, when turned or screwed down into the neck of the bottle, pierced a copper disc which in turn released gas and inflated the dinghy. Unfortunately, the constant leg movements on this bottle and cock had the effect of slowly wearing a hole in the copper disc, or at least wearing it thin. This could cause an unexpected discharge of the bottle and the dinghy to inflate in the cockpit. The pilot was thrust upwards and the central control column was pushed forward—the result of which was predictable. There were a lot of disasters before the reason was found, and then all pilots were issued with sharp, stabbing knives. It happened to me at night in the circuit over Manston. I was lucky, since I'd been on an op over France and was preparing to land when my dinghy inflated. I punctured it in record time with my knife but came very near to castrating myself. I was shaking a week later at the very thought . . .! Later, the inflation bottles were modified and put in a less vulnerable position.

The amount of personal equipment we used to carry on operations was really unbelievable. Apart from our uniform of blue battle dress, thick white socks, white roll-neck pullover (Navy type), fleece-lined flying boots, three pairs of gloves (one, white silk, then a woollen pair and overall leather gauntlets which were covered in something like varnish—fire-proofing), one leather helmet, oxygen mask-combined with microphone and heavy goggles; we had a yellow 'Mae West', a pack of escape money, iron ration pack containing glucose, barley sugar, an outfit for purifying water, small compass, a 'dirty' silk handkerchief (actually a map of France). Personal armament consisted of a revolver stuck down one boot and a Commando knife down the other. Under our battle dress we often had a civilian zipper jacket with a beret tucked away inside—though this was highly unofficial! We also had modified brass buttons on our trousers which could be used as makeshift compasses. Over all this lot one strapped on one's parachute/dinghy pack and somehow clambered into the Hurricane's cockpit. I've heard that the armoured knights of medieval times were hoisted on to their mounts by a sort of crane—I feel we could have usefully used something similar . . .!

Lastly, there was the task of landing a Hurricane. I'd like here to recall that a Hurricane was a 'first time' aeroplane, in the sense that you could not have dual instruction in it. Therefore, when you first landed, it was right after the time you took off and flew it for the first time. Instruction was all given on the ground before one got airborne. Once in the air you tried hard to remember all that you'd been told—though you usually forgot. Fortunately the undercarriage of the Hurricane was wide and very strong, unlike either the Spitfire and Me 109. It could be 'dropped' in without any undue harm. Nevertheless, it could at the same time be made to 'sit down' so gently that it became a matter of personal pride not to feel the aircraft touch the ground. And believe me, we used to operate from some rough old airfields—mostly grass, without concrete runways. I remember once during the summer of 1941 returning from a sweep escorting Blenheims and landing at Manston. A friend of mine, Sergeant Batchelor, had been badly shot up, particularly about the face and head. He flew his Hurricane back and landed it at Manston with the help of some squadron friends (who flew alongside him and talked him down) when he was almost blind. Later I heard that he became permanently blind. I saw all this whilst on the ground, resting beside my own aircraft. We were given lemonade by a party of Boy Scouts accompanied by a local vicar. (I wonder if any of those people still remember this . . .?)

As with the take-off, one actually landed a Hurricane in the final stages by looking at an angle from straight ahead. The technique was to close the throttle and glide at around 100mph (we used instruments graded in mph, not knots as they are today calibrated). One never came in straight in line with the landing path (or runway) but in a continuous slight left-hand turn, side-slipping if necessary. Then straighten up at the last moment, a split second before actual touchdown, looking to the left to judge height above the ground. It sounds slightly difficult but in fact, after a bit of practice, it became quite automatic. We normally took off and landed in formations of three and four aircraft at once and thought nothing of it.

They Also Served

FRANK HARTLEY

Mudlarks. A pre-1939 scene as a Hurricane of 17 Squadron is man-handled out of the soggy surface of a grass dispersal area, during field exercises.

The contribution of the toiling ground crews of the Hurricane squadrons—as with all other RAF fighting units—cannot be measured in terms of awards and victories. Yet without their loyalty, courage and devotion to the job, such epics as the Battle of Britain might never have been won. The erks—a universal RAF nickname for the maintenance men and women—gave an invaluable service, one which can never be over-estimated. Nor were their working conditions merely a comfortable sinecure, leaving the air crews to face all the dangers. Whether on a windswept winter dispersal in France, the barren rock-dust airstrips of North Africa, or the steaming sweatbath of a Burmese jungle strip, the erks were as much 'in the front line' as many of their airborne comrades. Possibly epitomising such conditions was Manston aerodrome in the summer of 1940. Well within range of marauding Luftwaffe fighters and bombers, Manston thoroughly earned its soubriquet, 'Hell-fire Corner'. Bombed, strafed and almost obliterated by continuous raiding, the airfield continued to provide a forward defence position for RAF Fighter command, despite almost complete lack of normal facilities. It was to Manston that Frank Hartley was posted just as the Battle of Britain had petered out.

Far left: Installing the oxygen bottles. The airman on the wing is carrying round his shoulders a Service gas mask —usually stuffed with a tea flask, NAAFI 'wads' (cakes or rolls), towel and soap—if the eagle eye of any officious NCO could be avoided!

Left: The men behind the men behind the guns. The anonymous but vital ground crews of the RAF— exemplified here by the erks of one of 242 Squadron's Flights at Martlesham Heath in the spring of 1941.

Bottom left: Radio check. AC1 J. A. Peterson checks the R/T of a 401 Squadron RCAF Hurricane IIb at Digby on July 24th, 1941.

Below: Pilot out. An American pilot of 71 (Eagle) Squadron climbs out as the ground crew takes over charge of the aircraft.

Bottom: 'Two Six'—the standard cry in RAF language for extra hands for any heavy job. The equivalent in Polish could have applied in this scene as airmen of 306 Polish Squadron (the 'Wild Ducks') shove Hurricane II, V7118, UZ-V back to its dispersal pan for servicing.

In January 1941 I was posted to RAF Manston, Kent, along with four of my colleagues. Situated within sight of the French coast, Manston had been under enemy attack many times and had earned the nickname, 'Hell-fire Corner'. When we arrived it was dark, but here and there we could see evidence of past enemy action, the empty shell of the Airmen's Mess, several flattened huts, the remains of a bombed wash-house, and the camp swimming bath which had once been a covered building—now resembling an open-air lido, except for the fact that most of the glazed tiles were missing and the bath was empty, probably no longer watertight. Next morning we set out to report to our new unit. We looked out expecting to see Hurricanes or Spits dispersed around the airfield, but our hopes were dashed—the only aircraft in sight were three Air Sea Rescue Lysanders. Walking round the aerodrome, and just before reaching our new section, we really thought we had 'struck gold' at long last. Passing a closed hangar, we decided to investigate and, peeping through a gap between the doors, one of my colleagues called excitedly, 'Look boys. Hurriboxes!' We squeezed through the gap into the hangar—only to find that the 'Hurries' were merely good decoys.

perhaps to attack enemy shipping. Many battles could be heard taking place out there, though these were usually too far away to see clearly. On one such occasion we were astounded to see a Junkers 87 circling the aerodrome with a mixture of Hurricanes and Spitfires, about six in all, spread around its tail. It looked as if the pilot, realising the hopelessness of the situation, had resolved to call it a day and land. He was actually making his approach when suddenly (or so it seemed) the Junkers' gunner decided to have a go, and as he opened up so did the fighters—and the Junkers crashed in a nearby field, killing its crew.

In the course of time our unit became known as No 2 R & R (Refuelling and Rearming) Party. Instead of dealing with just odd bods, we were handling several squadrons each day, as well as a goodly number of night bombers. On many occasions five or six squadrons of Spitfires and Hurricanes would land at Manston

Full Revs. Engine fitters give the Merlin of Hurricane IIb, Z3658, YO-N of 401 (*Ram*) Squadron RCAF full power. Digby, July 24th, 1941.

Centre: Air Vent trouble. Warrant Officer G. Carpenter (inevitably, 'Chippy') and Corporal K. Warren discuss the problem during a Major Inspection of a Hurricane IIb of 402 Squadron at Warmwell, February 9th, 1942.

Top right: Wheel change. LAC P. J. Turgeon attends to a faulty brake on the port wheel of a 401 Squadron IIb at Digby, July 24th, 1941, supervised by Sergeant Bob Fair.

Right: Corporal Trimble, 401 Squadron, Digby, doing a DI (Daily Inspection) on the instrument panel.

Our new unit proved to be a Servicing Flight—a group of ground personnel whose function was to attend to all visiting aircraft ie aeroplanes of all types which did not belong to Manston. Sometimes a fighter, sometimes a bomber, damaged in action or perhaps short of fuel, would lob in for attention prior to returning to base. Although by 1941, Manston was in a sorry state, it must nevertheless have been a welcome sight to many aircrews managing to 'just make it' back to British soil once again. We did not have to wait long before we saw some action, for it was only about our third day on the station when two Messerschmitt 109s flew low over the airfield. It was the first time I had seen a German low enough to see the black crosses and swastikas. It was also the first and only time I actually saw bombs leaving an aircraft. Fortunately the damage was of little consequence, just four small craters from light calibre bombs.

A few weeks after our arrival we were pleased to see a squadron of Hurricanes arrive. It was great to see them sweep low over the airfield, climb again and peel off before coming in to land. For a while this was Manston's resident fighter squadron and frequently they would go out over the Channel to protect Allied convoys, or

direct from their own bases. Our R & R Party would top up the fuel, oil and oxygen and thereby enable the planes to leave England brim-full of fuel etc to strike deep into enemy-occupied France, sometimes returning to Manston to refuel and rearm in readiness for a further sweep the same day, or perhaps just to return to their respective bases. In order to increase our fighters' range of penetration into German-occupied territory, the auxiliary (jettison) fuel tank was introduced. In the case of the Hurricane these cigar-shaped tanks were fitted under the wings near the fuselage. The idea was for the pilot to use the fuel in his jettison tanks first, then switch to his main tanks when the auxiliary supply was exhausted. If he met enemy fighters the pilot could, if necessary, jettison the auxiliary tanks and join in the fray or take evasive action unhampered. Speaking from memory, I think most of our machines returned to base complete with their jettison tanks—empty, but still attached.

Perhaps one of the greatest attributes of the Hurricane lay in its capacity to absorb punishment and still fly. The fuselage aft of the cockpit was fabric-covered and it was not unusual to find bullet or shrapnel holes in this area, which could easily be repaired providing that the interior airframe structure and equipment were undamaged. Similar damage to a stressed skin (ie metal-covered) aircraft, such as the Spitfire, needed more time to effect a suitable repair. I have a vivid recollection of one Hurricane landing with tail planes, elevators and rudder reduced to a mere framework, with pieces of fabric hanging loose. As we surveyed the damage I remember thinking that this kite had defied all the known laws of aerodynamics, as its pilot had coaxed it home. A day or so later the Duke of Kent visited Manston, inspected this aircraft and chatted with the pilot. Sadly it must be recorded that this same pilot was killed within the next few days when practice bombing an exposed wreck in the Channel, off Pegwell Bay; while the Duke of Kent lost his life in an air crash in Scotland a few weeks later.

As the war progressed so the frequency of our fighter sweeps over enemy-held territory increased, shooting up supply lines, bombing bridges, roads, railway lines, attacks on enemy depots and the like. One morning, having refuelled a Hurricane in readiness for a daylight sweep, I chatted to the pilot concerning the destructive power of his four Hispano 20mm cannons. He described a raid on a German depot. His squadron was to attack in threes, each group in turn peppering the building with cannon fire, and then circle and repeat this attack. 'As I made my second approach,' he said, 'the face of the building collapsed like a jig-saw puzzle and I could see some of the floors sagging.' Attacks by Hurricanes were by no means confined to the day time. There was in fact a period when a Hurricane night fighter squadron operated from Manston with great success, particularly in moonlight periods. Thinking back, I can recall the names of two pilots of this unit, Flight Lieutenant Stevens and Sergeant Scott.

A rather awe-inspiring incident occurred one morning when a Hurribomber was making an approach to land, complete with

Far left: Run-up. Hurricane XII, 5658, 'B' of the RCAF at Dartmouth, Nova Scotia on May 6th, 1943. The mini-spinner on the propeller was common to most Canadian Hurricanes of the period. Note unusual form of wheel chocks in use.

Left: Start up. The pilot of V7608, XR-J, of 71 Squadron about to run up his engine, Kirton-in-Lindsey, Lincolnshire in spring 1941. First of the three American 'Eagle' squadrons formed within the RAF, composed of 'neutral' Americans, 71 was formed at Church Fenton on September 9th, 1940 but only commenced operations as a unit in February 1941.

Below: 'Here they come'— the ground crews prepare to receive their pilots for a scramble take-off. Canadians of 402 Squadron race to their Hurricanes at Warmwell, whilst the airmen stand by with parachute harnesses at the ready, cockpit straps in position and trolley accumulators plugged in. Experience provided a silk-like co-ordination in teamwork, thus avoiding unnecessary time-wasting in getting the aircraft airborne.

two 250lb bombs under its wings. From the ground we could see that the undercarriage was not properly locked down, the starboard wheel swinging loosely in the breeze. We shouted and waved frantically, hoping to attract the pilot's attention—but to no avail. The Hurricane touched down on its port wheel, the starboard wing hit the ground, the propeller splintered and the whole aircraft spun round as the port wheel collapsed, nearly tipping the plane on its nose. We raced to help the pilot out of the cockpit. Fortunately he was unhurt but very shaken as he surveyed the wreckage—and was no doubt relieved mightily to see the two bombs, which had become detached, lying peacefully a few yards away! Another occurrence which remains vivid in my mind concerning Hurricanes at Manston was the occasion when a number of Messerchmitt 109s were reported somewhere in the vicinity and two Hurricanes took off *with* the wind! Very soon they were over the Channel and, after about 20 minutes, they returned. It was later reported that the Hurricanes had crept up behind the Germans, literally joined their formation, and at an opportune moment picked off three tail-enders before the enemy realised what was happening.

During 1941 Wing Commander T. P. Gleave took over as station commander of Manston. He was a very upright officer

There they go. 242 Squadron Hurricanes at Martlesham Heath in early 1941. In foreground is Z2588, a Mk II.

with a somewhat athletic carriage, but it was evident that he had suffered severe burn injuries. Naturally we were all curious to know something of his background. The Wingco was a very energetic man, always dashing from place to place, and it soon became obvious that he was happiest among the Hurricanes, whether they were stationed at Manston or just dropping in from ops. One day a lone Hurricane landed and as it parked the Wingco drove up to meet it. I believe he was out of his car before it had stopped rocking! The Hurricane was a 12-gun job and in a short time the Wingco was excitedly walking round it, trying out the controls—just like someone inspecting their first new car, though I should add

that this was by no means a new Hurricane. It transpired that this aircraft had been allotted for the Wing Commander's personal use and he was a very delighted man indeed. As a Wing Commander he was entitled to have his own initials on the sides of his aircraft in place of normal squadron identification codes, and it was my privilege to paint 'T.P.G.' on each side of the fuselage, plus a number of small swastikas below the cockpit—these indicating the number of enemy planes destroyed by the Wing Commander in combat. As the airframe fitter on this machine, I was frequently in personal contact with the CO, and many times he took off alone in the hope of bagging another German.

Start up. Flying Officer Sprague of 401 Squadron RCAF 'gives her the gun', Digby, July 1941. His personal insignia, just below the exhaust stubs, comprised a small cartoon serpent sitting in a champagne glass, centred on a coloured diamond shape.

174 Squadron's Hurri-
bombers at Manston in May
1942. Known as the
'Mauritius Squadron', XP-Y
is BE684 and XP-G is BE421.
Dieppe cost this unit dear,
nearly half of the participating pilots being lost.

Operation Jubilee

J. W. BROOKS

I was based at Manston in Kent with 174 Squadron and flew the 'new' Hurri-bombers. 'New' in the sense that the Hurricane was by then considered as out-classed by the new German fighters, so it was fitted with bombs—one 250lb under each wing. The squadron by then was fully operational and experienced in low-level work, and although the chop rate was high, there was no lack of enthusiasm. So when we were sent to Ford on a temporary posting, along with a number of other Hurricane and Spitfire squadrons, we knew something big was on. I see from my log book that I made an entry, 'To Ford, for what?' That was on August 14th.

We had no idea of what we were supposed to do, except that it was fighter-bomber work. However, it wasn't very difficult to reason out our target. Since we knew we were to operate from Ford, and knew our effective range, our most obvious destination was in the Dieppe-Fecamp area.

On the evening of August 18th we were all carefully briefed about what was to happen next day. We were told, amongst other things, that the German reaction was liable to be quick and massive. I personally can't remember very much of that briefing after all this time, except that this was not going to be *the* invasion but merely a 'try-out'. We were told that our job was

to cover the landings of Canadian troops etc. What did dismay our particular squadron was that we were to be the first lot in, before first light. We were also told that we were going to dive-bomb our targets at low level, and that we were to have two 500lb bombs instead of our usual two 250lb—just twice the weight. I was a Section leader at this time and was detailed with my three other pilots to dive-bomb some heavy naval-type guns which were emplaced to the rear of Dieppe on some high ground. These, we were told, could cover the beaches and sea approaches and it was essential to knock them out at first go. Which accounted for our early departure.

On the morning of the 19th we were called at some ghastly hour, although few of us had slept much that night. After a scratch breakfast served by the ever-ready WAAFs, we got into our aircraft already warming up on the airfield. Since we were taking off in the dark we had to have our navigation lights on to see each other, this being a real novelty to us. It was also remarkable that we had no collisions since we always took off in formation, four at a time. I believe there were three Sections to our squadron effort (12 aircraft) although there may have been another four aircraft on a separate job. My own Section formed up behind me in close formation

so that they couldn't lose me in the dark, and I kept a close eye on our new CO, Squadron Leader Fayolle, a Free French pilot, whose father was (I believe) an admiral in pre-war France. He had been with us just a few weeks. We flew in low since there was still a need not to alert the Germans of our approach—the first of our troops had not yet landed. .

It took us about 40 minutes to cross to the other side but long before we got there I could see a fire. This turned out to be a German ship which accidentally ran into the invasion fleet and had to be destroyed. Squadron Leader Fayolle naturally saw there was no need for us to continue on the deck, since the Germans obviously knew something was up, so we all climbed up to a couple of thousand feet in order to pin-point ourselves and to get sufficient height to dive with our bombs. It was quite easy to make out the coast and the town of Dieppe. The ship on fire lit up the whole scene clearly and the flak and fireworks were on a par with November 5th. My Section broke off from the CO's, who had other targets, and I swung away to the northern side of Dieppe. I dropped down to 1,500 feet and told the Section to drop back in line-astern, ready for diving. All this had been planned beforehand, needless to say, so that there was a minimum of R/T natter and less chance of confusion.

Dieppe Cover. The fighter pilots who provided the air umbrella for the Dieppe landings. The very nature of the operation demanded deck-level flying through curtains of deadly accurate flak—the losses were high.

Far left: The result of an argument. Hurricane BE394 after a mid-air collision with a Messerschmitt Bf 109. Its pilot, Flight Sergeant W. Merryweather of 174 Squadron, flew all the way back to base and landed without injury. He was lost in action later in the war.

The light flak was coming up thick and fast and we were flying at a very vulnerable height. I could see the 40mm stuff curving up towards us, for all the world like a strike of bright glowing beads on a string. It would flash past us and explode just above our heads—or so it appeared. Flak always looked worse at night. We were the only aircraft in the area so we knew it was meant for us alone. I was trying hard to remember the target details from our briefing, what it looked like and more important where it was. Then I saw it. Three or four big splodges of concrete surrounded by trees. I called up my Section and told them 'target ahead' although I found out later that they had seen it at the same time as myself, so they were ready for my 'Tallyho'.

Some light flak came up from the gun site but it wasn't really enough to put us off. My main concern was that we would all pull out and miss the surrounding trees— this being the first time we had done formation dive-bombing at night, and with 1,000lb of bombs apiece. I went down as low as I dared to release my bombs—I couldn't really miss. I could make out the heavy guns on their white concrete bases, along with some smaller gun sites and huts. It was these smaller sites from which the guns were firing at me, so I fired back as I dived down. This was a general tactic to make the people on the ground keep their heads down. Eight machine guns all going at once are quite noisy. I pulled out at a couple of hundred feet and saw the trees loom out of the darkness in front of me. I was weaving like mad now just above the tree tops with lots of machine gun and 40mm stuff quite thick all around me. My bombs had 6-seconds delay fuzes, whilst the boys behind me had 2-second fuzes. This was to prevent those behind me being blown up by my bombs. Nevertheless it meant a quick and co-ordinated run over the target even with such precautions.

After what seemed a very long time, I saw the whole site go up in a series of quick flashes and then felt the crump, which bounced my Hurricane about. On my left I saw one of my Section having a hard time with the flak. He was weaving like a madman just over the tree tops— then he must have seen me and pulled over, to our mutual comfort. It was 'Tommy'' Thomas. We were later joined by another of our Section and the three of us swung round to the south side of Dieppe. We all continued to machine-gun anything that moved on the ground. By then it was light enough to see and we all had a go at some German transport which disgorged its troops in a great big hurry. I could see a lot of activity on the sea and beaches. The German ship was still burning away merrily, although there were a lot of fires

89

in the town and on the sea front. The troops were now landing and I could see the landing barges and other sea transports quite clearly. I flew out to sea, giving the Navy a wide berth since those chaps were (understandably) trigger-happy and let fly at anything in the air. I joined up with some more from 174 Squadron and we all continued back to Ford. Half-way back it was fully light and I counted seven Hurricanes from our squadron. I knew who they were by their aircraft code letters—mine was usually 'G'.

There was a lot of activity when I got back to Ford. The Spitfire squadrons were taking off and forming up into Wing formations before setting out. I was somewhat short of fuel and lost no time in getting in. Some other members of 174 arrived back in twos and threes, but three didn't come in—the new CO, Squadron Leader Fayolle, and Flight Sergeant James who was in my Section, plus one from the other Section. I should point out that on operations of the sort that 174 was engaged in, the turnover of pilots was so great that sometimes you hardly got to know a new chap before he was killed or went missing. It was said that if you managed to survive your first three ops then you had a good chance of completing your tour. All of our aircraft were found to have holes in them. My own 'G' had a few through the fabric which the ground staff were hastily patching over with red dope. Our greatest worry was getting hit in the radiator. If a single bullet punctured this, things happened very quickly. Within minutes your engine either seized solid, caught fire or simply blew up. In any event you had to get out in a hurry. Unfortunately the low-level nature of our work did not give us much chance since we couldn't bale out, while if we pulled up we were sitting targets for the ground flak.

Another two Sections from our squadron went out, led by the senior Flight commander, Flight Lieutenant MacConnell, now acting CO. These pilots had not been in the earlier detail and we told them what to expect. We heard from the returning Spitfires that there was a lot of scrapping with the Germans, particularly with the St Omer and Abbeville boys. After being debriefed by our Intelligence officer, Flying Officer Tunks, we all went off for a second breakfast and a rest in the sunshine. Sometime after lunch we were briefed to go out again. This time our target was a concentration of tanks and guns which were apparently moving in from north of Dieppe. We were also informed that our troops were now pulling out and we were supposed to cover them as best we could. Flight Lieutenant MacConnell was

Sergeants I. J. Eady and B. E. Innes of 402 Squadron RCAF at Warmwell, February 9th, 1942— probably thinking that it was a long way to France, just to drop *that* little thing . . .

to lead our eight serviceable Hurricanes.

A different sight now met my eyes when we arrived over Dieppe. At 1,500 feet I had a panoramic view in the brilliant sunshine. There was an extraordinary amount of rubbish floating around in the water, quite some way off-shore. There were bright yellow dinghies which stood out against a surface of oil and sundry junk. The German boat was still there and still smoking. It was quite small, or so it appeared. There was a dogfight going on overhead and we all kept our eyes peeled for an attack. It was our job to avoid any conflict as this meant we would have to get rid of our two bombs and hence our mission would be wasted.

We went in two lines abreast as pre-arranged and I could see the targets right ahead. They were slinging everything at us, or so it appeared. In the daytime it was difficult to see the amount of flak being fired at you, so if you were sensible you kept jinking about, not flying straight and level for one moment, and getting down as low as possible. I saw one of our Hurricanes get hit and catch fire. He dived straight at a bunch of armoured vehicles and blew up. I think this was a friend of mine called 'Doofy' du Fretay, a Free Frenchman who loathed Germans. Then another friend, an Australian named Flight Sergeant Watson who had been to my home in London, blew up. I think one of his bombs got hit as he went in. I flew straight at some transport and troops with my guns going and skipped my bombs at them. I passed over the top at a couple of feet and brought back with me a souvenir—the whip aerial of a German tank, wedged in my radiator. I wasn't sorry to get out of that lot and, together with Murray ('Tommy') Thomas, joined up with Flight Lieutenant MacConnell and we then went on a strafing run up to the coast.

We formed up to go home (there were now just five of us) at about 200 feet, when I saw to my horror a big formation of Messerschmitt 109s and Focke-Wulf 190s flying parallel to the coast. They passed directly over the top of us at not more than about 200 feet. It was possible to make out the individual markings, and one I noticed had a big black oil streak underneath. I held my breath, as I'm sure the

others did, since we had used most of our ammunition in the ground attacks. Besides this we would have been slaughtered, being outclassed, outnumbered and short of fuel. I watched them disappear into the smoke and confusion to the north. Then there was a Junkers 88 attacking a destroyer but all his bombs missed and threw up great columns of water. He was too fast for us and got away. It was nice to see the

English coast again and even nicer to get down in one piece, because I was sure I'd been hit somewhere vital. In fact all I had was a lot more holes in 'G' and she was still flyable. We had been on the ground only a short time when a Ju 88, or a Dornier, came over Ford at very low altitude and dropped a stick of bombs straight across the grass. He ducked in and out of some low cloud which was coming in from the sea. He was a very brave man. I think he was later shot down by a Beaufighter. Around tea time we were stood down as the operation was considered over as far as we were concerned. We had lost Squadron Leader Fayolle, Pilot Officers du Fretay and van Wymeersch, Flight Sergeants Watson and James, and two others whose names escape me. We had begun the operation with (I think) 17 pilots, and we now had eight left and some very patched Hurricanes. Next day we flew back to Manston.

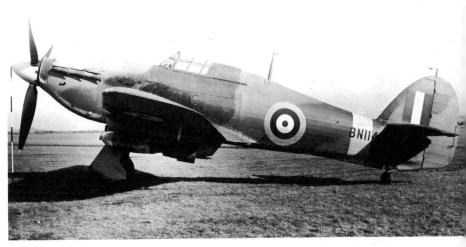

BN114, loaded with 500lb GP bombs. Though seen here at Boscombe Down in March 1942, this aircraft served later with 451 Squadron, RAAF in Cyprus and Egypt.

Bottom left: Replenishment. 250lb GP bombs are fitted to a Hurricane IIb for another sortie across the Channel. The wooden hand transporter was a 'local' aid constructed by the unit's armourers.

Malta Defender
FRED ETCHELLS

'Collie's Battleship'—L1669, a Hurricane I which was the only Hurricane in the Western Desert in June 1940, attached to 80 Squadron. So-named because it represented Air Commodore (then) Ray Collishaw's only modern fighter. Seen here in England, prior to leaving for Egypt.

Fred Etchells probably holds some form of record for longevity of Hurricane operational experience. He flew them from December 1940 until March 1945, interspersed with many other fighter types. And those four years included operations in virtually every main variety of Hurricane on sweeps over the Channel, Malta defence and intruder sorties over Sicily instructing in Egypt, defence duties in Iraq, the Persian Gulf and Palestine operations from Syria and Cyprus and, finally, back to the UK. Perhaps understandably, his affection for the Hurricane remains vivid even today—yet one more example of the feeling engendered by the Hurricane in its myriad pilots. After several months of operations with 242 Squadron, Etchells was posted to 249

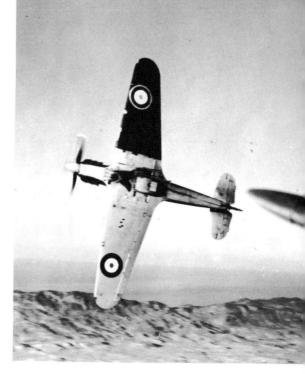

Right: Peel-off. An interesting study in underside markings (black and white) as a 213 Squadron Hurricane aerobats over the ill-fated island of Crete, 1941.

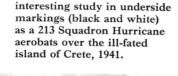

Above/right: Two views of 274 Squadron circa June–July 1940. Second pilot from right in first scene is Flying Officer P. G. Wykeham-Barnes (who eventually retired from the RAF as Air Marshal Sir Peter Wykeham), who played a leading part in the first two years of the desert air war, and ended the war as a Group Captain with 2nd TAF.

Squadron on May 7th, 1941, bound (ostensibly) for the Far East, and four days later flew in to Luqa airstrip on Malta Here, the squadron was 'retained'—the beginning, in Etchell's case, of some three long years of continuing service around the Mediterranean theatre of operations.

'Hullo my darling—third door on the right' was the greeting I'll never forget

from a very elderly-looking sailor on duty at the top of a gangplank leading from a Liverpool dockside to an opening in the side of the aircraft carrier, *HMS Furious*. RAF tales of naval personnel, which until then I'd considered fabrications, came rushing into my mind! Very heavily laden with kitbag, suitcase and sundry other items, I approached the open door with caution—and in about 10 seconds flat had received a yellow fever inoculation to add to my long list of jabs required to prepare me for overseas service. I had recently left Douglas Bader's squadron, 242, flying Hurricane IIs, and joined 249 Squadron, equipped with tropicalised Hurri Is fitted with long range tanks. This was considered a great come-down after flying Mk IIs, which were a considerable improvement on the old Hurri Is. We believed we were heading for Singapore, and our 24 Hurricanes had been dismantled, taken aboard *Furious*, reassembled and crammed into a hangar below the flight deck. I had not

heard of Hurricanes taking off from aircraft carriers, and was very intrigued. I'm sure that a blind faith in the Hurricane must have dismissed any fears.

Greenock was our first port of call, where we took on fresh water and were away again within an hour or so. Then Gibraltar, where we moored at the dockside on to *HMS Ark Royal* (which by then had been 'sunk' about three times by Dr Goebbels), and shortly after arrival we pilots helped push our Hurricanes over a bridge of planks joining the two ships. As soon as this chore was completed the *Ark Royal* cast off and headed west into the Atlantic (to fool observers in local trawlers etc who reported all shipping movements to the Germans—or so we were told). In the middle of the night a sharp turn through 180 degrees and through the straits of Gibraltar—briefing next day for the first leg of our flight (which was to be to Malta for refuelling and rest)—packing kit into ammunition recesses and any odd spots

in the fuselage we could find—then all set for the 'Off' at dawn.

All 24 of our Hurricanes were tightly, crowded at the 'blunt end' of the carrier and I remember even now my almost complete disbelief at the impossibly short 'runway'. *Ark Royal* then opened her throttles and headed into wind at something like 30 knots, which meant a further 30-mph by the aircraft would give us the 60-mph needed for take-off. Conscious of the heavily-laden state of my machine, I was grateful for the great height of the flight deck above sea level, which had made me quite dizzy when looking over the side earlier in the journey. It meant no immediate necessity to climb until adequate flying speed was gained. I still recall the joy of seeing the aircraft in front of me become safely airborne before reaching the end of the flight deck at the 'sharp end'. Many of our pilots swore they bent their throttle levers to ensure maximum possible revs!

First squadron in the Middle East to receive a complement of Hurricanes was 274, which reformed at Amriyah on August 19th, 1940 with a mixture of Gloster Gladiators and Hurricanes, under the command of Sqn Ldr P. H. Dunn, DFC. The squadron recorded its first combat victory on September 10th, 1940. This scene was at Amriyah in late 1940, the nearest aircraft being P2544, YK-T.

Below: P2627, another of 274 Squadron's early equipment, over the barren desert hinterland, November 1940.

Above: P3731, an aircraft of 261 Squadron at Ta Kali, Malta, 1941. This machine was one of the first Hurricane reinforcements for the island to arrive from the deck of HMS *Argus*.

Centre: Readiness at Ta Kali, winter 1941. 249 Squadron machines parked in the open, ready for take off (note trolley accumulators plugged in). Nearest Hurricane, XJ, is Z3580.

Top right: Scramble—249 Squadron get away from Ta Kali on receipt of a warning of an approaching Axis raid. Winter 1941.

Centre right: Malta reliefs. 249 Squadron's Hurricanes stacked and battened down on the flight deck of the carrier HMS *Ark Royal* on June 27th, 1941, bound for the beleaguered island of Malta. The apparent white 'markings' on wings are, in fact, webbing straps lashed to the deck.

Right: Wasted journey. A Hurricane II, Z3757, which crashed on arrival from an aircraft carrier on Ta Kali airfield, Malta, in August 1941.

Our Hurricanes were being led by a Fleet Air Arm Fulmar, which was forced to return to the carrier after 45 minutes with engine trouble. But before long a replacement Fulmar met us and we turned round and again headed for Malta. After almost five and a half hours in the air, during which time two enemy aircraft crossed our track heading for Tunisia from Sicily, we saw Malta ahead—in the middle of a bombing raid by Italians from Sicily. We had been briefed to circle a small island off the south coast called Filfla, in order to identify ourselves, but the state of our fuel gauges decided the issue and we flew straight in to land at the first aerodrome sighted—Luqa in my case and several others, though others landed at Hal Far and Ta Kali. The anti-aircraft defences were firing at maximum rate and we were lucky to escape any hits on the squadron. 'Heads down' was the first desire after landing and taxying as close as possible to the nearest slit trench, where we hurriedly joined the RAF ground crews to whom air raids had become part of everyday life. After the raid we were gathered together and informed that instead of refuelling and continuing our journey to the Far East, we were needed more in Malta, and our base would be Ta Kali. The official promise was that we would do 12 months on the island and then return to the UK. For several of us it was to be three and a half years before we saw home again . .

Malta's air defence was in poor shape, and most of 249's pilots felt they were just the boys to remedy this defect, and morale was high. Our Hurricane Is were in good

shape and we dreamed of meeting flocks of Stukas and slow, outdated Italian bombers, unescorted. The Axis, however, appeared to decide that as Malta had been reinforced, they would stiffen their aggression by adding Luftwaffe units to the Italian air forces, and we soon found Messerschmitt 109s to be more aggressive than the Macchi 200s as bomber escorts. The Junkers 88 was a superb aircraft for its purpose, and we found that if we intercepted a high raid after they had bombed, we could not catch them after they had their noses down by about 10 degrees, and they were soon back over the 60 miles of sea separating Malta from Sicily. After considerable losses on both sides, activity by the enemy was greatly reduced, which was fortunate for 249 Squadron in particular in view of the small number of Hurricanes available for duty. Towards the end of June 1941 we received reinforcements in the shape of Hurricane IIs, with fresh pilots to replace our casualties. The Mk IIs still could not cope with a nose-down Ju 88, but we had a much-improved performance at higher altitudes, which gave us a far greater chance of attacking raids from above.

Late summer saw some of our Hurri IIs fitted with Light Series bomb racks, holding four 40lb bombs under each wing, and a number of raids were carried out during moonlight nights on airfields in Sicily. The bomb racks appeared to upset the magnetic compasses and arrival at any intended aerodrome target was mainly a matter of luck. Nevertheless, enemy airfields were bombed and strafed. The Hurri

II had heavy fire-power in the shape of four 20mm cannons and obtained good results in many cases—setting fire to aircraft on the ground, petrol bowsers and buildings. One such raid gave rise to an eventual joyful reunion at a much later date. A fellow Flight Sergeant pilot was thought to have been shot down whilst strafing an airfield, and as no news came through to report his being taken prisoner, we mourned the loss of another comrade. Ten years later I was a guest at a golf club dinner, when the sight of my 'late' comrade, alive and well, brought me to a fully sober condition in one second flat! It appeared that whilst strafing what he considered to be the enemy's officers Mess from across the airfield, he touched the ground with his propeller, which disintegrated. He skidded across the airfield, coming to a halt just short of the building

he'd been attacking, and thus quickly changed his status to that of PoW. A very joyful reunion, indeed.

The boredom-cum-nervous tension of standing by ready to 'scramble', kitted up in flying suit and 'Mae West', was interspersed with some moments of extreme excitement which were enjoyed more in retrospect than at the moment of happening. One such occasion was an intended arrival, exactly at dawn, over a railway line in Sicily which was considered important enough to be attacked frequently. I was one of four pilots due to take off 20 minutes before dawn from Luqa. Unfortunately, the armourers bombing up my Hurricane found a technical snag, and it was almost dawn by the time I was able to take off, the other three being long gone. As I was

more than half asleep, I suppose I must have expected the same to apply in Sicily, for after dropping my little load and strafing the railway target, and on gaining height again, our wonderful and normally unflappable controller, 'Woody' Woodhall, was almost screaming over the newly-fitted VHF radio for me to get home 'without delay'. I believe the plot on our radar showed something like 170 enemy aircraft airborne and headed for Malta, but the tone of our controller was sufficient to cause another throttle lever to be 'bent'. Being winter, there was a reasonable cloud cover which I used thankfully, but disliking instrument flying and wishing to see if I was nearing the island after some time in cloud, I descended—and found a Macchi 200 on my left and very close!

Indeed, he was close enough for me to see that the pilot was wearing white goggles and had his cockpit closed. A little further away to my right was another Macchi. I don't believe either of them noticed the 'intruder' in their formation, and I was back up into cloud and changing course in a jiffy. All my ammunition had been used in strafing, and I blessed the Italian pilots' poor airmanship for possibly saving my life.

A completely clear field of vision through 360 degrees was, I believe, only second in importance to having a good and thoroughly reliable aircraft, and although slower than one would have wished, our Hurricanes were certainly reliable. A minute or two after veering away from the Macchis, I cautiously broke cloud cover again. No enemy visible, so I nipped down to sea level, over the coast at just above rooftop height and straight into land without the formality of a circuit at Ta Kali. After a tail-up, high-speed spot of taxying to the nearest slit trench and head down, I felt able to breathe again and waited for the strafing to stop.

Although superbly manoeuvrable despite slightly heavy controls, we had to admit reluctantly that the Hurricane did lack speed, but I don't think I ever heard a word spoken against the aircraft. Somehow one loved the Hurricane without either realising or expressing it, and it was only after flying Spitfires with controls light enough for a five year old to handle that one came to realise the strength required to throw a Hurricane about the sky.

Landing on the rock surface, interlaced with stone walls and buildings, was never an easy prospect for the Malta pilots. One casualty (an overshoot) was Z4356, thought to be a 261 Squadron machine.

I joined 6 Squadron on June 22nd, 1942 at its base camp at RAF Shandur on the Suez Canal. I'd recently been promoted to substantive Squadron Leader as an instructor in South Africa and, being 'surplus to requirements', had been posted to the Middle East under a two-way exchange scheme. AHQ selected me for the post of second-in-command of 6 Squadron, under Wing Commander Roger C. Porteus, who was an old friend of mine from Army Co-operation days. By that date the squadron had already been in operations with its Hurricane IIDs during the latter part of the 8th Army's retreat to the El Alamein line, and were presently based at Landing Ground (LG) 91 in the desert west of Alexandria. The Hurricane IID was, at that time, a secret weapon. It was in fact a Hurricane II fitted with two Vickers 'S' guns of 40mm calibre, slung one under each wing, and two .303 inch machine guns. It was created for the prime role of tank destruction from the air because our own tanks were under-gunned compared with the Germans and invariably came off second-best in a tank-versus-tank engagement. The 'S' gun was (with one exception) the biggest calibre weapon to be carried in any RAF aircraft, and the Hurricane had been found to be the best aerial platform upon which to mount it.

Tank-Busters
D. WESTON-BURT

Working up. A 6 Squadron
Hurricane IId during the
unit's training period at
Shandur, 1942.

It had (as I recall) 20 rounds per gun contained in drums. They were armour piercing and designed to break up into fragments on emerging inside the tank, so as to achieve as much damage as possible to the tank's intestines and the crew. The guns were mounted parallel to the fore and aft axis of the aircraft, unlike a fighter which had the guns set to fire four degrees upwards to enable it to get under its prey from behind. The IID, which made its attack at very low level, could not therefore (in theory . . .) fly into the ground, whereas a fighter would, if the gunsight were kept on the target. The rounds could be fired in a burst but this so depressed the nose that in practice they were fired in single pairs, bringing the gunsight back on to target for each pair. It took not much more than half a second to get each pair away.

Training on the type was carried out at Shandur on a captured German tank located in an isolated piece of desert. The attack was started from something like 5,000 feet, putting the aircraft into a dive to achieve 254mph, which with full throttle could be maintained during the

run-in at about 20–40 feet above the ground. Opening with the first pair at about 1,000 yards, two more pairs could be got away accurately before breaking off the attack. It is no exaggeration to say that any good pilot would guarantee to hit his target with one or more pairs on each attack. The tank had little chance of retaliation. Many were equipped with one external machine gun fired from the open turret, but it took a brave man to fire at a Hurricane screaming in at 254mph with two machine guns blazing and a slow crack, crack, crack from its big guns. Normally they battened down and took their punishment. Later in the campaign they dug a slit trench at the side of the tank when stationary and mounted the machine gun vertically in the trench. As the Hurricanes came over, the gunner kept his finger on the trigger, sending a stream of bullets straight up into the air. This was not as dangerous as it might sound, as the aircraft would collect only one or two rounds, but a bullet in the glycol could bring the aircraft down, and once we knew about the trick we made a point of banking away just before the tank.

The two Flight commanders at that stage were Pip Hillier and Julian Walford. Pip Hillier had put up a score of about nine tanks hit and destroyed or put out of action during the retreat. The fitters used to paint a small tank silhouette alongside the cockpit for each tank claimed. Claims were largely unofficial, unlike those of fighter pilots, due to the difficulty of assessing the damage done to the tank or, indeed, how many pilots may have hit the same tank, but later it was fairly reliably assumed that the squadron had destroyed the equivalent of two panzer brigades, which was all there were in the desert, the 19th and 21st. Unfortunately, during a demonstration laid on for the benefit of senior army officers against our tame tank on September 6th, 1942, Pip Hillier banked away too steeply at the end of an attack, did a high speed stall and was killed. Julian Walford, doing searchlight co-operation with the army over Suez on the night of October 2nd, 1942, was blinded by the concentration of light and crashed into an Arab encampment in Sinai. I had done some searchlight co-operation the night before and realised the danger

Above: Splendid underview of a 'tank-killer', fitted with faired Vickers 'S' guns.

Above left: Tank-buster. Z2326, originally built as a Mk II, but converted to become the Mark IV prototype. Fitted here with twin, unfaired 40mm Vickers 'S' cannons.

Left: Can-openers. Close-up view of the sharp end of the twin Vickers 'S' 40mm cannons, so effective against German panzers in the desert war. An aircraft of 6 Squadron, taken possibly at Shandur, 1942

103

without screens fitted to the fuselage beside the cockpit. I was called up to the advanced landing ground and left Walford in charge of the base camp, and on departure I advised him not to undertake any more co-operation, but he ignored my advice.

I had joined the operational squadron, now on LG89, on July 22nd and had participated in a number of operations, but these were not very notable. One of the first principles of tank-busting was to catch the enemy tanks in the open, away from their second echelon, the backing-up vehicles and defensive anti-aircraft armament. They were then at our mercy, but this state of affairs did not occur often during the preparatory stage leading to the battle of El Alamein. We were forbidden to endanger the valuable aircraft by attacking targets other than tanks and it was wasteful of the heavy ammunition to use it against thin-skinned vehicles. The wisdom of this was brought home to me one day when returning from an abortive sortie, alone except for my No 2, I saw a lone lorry in open country with sandstone hills rising on either side. I came down and gave it a burst with the small guns but in return got a burst of machine gun fire from a gun ensconced in the hills to the right. There was no real damage to my aircraft, but one round hit the armour plating behind my back, and although it could not possibly have hurt me I developed an

induced pain at the spot where the bullet struck.

The battle of El Alamein was heralded at 11.00 hours on the night of October 23rd, 1942 by the largest artillery barrage the world had ever known. From our airfields we could see the whole western horizon lit by thousands of gun flashes. The following morning I was sent off with six Hurricane IIDs on a target of 15 tanks and two half-tracks. We found them, attacked and did considerable damage. I personally claimed three tanks definitely hit. Again, on the 28th, I led six IIDs against a reported target of 15 tanks but on arrival at the map reference could find no tanks. However, as we had come down to ground level for a possible attack, we did fire at anything in sight and my log book tells me that I claimed an ambulance set on fire and a lorry. On November 1st we went out looking for four reported tanks but were recalled in mid-air. On November 3rd we were let loose along with all the other squadrons to play as much havoc as possible with the now retreating German and Italian forces. Again, my logbook states that I claimed four mechanical transports hit (two flamers) and two tanks. I also recall one bus which spewed forth several dozen Italians which we gleefully and callously mowed down as they ran for their lives across the coverless desert. The German forces were by then in full retreat and the Italians, who chivalrously allowed the Germans to take their transport, were to a large extent happily captured. In early December, 6 Squadron was brought back to Edcu, east of Alexandria, and issued with a number of Hurricane IICs in addition to their IIDs and given an additional role of convoy patrolling.

On Christmas Day, following tradition, the officers moved down to the airmen's Mess to serve them their Christmas lunch. The air liaison officer, a major, picked up a number of young pilots in a Jeep, with which he proceeded to do tight turns on the sand airfield. Being naturally top-heavy, the Jeep turned over and the major was killed, while one of the pilots suffered a broken jaw. At about this time I inadvertently hit a tram standard in Alexandria one night with my staff car and suffered some slight concussion. The medical authorities would not let me fly again without a medical check at the general hospital at Heliopolis, outside Cairo, so on January 21st, 1943 I got into a Hurricane IID, flew to Heliopolis, got checked out and flew back 'fit for flying duties . . .' It was perhaps only possible to do this because I was now commanding officer of 6 Squadron, Roger Porteus having been posted to the Staff College in Palestine. I was not to see him again. Years later I was at an airfield in occupied Germany on a special mission. There was to be a dance that night and guests were arriving by air and road. We heard in the Mess that a DH Vampire had crashed on its approach, killing the pilot. Shortly afterwards the news came that it was Wing Commander Porteus.

On February 22nd, 1943 the squadron was moved westward to Bu Amud, equipped still with IIDs and IICs for convoy patrol duties. At that time the convoys through the Mediterranean were liable to be harassed by German U-boats and some ships were being sunk. Our task was to try to spot the U-boats from above, radio for assistance and in the meantime endeavour to distract the U-boat with some small bombs we carried. There was also the chance of Italian long range small bombers trying their luck, and an incident occurred on February 15th which might bear recounting. The early warning radar chaps in our area had detected blips in the early morning indicating that enemy aircraft were penetrating close to the coast, obviously on anti-shipping sweeps. They suggested that we put up two aircraft before dawn to hang around and wait for them. I took a No 2 with me and patrolled for four and a half hours in rather cloudy conditions until, about to give up, I came down to sea level and saw, also skimming the waves, two Savoia SM79s. We gave chase but they were a match for us in speed. We were flying IIDs and I called up my No 2 to try lobbing the big shells at them. We tried this for a bit with no obvious success and then, consulting my fuel gauges, I realised we had little enough fuel to get us home. I turned and headed for base gaining height slowly and in due course landed with one and half gallons in the tanks. The following day an enemy aircraft was reported in the water and I was told that I would be credited with the kill, but I never had any confirmation. The squadron was now instructed to move from Bu Amud to Castel Benito in Libya, and the move was made on March 3rd, 1943, the aircraft flying up in one day, leaving the ground crews to follow by road. On arrival there seemed to be some slight misunderstanding somewhere, and there was no space for us. However, we were quickly found an airfield called Sorman on the coast. We were now back in our proper role of tank buster and were being brought in to assist in the coming difficult battles envisaged in the vicinity of Gabes, where the mountains would assist Rommel in making a stand.

For some many weeks prior to this, General Le Clerc of the Free French had been leading a force of around 200 white and 2,000 native troops across the Sahara from the vicinity of Lake Chad. It was known as the Lake Chad Expedition. It was not all that formidable as a force, being armed mostly with small arms and machine guns, but nevertheless it was a creditable effort on the part of the Free French to assist in the campaign. On arrival south of the mountains near Gabes, General Le Clerc was asked to establish his camp there and to use his men to prepare a route which General Montgomery could utilise in one of his now-famous outflanking movements, skirting the mountains and returning to the coast to the west of Gabes and, with luck, bottling up a proportion of Rommel's army. The Germans discovered the presence of this French force south of their positions and despatched a strong armoured column of tanks, armoured cars and supply vehicles, possibly 50 in total, to round up the French and bring them in. However, the 8th Army, on the 'Y' Intercept, became aware of the German plan and called on the RAF to intervene. This was a job for 6 Squadron.

On March 10th we were called up to a small advanced LG known as Hasbub Satellite. We could muster 19 Hurricane IIDs and pilots. On arrival we landed and dispersed the aircraft in the open, and soon discovered that we were under shell-fire from some heavy guns located high in the mountains to the south-west. We huddled behind some sand dunes where we found a solitary RAF wireless operator and his equipment. After a while our group commander, Group Captain Atcherley flew in, joined us behind the sand dunes and brought us up to date on events. Apparently a SAAF reconnaissance squadron was sending out sorties to try to locate the German column, but had so far failed to do so. As the day drew on, with no new developments, I suggested to Group Captain Atcherley that, as I was an ex-Army co-operation pilot, I had as good a chance as the recce pilots of finding the German column. He agreed and sent out a call for two squadrons of Spitfires as cover to escort us. When these appeared in the sky, we took off, 13 of us for the first attack, leaving six in reserve. I headed south to the extent of the German lines, turned west and then north again behind the German lines.

At the position where the column was reported to be I looked down and, with considerable surprise, saw them almost immediately beneath us. We were not in a good position to attack. We liked to espy our target from some distance, dive and come in at very low level hoping to achieve some measure of surprise. As we had been seen I decided to go straight down into the attack, and in so doing received a large shell in my port wing. I did not know until then that in diving straight at a gun firing towards one, one could see the shells coming up. For some five minutes we flew to and fro across the column, dealing out savage destruction. Each time a tank went on fire there were shouts of exultation over the R/T. When I thought we must have knocked out every tank and vehicle, and having seen none of our aircraft go down, I thought I would not push our luck too far, and called the squadron together and headed for home. The fighter cover, unable to resist the temptation, carried on ground strafing the remnants, and the Group Captain, no doubt hearing it all over the R/T, des-patched the remaining six IIDs under my senior Flight commander, Flight Lieu-tenant Bluett, to give the *coup de grace*. On arrival at base, Sorman, I resisted the impulse to do a low victory roll to indicate to those on the ground the success of our mission. It was as well that I did, because after landing I found I had a nine inch hole in the ten inch main spar of my left wing . . .! We subsequently learned that General Le Clerc was able to witness the whole attack from his entrenched position, and a very relieved officer he must have been. He decided to give the *Croix de*

Guerre to the three squadron leaders of the first wave and Flight Lieutenant Bluett. The Germans sent out tank recovery vehicles and removed some of the tanks, but a ground reconnaissance proved that our claims of almost complete destruction of the column were no exaggeration.

By March 22nd the Allied forces were well advanced in their outflanking movement but had come up against resistance from the Germans, including the 21st Panzer brigade, and 6 Squadron was called upon. We found the tanks facing each other in fairly open country and attacked, making several passes to and fro. We inflicted considerable damage. I recall one pilot flying straight over his victim and receiving a hunk of tank in the underbelly of his aircraft. Having returned to base we were sent out again on the same target as soon as we had refuelled and rearmed. On March 24th we did a sortie but it could not have been of much import as my log book merely records, 'hit in Browning' and 'Sgt Harris killed near El Hamma'. Which leads me to digress

slightly regarding Sergeant Harris. He was a very young newcomer to the squadron and on his first operation he was hit by anti-aircraft fire and had to land wheels-up in the desert. This was not a particularly unusual occurrence, and when his turn came up he went on his second operation. Again he was hit, landed and returned safely to the squadron. This must have been enough to shake any man's morale and I realised he needed careful handling. I decided to let him do one more operational flight and, assuming he returned safely, to recommend he be stood down for a while. However this time he was shot down and killed. I felt he had well deserved a decoration, but on consulting King's Regulations I discovered that only the Victoria Cross and Mentioned in Despatches could be awarded posthumously. I duly recommended him for an MiD, which was in fact awarded.

The two armies were by now operating in very hilly and even wooded country and it was difficult to get good targets. On April 6th we were out looking for a reported

Briefing. Pilots of 6 Squadron being briefed by the unit commander, Squadron Leader R. Slade-Betts, DSO DFC **(far left)—a photo taken late in the war, but wholly representative of hundreds of similar occasions in the desert.**

assembly of tanks but in the wooded ravines they had excellent cover and we were subjected to considerable anti-aircraft fire from gun positions we could not see. My particular friend, Flying Officer Zillessen, did not return from this mission, and we assumed him dead. Many weeks later we had news that he was a prisoner of war in Italy. How he got his Hurricane down in one piece in that country I shall probably never know. On April 7th we did an armed reconnaissance which yielded nothing and then we were sent out on what was thought to be an excellent target of tanks in the sandy country near the coast. I had decided that it was about time I allowed my Flight commanders to lead the odd sortie, and had already let Flight Lieutenant Bluett lead one, whilst I led the second six aircraft. This time I instructed my other Flight commander to lead. I led the second six. He proceeded westwards several miles inland of the coast, searching to the north towards the Mediterranean. He saw some tanks and no doubt recognised them as American Shermans, but what he did not notice was that they were proceeding *eastwards* towards our lines. A short distance further on he sighted a conglomeration of vehicles, assumed they were German tanks facing the Shermans, and immediately dived to the attack. What in fact had happened was that the Germans had captured the Shermans from the Americans on the 2nd Army front and brought them down against the 8th Army. We were attacking the second echelon of this force (normally we never attacked tanks unless they were divorced from their second echelon). As we came in at low level the flak came to meet us. We crossed slightly in front of the second echelon of tanks so that the flak came from our port side. The leading aircraft flew straight through it. Being behind and hugging the ground, I realised there was no chance of getting through this murderous curtain of fire. There were tracers in the belts, so that it was possible to see the direction and concentration of the flak. It was impossible to get under it and suicidal to fly through it.

There was only one chance. I kept my Flight low on the deck until we were about to enter the worst of the flak. Then,

pulling back hard on the stick, I lifted the aircraft over it, hoping the others would follow suit. I then headed at full throttle out to sea. There was no sign of any of the rest of the squadron so I returned cautiously to land. I saw one of my aircraft, a ball of fire as a result of the fuselage tank having gone up, slowly fly into the ground and explode. I could find no others and returned to base. To add insult to injury, a British army gunner had a go at me as I flew over his position.

Only six of us came back by air. Three walked in later, but three had been killed, Flying Officers Walter and Clarke and Sergeant Hastings. This was our most tragic mission. Since El Alamein we had lost only six pilots killed and one captured, and three had gone on this one operation. Admittedly we had been incorrectly briefed. We were told to expect German Tiger tanks, but the real cause of the failure was inexperience on the part of the leader, and foolhardy courage in leading his squadron into a dangerous position. Shortly after this I was posted to a Kittyhawk Wing, with a view to taking it over, but that is another story. Apparently I was staying alive too long and holding up promotion in the squadron . . .

Left: Unusual view of the tank-busting Hurricane's armament. Jacked and (necessarily) braced, this aircraft was about to have its Vickers 'S' guns butt-tested.

Below left/below: At the receiving end—two views of a German tank which was devastated by the pin-point accuracy of a pair of Vickers 'S' cannons — just one of 6 Squadron's many victims.

109

Alamein by Night
GRAHAM LEGGETT

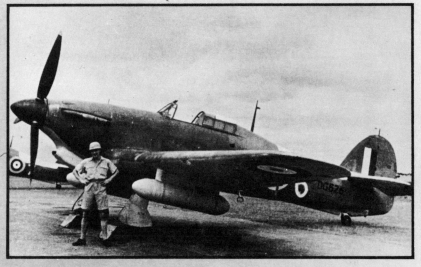

DG626, a Hurricane IId, marked '6' on fuselage, awaiting a delivery flight from Takoradi, late 1941 or early 1942. Standing by its nose is Sergeant L. Davies.

Supplies of aircraft to the DAF came (necessarily) by a long and tortuous route via West Africa for much of the time. One central 'depot' which received them from England, built and serviced, and then flew delivery flights clear across the African continent, was established at Takoradi. This equivalent of an RAF Maintenance Unit was (literally) hacked out of an equatorial jungle and soon became the major focal half-way stage for the DAF's re-equipment. In this view a line of Hurricanes is being fuelled (the hard way . . .) in preparation for a delivery shuttle flight. Second from left is BE715 which served with 250 Squadron in mid-1942.

Above: TAC-R. The value of tactical reconnaissance was first shown vividly during the early stages of the North African campaign. On-the-spot development of the photos brought back by roving Tac-R Hurricanes was necessary if results were to be of any help to local commanders. One 'instant' developing 'dark room' is seen here.

Right: The Desert Air Force (DAF) was composed literally of every Allied nationality to take part in the war. Such a conglomeration of languages, creeds and widely-differing backgrounds amalgamated astonishingly well in the desert 'team'. Here, two aircraft of 237 (Rhodesian) Squadron are taking-off, May 12th, 1942.

On October 27th, 1942, for the fifth night in succession, the western skyline was ablaze with the flashes of a thousand guns, their thunder trembling through the ground to set the cocoa mugs chattering on the table of 73 Squadron's pilots' Mess tent. Earlier that evening the pilots had flown their black-painted Hurricane IICs from their desert strip south-west of Alexandria to the advanced landing ground (ALG) at Burg-el-Arab (sometimes known as 'Bugger-the-wog' . . .). Then at dusk the first aircraft had taken off on a night-long programme of individual sorties where planning, stealth and precision meant the difference between success and disaster. All our pilots were experienced; mostly from day-fighter squadrons. Some had fought over Malta, others had hunted Germans in the night skies of Britain, a couple had been flying instructors. Now together they formed one of the most unusual Hurricane squadrons of the war—hitting the enemy behind his lines at night

and keeping the Luftwaffe away from ours. Many an Afrika Korps driver, feeling safe on a dark road miles from the fighting front, had been hit from apparently nowhere by the four 20mm cannons of these night prowlers. But on this night the essential task was to prevent the enemy aircraft from attacking the 8th Army, to which end the squadron was to maintain standing patrols over the battle zone. The turning point at the north end of our patrol lines was a tiny village, then unknown, called El Alamein.

Even under the light of a bright desert moon it required little navigational skill to find one's way to the patrol line. One simply took off, spiralled quickly up to a few thousand feet and then set off along the coast in the direction of the battle. It took only a few minutes to reach El Alamein and the whole incredible scene was set out like a huge illuminated map. To the east and reaching away southwards, the countless guns of the 8th Army kept up

Bottom left: Aussie Hurris. Line up of 451 Squadron RAAF, nearest machine being Z4036.

One of the more daring operations of the desert air war was the four-days 'detachment' of No 243 Wing (213 and 238 Squadrons), led by the legendary Wing Commander Johnny Darwen, DSO, DFC, November 13th to 16th, 1942. A total of 36 Hurricanes, supported by Lockheed Hudson transports, were established secretly on a bald landing area, some 140 miles *behind* the Axis front lines, titled Landing Ground (LG) 125. The object was to harass retreating Axis ground forces along the Libyan coastal strip, following the

successful battle of El Alamein. In four short days the Wing destroyed or knocked out of action over 300 vehicles (and their human contents), 15 aircraft on the ground and two more in the air—all for the loss of three Hurricanes missing in action, plus four more abandoned on return to 'friendly' territory. Seen here is a 213 Squadron Hurricane IIc, HL887, AK-W, with one of the Hudsons which 'lifted' supplies and personnel to and from LG125.

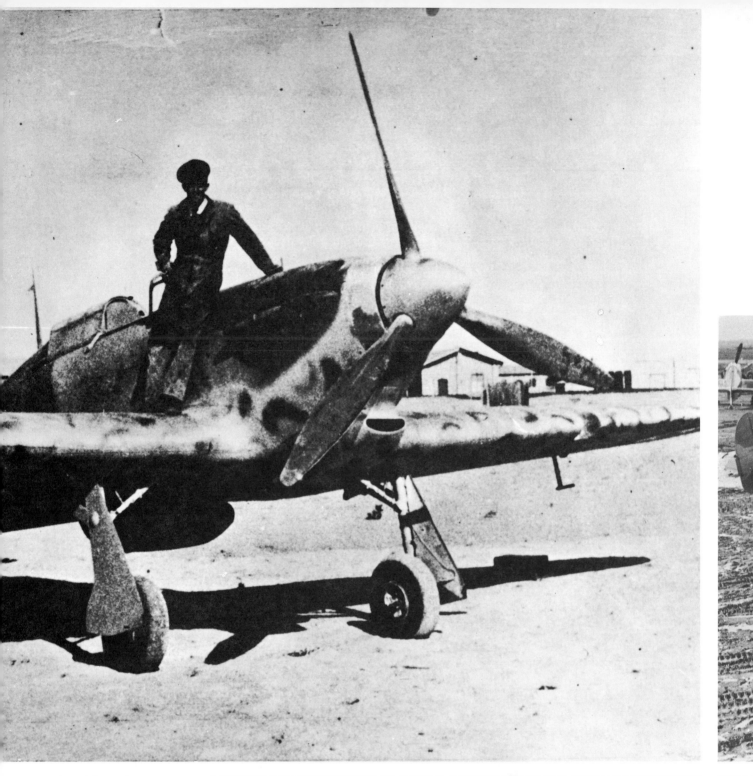

Right: Pick-up. Captain K. A. Quirk, SAAF, who on May 16th, 1941 landed behind the enemy lines to help a squadron comrade, Lieutenant Burger, who had been forced down. Sitting on Burger's knees, Quirk took off again and flew back to base (as illustrated here). Quirk was later awarded a DSO for this the first of many such 'two-some' rescues by fighter pilots throughout the desert campaign. *Babs*, painted on the cockpit panel, was Quirk's pet name for his wife.

their relentless barrage of fire, flash following flash so closely that the surrounding terrain stood out in sharp relief, betraying positions and emplacements. From the west came the replying fire of enemy guns, less numerous perhaps, but nonetheless insistent. And among the positions of both sides, which at places was impossible to divide, the sudden flash of bursting shells of every calibre, gleaming briefly through the dust clouds. Nor in the night did the enemy find relief from his hammering from the air for, like great smoky candles in the sky, parachute flares drifted slowly downwards upon his lines, adding more light to the scene and enabling our night bombers to pile even more discomfort upon the men beneath. Not that the enemy was taking it lying down—red and green tracers arched upwards and amongst the fluffy white clouds heavy AA shells flicker and puffed.

From the snugness of my cockpit, with the instruments glowing softly, a voiceless R/T hissing in the earphones and the contented roar of the Merlin drowning all other sound, it was difficult to imagine what was really happening down there on

Far left: Spaghetti Paint. A 3 Squadron RAAF Hurricane at Benina airfield in 1941, with unusual 'camouflage' markings applied to its nose and wing leading edges, fairly similar to the contemporary Italian camouflage paint schemes.

Left: The desert was not always 'burning sands'. 32 Squadron's Hurricanes, seen on Maison Blanche airstrip in early 1943, could vouch for the 'English weather' often encountered in North Africa.

Below left: No 94 Squadron, based at El Gamil in late 1942, was equipped with Hurricane IIc four 20mm cannon versions. Included were three of four presentation Hurricanes, paid for by Lady MacRobert in memory of her three sons—all killed whilst flying. All three aircraft are seen here. From front: BP389 (GO-C); BP387 (GO-J); HL851 (GO-P, *Sir Roderic*); HL735 (*Sir Iain*); HL844 (*Sir Alasdair*). The fourth MacRobert Hurricane was titled *MacRobert's Salute to Russia*; whilst earlier Lady MacRobert had 'presented' a Short Stirling bomber to the RAF—*MacRobert's Reply*. In this view the Hurricanes are fitted with two cannons only, in the interests of better performance.

Above: Off to the war. Z4769, '3' en route to the Middle East operational theatre from Takoradi, August 1941.

Top: Greek warrior. HW798, AK-P, of 213 Squadron, pictured at Paphos, Greece, in September 1943. Note the medium-range 'cigar' petrol tanks fitted externally under the wings.

Right: LF498, a Hurricane Mk IV of 6 Squadron, landing at Tatoi, Greece in late 1944. This aircraft destroyed a rail bridge at Spuz 'single-handed' with a rocket attack in November 1944, during the Balkan campaign.

the battlefield. On occasion men on the ground have spoken with admiration of those who fought their war in the air. What is seldom realised, however, is the sense of detachment with which most airmen went about their business. A target was simply a target, be it an iron-crossed aircraft, a ship at sea, a truck in the desert or a pinpoint on the ground. Rarely does an airman catch more than a glimpse of other humans manning such targets, and hardly ever does he witness the remains of his comrades or those he has destroyed. So it was with a sense of unreality that I watched history being made in this wilderness of rock and sand—so aptly described as a place only fit for war.

During that crucial night, enemy air activity seemed to be minimal. It was not until my tanks were emptying and my relief already on his way that the R/T provided news that a 'bandit' was about. Suddenly it was my war again. Hood open to improve visibility—check gunsights—increase revs—tighten straps—search the night sky. But then control called my

Above: Mixed load. A Hurricane with four 3 inch RP under one wing, and a medium-range fuel tank under the other, belonging to the Balkan Air Force, taxies out for take-off in Greece, watched by a gaggle of Spitfire pilots.

Left: West African Defender. A Hurricane of 128 Squadron, sporting a red/white/blue spinner, being serviced at Hastings, Sierra Leone—a unit formed specifically for defence of the Allied ports and bases in West Africa, and commanded initially by Squadron Leader Billy Drake, DSO DFC, a veteran of the desert air war in which he commanded 112 (Shark) Squadron.

relieving colleague and proceeded to vector him towards the 'bandit'. My orders —'Pancake'. Reluctantly easing back the throttle, I started to descend, peering along the coastline to identify a point at which to turn inland towards the airstrip. At that moment the cockpit exploded in a blinding sheet of white light! The speed with which the computer brain analyses

alarming rate. Then, as I turned for a second attack, the flare broke up and plunged earthwards, trailing sparks as it went. By then my colleague was chasing the German out to sea, but the night's adventure was not quite over for, still dazzled, seeing detail on the ground was most difficult. With tanks running dry I finally found the marker flares and then searched feverishly for the tiny glim lights of the flare path. Then, with remaining flying time reduced to bare minutes, and visions of a belly landing coming closer, a double red Very light soared upwards a few miles eastwards. God bless our vigilant OC Night Flying..! Within moments I had completed final actions and settled the wheels rather firmly on the sand. Taxying in, I was happy to find my night vision beginning to return. To the west the horizon continued to flicker into the night and I reflected on the spectacle I had just observed from a grand-stand seat. For myself, for a few hours at least, the war was less immediate, and on pulling back the flap of the intelligence officer's tent, I answered his questioning glance with my report—a 'flamer'.

Above: Big Lift. Using a Coles crane, an R & SU party swings the fuselage of BD930, from 73 Squadron, on to the trailer of a 'Queen—Mary'. The squadron insignia comprised a central yellow 'dart', bordered by two blue.

Right: Delta Convoy. Three battle-damaged Hurricanes aboard 'Queen Mary' transporters en route to a Maintenance Unit south of Cairo, near the Tura foothills. In background can be seen two of the well-known Gizeh Pyramids. Nearest Hurricane is Z4967, 'D' of 229 Squadron.

Top centre: The state of some salvaged aircraft was so bad that a new maintenance 'instruction' was jokingly introduced by the indefatigable ground crews—'Item 1. Sit fresh pilot in middle of dispersal and commence building aircraft around him . . .!' A typical scene was this view of a repair gang at work at Maison Blanche airfield, Algiers.

such moments is remarkable. In a split second it compares all known facts, examines technical data and proceeds to supply answers. Surely an AA shell? But at such close range, why no apparent damage to me or my machine? Then I realised I could see very little except for a very bright white light, reflected, as I then realised, in the rear-view mirror. Banking gently into a turn, I could focus upon it more easily—a parachute flare. It must have burst immediately over my cockpit, presumably having been dropped by the reported 'bandit'—who, in this light, must surely be visible. Holding the Hurricane in a series of 360 degree turns, I scoured the night sky. But with my night vision temporarily (I hoped . . .) impaired, I could see nothing except the glare of the flare—which, incidentally, our troops on the ground would not be feeling too happy about.

I soon discovered that ranging on a flare was not especially easy. It tends to hang motionless at a considerable distance, and then rush into the gunsight at an

Above: Repair and Salvage. A substantial contribution to the DAF's final superiority in the air over the desert war was made by the unpublicised R & SUs—the Repair and Salvage Units of the RAF. Living away from any 'base' airfield for weeks at a time, these parties of ground crew literally scoured the sands for crashed aircraft and brought them back for reclamation, repair and re-issue to the front-line units. A measure of their tremendous effort is the fact that in one four month period alone, they recovered just over 1,000 crashed aircraft, and were able to send some 800 of these back into battle. A typical 'scavenging crew' is seen here on its way to the Allied back areas with its latest 'collection' of salvageable Hurricanes, strapped on the trailers of their 'Queen Mary' lorries, and stopping for a traditional 100-mile brew-up. The mixture of parent units of the aircraft is evident from the various code letters.

Hurricane pilots who were employed in the day fighter role, and had the necessary night flying experience, were frequently called upon to undertake missions which were outside the normal span of daylight operations and which, later, were more appropriately allocated to the night, all-weather fighters equipped with sophisticated airborne radar and a second crew member employed as a radar operator. Thus, although never officially designated a night fighter pilot nor specifically trained as such, I was often called upon, in common with other 'suitably qualified' day fighter pilots, to fly Hurricane sorties either in darkness to augment the night fighter forces, or in the grey hours of dawn or dusk which could not readily be defined as belonging exclusively to day or night fighters. These missions varied widely in character but not in probability of success. Although few were prepared to admit it at the time, it is clear (in retrospect) that the odds against any tangible success were extremely high. Nevertheless, there is some evidence to suggest that the very presence of fighters, whether day or night, patrolling over likely targets or being directed on to

Vigil by night. A Hurricane stands ready for a night patrol. The pilot's flying helmet is 'hung' over the gunsight—a fitter carries out final cockpit checks.

Night Fighters

G. A. BROWN

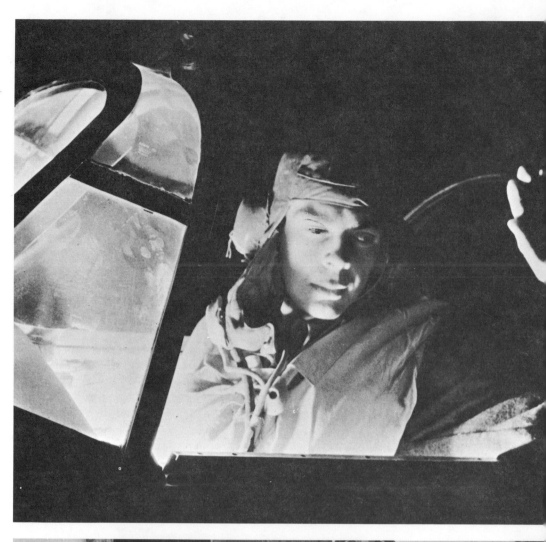

Right: Chocks Gone. A night fighter pilot gives a wave of the hand to acknowledge the ground crew's call and prepares to taxi. Cockpit lighting is on full here, but will be subdued within a few seconds.

Right: Night Stalkers. Pilots of 85 Squadron relax in the Readiness hut, prior to another night's work, their eyes protected by 'dimmer' glasses in order to assist their night vision. Second from right is the squadron commander, Squadron Leader Peter Townsend, DFC, with his pet Alsatian 'Kim'.

enemy aircraft, acted as a deterrent and possibly resulted in the otherwise un-explained jettisoning of lethal bomb loads on open ground or in the sea, or in raiders turning for home before reaching their targets and discharging their bombs.

My lasting impression of my own night fighter activities is one of utter impotence and frustration, arising from my abject failure ever to see anything of the enemy except perhaps, a fleeting glimpse of the shadowy form of an aircraft hurrying across my flight path, or flashing past in the opposite direction. In either event one was faced with the awful choice between, on the one hand, trying to guess the right course to steer to re-establish contact, followed by a long and probably futile chase; and on the other hand, ignoring the sighting and hoping for another contact giving a more favourable attacking posi-tion. The sad truth is that the accuracy of the ground control organisation, which proved reasonably adequate for daylight interception in conditions of average visibility, was not of a sufficiently high order in darkness or poor visibility to ensure that the single-seater fighter pilot, with no airborne radar and only one pair of eyes at his disposal, would be brought into visual contact with his quarry or, if he was, that he would be in a viable position to lainch an attack. In average visibility

by day the pilot's position in relation to the target when he made visual contact was not nearly so critical as it was in poor visibility or darkness. Generally speaking, if he had superiority in height and/or speed and was not put on a head-on collision course with the target, the day fighter pilot would be quite happy and capable of manoeuvring himself into the most advantageous attacking position. Visual contact in the shortest possible time was the main ingredient of a good daylight fighter interception. Assuming the normal speed superiority of the fighter over a bomber, relative course was of secondary importance. By these criteria, ground controllers could claim a fair measure of success in daylight operations. But there is at least a suspicion that they used the same criteria by night whereas, of course, speed of interception and visual contact were meaningless aims unless the fighter was in a position to launch his attack without losing that all-important visual contact.

There is also reason to believe that the controllers, accustomed to day fighter pilots reporting sightings of aircraft at great distances in daylight, over-estimated the visual acuity of a pilot's eye in darkness. It was possible for a pilot to improve his visual efficiency at night insofar as he could train himself to search the sky

The pause before opening up to full power for take-off. Wing tip lights on, the pilot's cockpit thrown into sharp relief by a background searchlight along the runway, a night owl is about to make its run.

Airborne. A Hurricane IIc, PZ869 starts its climb towards its patrol area.

systematically and thus improve his chances of acquiring a target. There were those who, like John Cunningham (known as 'Cat's Eyes'), had perfected their night visual capability to a high degree and achieved remarkable success in night fighter operations, even managing to bring off the occasional freelance interception. But I am still convinced that these successes owed more to an uncanny instinct or sixth sense than to any extraordinary physical attribute, and the claim by journalists and others that a diet of carrots or special vitamins was beneficial to night vision was entirely fanciful. In summary, until the advent of GCI (Ground Control Interception) radar and airborne radar, fighter control, relying as it did on early warning radar and Royal Observer Corps reporting, was just not accurate enough in darkness or poor visibility to give a pilot more than an outside chance of successful interception and attack.

Perhaps in recognition of the limitations of close control from the ground, we Hurricane pilots were only rarely scrambled at night to intercept or investigate specific targets. Even so, these sorties proved all too often to be completely

124

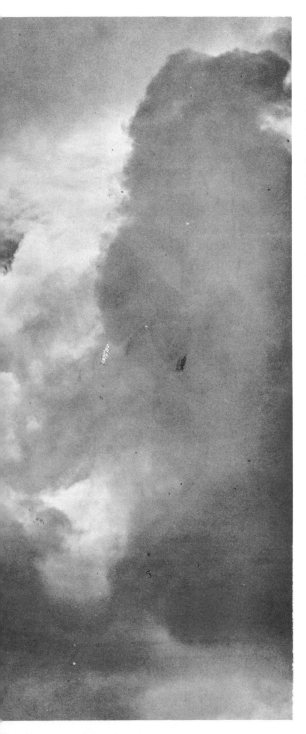

abortive, with the plots themselves sometimes fading mysteriously whilst we were ostensibly in full pursuit of a quarry. On one such notable occasion, after using most of my fuel chasing an alleged hostile plot, I was informed apologetically by ground control that the source of the plot reported by the ROC had in fact been identified as an army lorry manoeuvring in the area! Thereafter, whenever we were scrambled on what we suspected to be a false errand, the catch-phrase 'Sorry, lorry' was yelled in chorus by all in the crew room . . .

More usually, we were employed in a freelance role on standing area or line patrols covering vulnerable targets such as major towns and cities, bomber bases or other military installations and, occasionally, sea convoys. On this type of mission we were under a very loose form of control from the ground, receiving only snippets of information from time to time about hostile movements in our area. Otherwise, we were left very much to our own devices, initiative, instinct and, perhaps most of all, to the whims of pure chance. There were several variations of the standing patrol, some involving integration between day fighters and AA guns, or night fighters, or both. I recall one such night operation in particular which was mounted during a fairly heavy bomber raid over Sheffield. On this occasion Defiants and Hurricanes were 'stepped' upwards at 500 feet intervals from 12,000 feet, below which the AA guns were given freedom of action, I was allocated a height band of 18,000 feet with the Defiants patrolling below. An esti-

Suez Defence. Soot-black Hurricanes of 213 Squadron revving in unison during 1941, when the unit was charged with the defence of the Suez Canal area in Egypt. Based (ostensibly) at Nicosia, Cyprus, the unit was split into several detached Flights along the Canal area and in Cyprus— the Flight pictured here being (it is believed) at Ismailia, Egypt.

mated 20-plus bombers were reported over Sheffield at the time and the effects of their attack were clearly visible and most spectacular. There were many fires caused by incendiary and high explosive bombs providing a brilliant back-cloth against which aircraft were occasionally silhouetted Yet, even in these seemingly ideal conditions contact was so fleeting that positive identification was virtually impossible and pursuit futile. The strange thing was that, with three fighter squadrons operating over Sheffield that night in better than normal visibility because of the ground conflagrations, not one successful engagement was reported. Perhaps there is some consolation in the fact that, with collision more than a remote possibility, all our fighter aircraft reported safely to base, but our inability to provide Sheffield with any respite from the bombing, or restitution against the bombers was extremely frustrating and saddening.

On another occasion I was scrambled on a dark night with Squadron Leader (later, Air Marshal Sir) David Atcherley to patrol Hull, which was being subjected to sporadic attacks by German bombers. Again, we were given freedom of action above 12,000 feet with the AA guns operating below that height. There was comprehensive searchlight cover in the area and we were hoping for some successful co-operation with them. We were able to observe fairly frequent bomb bursts on the ground and heavy AA response, but in

spite of intense searchlight activity, we never saw a single German bomber illuminated by them. Eventually David Atcherley asked for authority to reduce height so that we could operate where we judged the German bombers to be flying, approximately at 8,000 feet. This authority was given after the guns were silenced, but immediately we descended to this new height we were picked up by the searchlights and relentlessly held by them, although we repeatedly asked our controller to order them to be doused. The glare from the multiple criss-cross of searchlight beams reduced our visibility outside the cockpit to nil and made instrument reading inside the cockpit virtually impossible because of reflection. At last, in desperation, David Atcherley pulled out his trump card. He told the fighter controller that unless every searchlight in the area was immediately doused, he would bail out, and added that although it was impossible accurately to pinpoint his position, he believed he was over the centre of Hull. Needless to say, within five seconds every searchlight within sight was extinguished, leaving an inky blackness which by contrast was even more impenetrable than the glare of the searchlights. With friendly guidance from our controller, however, we returned safely to base after yet another abortive and frustrating night fighter defence sortie.

These accounts, illustrating the limitations of the Hurricane in the night fighter

Touch-down. Squadron Leader Ian Gleed, DFC, OC 87 Squadron, landing his personal Hurricane, P2798, LK-A, at Colerne on February 6th, 1941. Painted overall black, except for his personal nose marking (in pale blue) and rudder striping.

role, do not imply any general criticism of the aeroplane which endeared itself to most fighter pilots as a robust, efficient and viceless fighter, although somewhat lacking in performance as compared with its contemporaries. I flew both Spitfires and Typhoons as well as Hurricanes on fighter defence missions at night, and although the Hurricane, and to a greater extent the Typhoon, were probably potentially better night fighters than the Spitfire (which I preferred as a day fighter), none was really up to the task with the ground environment and airborne equipment then at our disposal. One of the serious limitations of the Hurricane at night was brought home to me when, as a Flight commander, I was scrambled from Martlesham Heath with two pilots from my Flight to combat a German bomber raid over Ipswich. My instructions were to patrol over the town at about 12,000 feet and, again, on this occasion there was searchlight and AA activity but I was unable to detect any bomb bursts. Needless to say, I saw no other aircraft, friend or foe, and after about an hour I was recalled with perhaps enough fuel for an emergency diversion if necessary. On arrival over base I was told that there was a hostile aircraft lurking in the vicinity and was ordered to provide cover whilst the other two Hurricanes were landed. I was given a couple of tentative courses to steer in the hope that I might pick up the 'bandit' but saw nothing and was then ordered to land, with (by that time) just sufficient fuel for a circuit and perhaps one

Above: Night Intruder. Squadron Leader J. A. F. MacLachlan DSO, DFC, commander of No 1 Squadron RAF during the period it was engaged in night intrusion operations over Occupied Europe. A veteran of Malta and the desert war, 'Mac' had his left arm amputated after being shot down over Malta, but flew with an artificial arm instead. His war total was 17 victories before his death in July 1943.

Above left: *Night Fighter*—a drawing by Eric Kennington, which portrays one of the greatest Hurricane night 'aces', Squadron Leader Richard Playne Stevens, DSO, DFC. He claimed a total of 14 victories by night with 151 Squadron, without the benefit of radar, but was lost in action eventually on December 15th, 1941, whilst serving with 253 Squadron.

overshoot. Almost inevitably (it seemed) as I was making my circuit the airfield controller announced that he had received instructions to extinguish all airfield lighting because of the close proximity of an unidentified aircraft. Thereupon the airfield was plunged into darkness but I had no alternative but to complete my circuit and land as best I could without any form of lighting. Fortunately, I was not restricted to a runway, my circuit pattern was well established by then and I was able to distinguish sufficient features in the final approach to judge my touch-down point. Nevertheless, I was a little apprehensive about the final landing and the

aircraft appeared to spend an unduly long time in a stalled condition before finally reaching the ground with a resounding thud, though with no apparent ill-effects. This episode, although otherwise unproductive, brought home to me the Hurricane's general unsuitability and lack of flexibility in particular in the night fighter role. An aeroplane which could not spend an hour on patrol, including a period of full throttle combat, and still be capable of a diversion hardly deserved serious consideration as a night fighter.

This is certainly not to say that the Hurricane was never used to good effect at night during the war. Indeed, there was

Black Beast. BE500, the personal Hurricane IIc of Squadron Leader Denis Smallwood, commander of 87 Squadron from November 1941 to September 1942. His rank pennant is displayed just below the windscreen.

a small and elite band of extremely skilled and adventurous Hurricane pilots who achieved remarkable success in night intruder operations, attacking and destroying enemy aircraft within their own airfield circuit. These extraordinary and highly individualistic exploits however did nothing to vindicate the Hurricane in the night fighter defence role. Rather did they emphasise the validity of that most fundamental of all military doctrines which asserts that attack is the best form of defence. They also demonstrated how the Hurricane could more profitably have been used to counter Hitler's night offensive against Britain. Where better, in

other words, to seek out and attack the enemy raider than over his own base, particularly at night when everything favours the intruder?

Nor is the Hurricane's indifferent record in the night interceptor role any reflection on the calibre and training of the pilots, many of whom went on to make highly successful night fighter pilots when flying suitably equipped multi-seat aeroplanes. In the days of intensive training prior to and after the outbreak of war, night flying was practised regularly and assiduously by all day fighter pilots for, apart from the Blenheim Is which were just assuming the role and, later, Defiants there were no specialised night fighter aircraft. It was in fact generally understood that the single-seat fighters would have to bear the brunt of night fighter defence. One of the most important training exercises then was night formation flying and the more experienced of us also tried simple aerobatic manoeuvres in formation, tail chases and dogfights. Needless to say, all such manoeuvres were carried out with navigation lights burning, but it gave one great confidence in handling the aircraft at night and helped enormously in judging distances, approach speeds, ranging and sighting of guns. Without the benefit of navigation/identification lights, visual acquistion, judgement of closing speeds, sighting and ranging became operations of exceptional skill which few mastered, and only then after much experience and practice. It was also quite hazardous and recognition of the fact is implicit in the popular belief at that time that premature baldness amongst fighter pilots was due to one or other of two nocturnal activities— the more likely being dogfighting at night without navigation lights!

It is a melancholy and, to many, a perplexing thought that the Hurricane which proved such an excellent all-purpose day fighter, and whose effectiveness as a bomber destroyer, especially, had been proved beyond doubt, should have made so little impact on the Luftwaffe's night offensive against Britain. Had the sophisticated ground environment and pilot-operated airborne radar equipment subsequently developed been available then, perhaps quite a different story could have been told.

Over the Chindwin.
BP704 of 28 Squadron
patrolling along the
Chindwin River in
Northern Burma, 1943.

Burma Bomber. A
Hurricane IIc (unit
unidentified) on the Arakan
front receiving its ration of
500lb GP bombs, and re-
arming of its four 20mm
cannons.

Jungle Fighters
E. D. C. LEWIS

The chronicles of the Hurricane in the Far East theatre of operations deserve a book unto themselves. From the debacle of Singapore in early 1942 until the final defeat of Japan in August 1945, Hurricanes played a leading and vital part in the 'Forgotten War'. Due to vacillation and jingoistic complacency on the part of the contemporary British government and military high command, when the Japanese finally invaded Singapore—that 'impregnable British fortress' as Winston Churchill so naively termed it—a mere handful of Hurricanes (51, mostly crated, and without sufficient trained pilots) were available to spearhead the outmoded RAF fighters stationed there. During the desperate and bitter fighting retreat through Java, Sumatra and Burma to India,

driblets of Hurricanes were thrown into the struggle, and lost unnecessarily because of sheer weakness in overall air strength.

The long trail back from the Indian border to final victory owed a not inconsiderable debt to the Hurricanes and their determined crews. By June 1943 a total of 23 squadrons were equipped with Hurricanes, almost exclusively Mark IIs, although a few Mark IVs had just arrived in Ceylon—a total of nearly 700 Hurricanes for the imminent land offensive by the Allies. By the following year a further 14 squadrons were operating Hurricanes (including the Indian Air Force). And it is probably not too much to suggest that the bulk of close support and tactical reconnaissance for the advancing 14th Army during the years 1943–45 was carried out by the ubiquitous Hurricane units. The aircraft's rugged construction, superb stability and extreme versatility proved nearly ideal in the almost primitive fighting conditions of the jungle war.

In the offensive role Hurricane IIBs and IICs, bearing clutches of high explosive bombs and rockets to supplement their gun and cannon armament, proved to be deadly effective close support to the jungle-bound infantry. As will be seen in the account following, the critical Allied stand at Imphal—which, with the legendary siege at Kohima, was to be the key turning point of the campaign in Burma—owed a large part of its success to air

support, provided as ever by the sturdy Hurricanes. By late 1944 most Hurricanes in Burma were being replaced by the seven-ton Thunderbolt fighters, yet on VJ-Day (August 15th, 1945) three RAF squadrons (17, 20 and 28), plus eight Indian Air Force squadrons—all battle-hardened veterans of the Far East war—were still flying Hurricanes. Thus from September 3rd, 1939 until the last day of the global war, Hurricanes served in a first-line operational capacity.

The account which follows was originally written by Flight Lieutenant E. D. C. Lewis in 1945, and describes his opinion of the work of the Hurricanes during the Imphal siege of March–April 1944. Imphal reputedly the original home of polo, stands centrally in a wide plain and athwart the main route from Burma to India. Its

Left: Beat-Up. A trio of Hurricanes of 258 Squadron beating up the remainder of the unit's aircraft, probably when the unit was based in Ceylon, 1942. Nearest two Hurricanes are BN125 and HV774 (S).

Below: Canadian pilots of 30 Squadron at Ratmanala, Ceylon, in August 1942. From left: Sgt C. I. Nuttbrown, Plt Off D. A. McDonald, Sgt Jack Hurley, Plt Off Jimmy Whalen (killed in action April 18th, 1944), Sgts Grant Bishop, G. Murray and G. G. Bate. The aircraft is Hurricane BG827, (RS-W), named *Bitsa*, the personal aircraft of Jimmy Whalen at the time.

Above left: Fine aerial view of a Hurricane IIc (minus its cannons) in Bengal skies. Judging by the markings, and lack of armament, this was probably a training machine.

Right: Fighter Leader. Wing Commander Frank Carey, of whom an official historian wrote: "He was the back-room boy of the Burma victory in air supremacy, the man whose refresher courses in gunnery and tactics at his school (the Air Fighting Training Unit, Calcutta) produced some of the most ingenious fighter pilots of the war. In Burma it was said that a remarkable proportion of enemy fighters brought down were destroyed by pilots listening to the echo of Carey's voice and obeying his teaching.' Carey's final war tally of victories has never been fully confirmed, a minimum figure of 28 being usually quoted, though reliable evidence suggests this figure is far below his real tally.

heroic defence was partly responsible for nullifying the Japanese intended invasion of India.

During the siege targets were almost in Imphal itself and many were north of the Manipur capital, indicative of the seriousness of the threat from that direction. With the clearing of the Japs from that area, the Battle of the Tiddim Road got under way. The progress of the army could be followed by noting the movement of line from milestone to milestone as one after another the enemy pockets of resistance were obliterated. Then the 40-hairpin bend—the 'Chocolate Staircase'—was dealt with, followed by Tiddim, the much-bombed Vital Corner, Kennedy Peak No 3 Stockade, Fort White, the Hurribombers cleared the way for the army. Brief one-line sentences announce nonchalantly, 'All bombs in target area. Fires started. Fires spreading. Explosions seen.'

Bridges, transports, troops, foxholes,

Left: Close Escort. A Hurricane IIc tucks in close to its bomber 'charge' during a raid among the Burmese hills.

Bottom right: Indian fighter. Hurricanes of the Indian Air Force (the prefix 'Royal' was not conferred until March 1945), fitted with long-range fuel tanks—the virtual backbone of Tac-R missions in Burma. Built up solely as a tactical air force, the IAF seldom received any of the more 'glamorous' aspects of the Burma air war; yet the total of merely nine squadrons (all types of duty) flew over 16,000 operational sorties and 44 members were decorated for superlative gallantry and services. At least 50 IAF pilots were lost in action over Burma alone, apart from other casualties.

135

Top right: Recce. A reconnaissance patrol Hurricane crosses the Irrawaddy River, alongside the Aya Bridge, in Mandalay, whilst 'scouting' for the 14th Army.

Right: Calcutta Guard—YB-L of 17 Squadron lifts off Red Road, Calcutta—an unorthodox, if practical runway.

Far right: Another mission Starts. Flying Officer J. H. Slimon, RCAF, takes off on the Arakan front, July 7th, 1943. Only two of the usual four cannons are fitted—a slight boost to performance and handling qualities.

supply dumps were destroyed, and hundreds killed in the monsoon months that the enemy had calculated on as a rest and rehabilitation period. From the beginning of March and on through the monsoon, the Hurricanes had only missed hitting the enemy on a small number of days. In that vital period, nearly $5\frac{1}{2}$ million pounds of bombs were delivered with pinpoint accuracy in the course of 12,252 sorties. The greatest effort of any month came in April, when the enemy regarded Imphal as a halting place on the road to Delhi. Over 1 million pounds of bombs raised the first doubt as to whether their destination would be reached. The army displayed an enthusiasm for Hurri-bombers as of no other combat aircraft in the India–Burma theatre. From the despatches of commanding generals to the private mail of the men fighting in the jungle, have come messages of praise for Hurri-bomber attacks pressed home at the appropriate moment. It is the proud boast of the pilots that they have never failed to give prompt aid when called upon by their comrades fighting on the ground. Indeed, one of the squadrons, which stayed in the valley through the siege, is proud of the number of 'strawberries' it has received from the army and other sources arising out of its most successful partnership. Today the army has come to look upon the Hurri-bombers as an extremely adaptable artillery arm hitting the enemy at long range or within a few yards of the British front line, whichever hurt him most. The vast majority of bombs dropped have been 250 pounders, but that eggs of double the weight could be carried over the treacherous mountain terrain and through some of the most dangerous air currents in the world was established in July, when a small force hit the 420ft long Yanan bridge near Tamu,

an extremely vulnerable link in Jap communications, and blew out three spans.

Indian Air Force, RAF and men of the Empire air forces have piloted these formidable weapons, and, in the days when the Japanese were ringed around Imphal, were often bombing targets within five miles of their strip. Machines were serviced, re-armed and refuelled within range of enemy mortar and shell fire, and marauding parties of Japs penetrated frequently to within a few yards of the airstrip. On one occasion a patrol was surprised less than 100 yards from the pilots' sleeping quarters. Ground crews, for the first time, could watch the effect of the bombs they had risked their lives to load—in fact, the Sunday lunch-hour calm of an RAF Group HQ was once disturbed during the siege with terrific explosions from the nearby hills. It was a Hurri-bomber squadron blasting hideouts overlooking the headquarters of the airstrip, and the diners had a grandstand view. Hurri-bomber pilots rated monsoon weather a more formidable enemy than the Japanese as they flew in and out of mountain gorges half obliterated with thick cloud to burn out some particularly troublesome strongpoint, but they were proud of the way their aircraft had stood up to the buffeting and they would readily recount how on one occasion the monsoon outsmarted them. Crews were briefed to destroy the Hpaunzeik bridge west of Kalewa. They flew to the scene and found the bridge had gone—the monsoon had got there first and destroyed it for them!

Far left: 40-Hour Inspection. Leading Aircraftmen Ivor Lillington, H. Wollett, W. 'Dusty' Miller and R. Francis overhauling a Hurricane IIc in March 1945. As in every other theatre of air operations the ground crews were a vital section of the 'team'.

Left: Overshoot. BG802, thought to be from 28 Squadron, decides to park in its own fashion, Cox's Bazaar.

Below: A mixture of uniforms and Services, in this case, 28 Squadron, typifying the supreme teamwork of all three allied Services which made final victory in Burma possible.

Men and Markings

Squadron Leader Billy Drake, DSO, DFC, with the Hurricane he flew as commander of 128 Squadron at Hastings, Sierra Leone, West Africa, winter 1941–42. The spinner was hooped in red, white and blue.

Above: Canadian John Kent, pictured when a Flight commander of the Polish 303 Squadron at Northolt, 1940. High on the Hurricane's fuselage is the 'Kosciuszko' badge carried on all 303's aircraft. Kent finished the war with a credited total of 21 victories, and eventually retired from the RAF as a Group Captain, DFC, AFC.

Top centre: The Joker. Ornate insignia of Squadron Leader John W. C. Simpson, DFC when he commanded 245 Squadron at Aldergrove, Northern Ireland, late 1940. An ex-43 Squadron pilot, Simpson was the subject of the book, *Combat Report* by Hector Bolitho.

Right: Lucky Tuck. Squadron Leader R. R. S. Tuck, DSO, DFC, when commander of 257 Squadron at North Weald, November 1940, strapped into the cockpit of Hurricane V6864, DT-A. The Burmese 'flag', a standard blue ensign, was in honour of the fact that 257 had been 'adopted' by the Burmese government (pre-Burmese independence). Tuck finished the war with a credited total of 29 victories in the air.

Right: Irish Tally. Squadron Leader J. I. Kilmartin, DFC, who fought in 1 Squadron during the 1940 French campaign, and with 43 Squadron in the latter stages of the Battle of Britain. In the spring of 1942 he succeeded Billy Drake in command of 128 Squadron in West Africa, and by 1944 was Wing Commander of a 2nd TAF Typhoon Wing. His final tally was at least 15 victories.

Bottom centre: Under Two Flags. D. L. du Vivier, a Belgian, who fought through the battles of France, Britain, North Africa, Tunisia and Italy, and survived the war. Seen here as commander of 43 Squadron (the 'Fighting Cocks') in early 1942, with a panel showing the RAF and Belgian flags and 43 Squadron's black/white dicing marking.

Below: Line-Shoot. Sergeant G. D. Robertson of 402 Squadron RCAF proudly displays his 'duck-breaker' (first victory symbol) at Rochford, September 22nd, 1941.

Left: Belgian Thistle. Captain Gerard, a former World War I pilot, standing by a Hurricane of the 2nd Escadrille, BAF, March 1940. This unit badge was a continuation of the insignia carried by the unit during the 1914–18 war.

Right: Dumbo—a Hurricane IIb's insignia on the Arakan front in Burma, July 21st, 1943. The pilots (all Canadians) are Plt Off N. M. Scott, Flt Sgt W. Thompson (who flew this aircraft) and Plt Off Lloyd Miller.

Bottom right: Flying Officer Roy Dutton poses in front of two of 111 Squadron's Hurricane Is, 1939. The unit's coding, JU, can be seen on L1730 in background. The equal-division black/white undersurfaces show to advantage.

Bottom centre: Butch the Falcon—the unit insignia of 402 Squadron RCAF at Warmwell, February 9th, 1942. Aircraft is a Hurricane IIb, AE-Q, and the NCOs Corporals Graham and T. Ryland.

Bottom left: Burma Squadron. Squadron Leader Francis J. Soper, DFM, in command of 257 (Burma) Squadron in the autumn of 1941, and a Hurricane displaying the Chinthe (Burmese effigy) which figured in the official squadron badge. With a credited total of 15 victories, Soper failed to return from a sortie on October 5th, 1941.

Above: *To the Memory of . . .* Hurricane IIc, HL844 of 94 Squadron, El Gamil, Egypt, 1942, with its dedication to Sir Alasdair MacRobert who was killed in a flying accident at the Redhill Flying Club on June 1st, 1938. Two brothers, Sir Iain and Sir Roderic, were also killed whilst flying—all three being commemorated by similar inscriptions on Hurricanes of 94 Squadron (with which unit Sir Roderic had served as a Flight Lieutenant in early 1941).

Right: *Dodie*—the girl-friend of Sergeant J. R. Scott of 402 Squadron, RCAF is suitably honoured. Warmwell, February 1942.

Below: *Our John*—another Hurricane bearing a dedication to a lost son. Hurricane IIb, BN795 of 174 Squadron, with its pilot, Flt Lt J. R. Sterne, DFC at Odiham, January 1st, 1943. This was one of three Hurricanes similarly inscribed, 'presented' to the RAF by Mrs Gillan, the mother of Wing Commander John Gillan, DFC, AFC, the one-time commander of the first Hurricane unit, 111 Squadron, who was killed in action, flying Spitfire V, W3715, on August 29th, 1941.

Above: Squadron Leader G. A. Butler, DFC, who commanded 11 Squadron in Burma during the last six months of the war. The Norwegian insignia on the nose of this Hurricane is presumably a reference to the aircraft's individual 'owner'. Believed taken at Sinthe airstrip.

Left: Whatever the 'book' said, there were times when simple muscle power was more convenient. LACs R. Finney and W. Jones roll a 250lb GP bomb to *Hellzapoppin*, a Hurricane IIc, in Burma 1945.

Top centre: *The Isobelle A*—motif of Pilot Officer J. Muff's Hurricane with 28 Squadron, Burma. The pilot's Canadian origins are exemplified by the added maple leaf marking.

Above: Veterans. Hurricane pilots of 80 Squadron at Eleusis, Greece, early 1941, where they were part of the pitifully few RAF fighters who fought an outstanding air campaign against vastly superior numerical odds. From left: Plt Off 'Keg' Dowding; Plt Off 'Ginger' Still; Sgt C. E. 'Cas' Casbolt (eventually commissioned, awarded a DFM and credited with at least 13 victories); Warrant Officer M. 'Mick' Richens; Sgt E. W. F. 'Ted' Hewitt, DFM (who ended the war as a Squadron Leader with 21 victories); and Fg Off 'Twinstead' Flower.

Left: Bulldog Breed. The ferocious figure carried by a Hurricane of the RCAF, 135 Squadron, at Patricia Bay, British Columbia on January 6th, 1943.

Right: 73 Squadron pilots in France, May 1940. From left; Sgt Pilkington; Fg Off H. G. 'Ginger' Paul (15 victories); Fg Off O. 'Fanny' Orton, DFC (25 victories, killed in action September 17th, 1941); and Fg Off E. J. 'Cobber' Kain, DFC (17 victories, killed in flying accident June 1940).

Above right: Deadly Duck. An aggressive Walt Disney Donald Duck which adorned the Hurricane IIc flown by Sergeant Jack Pollock of 30 Squadron, Ceylon, July 11th, 1943.

Left: Fighting Cocks. Pilots of 43 Squadron's A Flight at Wick, 1940. From left: Sgt Buck; Fg Off C. A. Woods-Scawen, DFC (killed in action September 3rd, 1940); Flt Lt Caesar Hull, DFC (killed in action September 8th, 1940); Fg Off Wilkinson and Sgt G. W. Garton (who ended the war as a Wing Commander, DSO, DFC).

Left: False Colours. V7670 in German markings, which was recaptured on Gambut airfield, North Africa, in January 1942. Personnel here are (from left) Flt Lt Whittard, McKenny Paul Rylands.

Bottom left: False Colours. JS327, a Canadian Sea Hurricane of 808 Squadron, FAA from HMS Chaser, which force-landed at St Leu, Algeria on November 8th, 1952, just after the initial Operation 'Torch' Allied landings there.

Right: An Ace meets his King. Flight Lieutenant Geoffrey Allard, DFC, DFM, receives his DFC award from the hands of King George VI, at a hangar investiture, early 1941.

Below: Silver Warrior. AG244, an ex-Desert Air Force Hurri-bomber which was relegated to training duties with the Central Flying School, Norton, (No 33 FIS), Southern Rhodesia, in 1945. Finished all-silver (reminiscent of the Hurricane prototype), the rear fuselage band was in red, edged with blue. Its ignominious end came in 1948 when, with about 50 DH Tiger Moths and Airspeed Oxford trainers, it became one section of a huge bonfire. . . .

In Many Forms

Cannon Sextet. Immaculate
echelon of 3 Squadron's
Hurricane IIcs in 1941.
Identifies include: Z3069 (F);
Z3092 (T); Z3094 (R);
BD869 (P); Z3464 (Z); and
BD867 (Y).

Above: Advanced Trainer. P3039, a Hurricane I belonging to Squadron Leader (later, Group Captain) W. D. David, DFC, whilst instructing at No 55 Operational Training Unit in 1942. Just below the engine exhaust stubs can be faintly seen the name *Joan*.

Top: Canadian Trio. Hurricane XIIs of No 1 OTU, RCAF at Bagotville, PQ, on July 31st, 1943. Nearest aircraft, 'L', is serialled 5470. Note the mini-spinners common to the majority of Canadian built Hurricanes.

Top right: Sea Boots. Early Sea Hurricane Ibs aboard a Fleet carrier.

Right: Sea Hurricane with problems. One of HMS *Argus*'s brood which suffered a port wheel blow-out on landing, skidded towards the 'drink', but was saved from a dunking by the out-rigged safety nets.

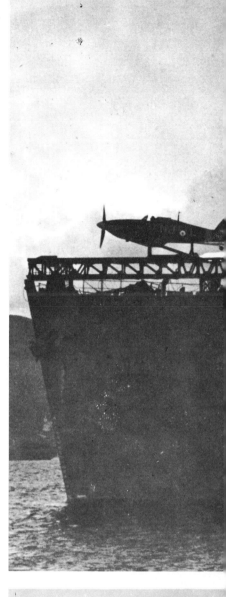

Top left: Tandem for two. The Hurricane IIc (ex-KZ232) two-seat conversion supplied to the Persian Government in 1947. First flown at Langley, on September 27th, 1946, the trainer is seen here with its original rear cockpit configuration, before the hood was modified for more comfort. Bearing the Persian serial ('2-31'), it was delivered to Doshan Teppeh FTS initially.

Centre left: Ski Boots. Hurricane XII, 5624 of the RCAF, seen at Rockcliffe, Ontario on January 1st, 1943.

Left: Catafighter. V6756, NJ-L, a Hurricane I of the Merchant Ship Fighter Unit, being blasted away from the CAM ship, *Empire Tide*.

Bottom left: Naval Threesome. Sea Hurricane 1As P3090, Z4922 and V6700—the latter having served with 504 Squadron AAF in 1940.

Below: Hurricane IIc, NF672 of 835 Squadron, FAA which hit the deck barrier of its carrier, June 27th, 1945. Just below exhaust stubs is the nickname *Nicki*.

Bottom right: Last of the Many. PZ865, the ultimate Hurricane to be produced by Hawkers, was never issued to the RAF but bought by its parent firm off contract and retained by the firm. After the war ended it was registered as a civil aircraft, G-AMAU, its armament removed and the splendid livery (seen here) of royal blue and gold was applied. Entered in several air races until 1960 (it is pictured here in September 1950), it was then repainted in military camouflage.

Requiem

A scene which was repeated
thousands of times, in
virtually every operational
theatre; pilots sprinting to
their Hurricanes for a
Scramble take-off.

Photo Credits

The illustrations in this book were obtained from the following sources:

AELR Air Museum Brussels: 26TR, 28B, 31TL, 32

Aeroplane: 67BR

Air Ministry: 127L

R.C.B. Ashworth: 41, 96L

Associated Press: 43BR

K. Atkinson: 157TR

W. Baguley: 151B

British Official: 25, 29T, 56L, 57R, 58C, 58B, 59R, 59L, 64BL, 68T, 69B, 90B, 95T, 95BR, 103TR, 110, 112T, 114B, 115T, 117B, 124, 143TR, 155B.

J. W. Brooks: 88

Charles E. Brown: 46T, 47T, 128, 156B.

J. H. F. Cutler: 135B.

J. B. Cynk: 51T, 79B.

Czechoslovak Inspectorate: 121

Group Captain W. D. David, CBE, DFC, AFC: 154B.

Air Commodore R. G. Dutton, CBE, DSO, DFC: 145BR.

F. A. Etchells: 84, 97B.

Flight International: 12T, 12B, 13T, 14, 15B, 15T, 18, 19, 20, 21, 23T, 78T.

Fox Photos: 36, 53, 61, 63, 78TR, 82B, 127R.

Graphic Photo Union: 89.

Hawker Siddeley Aviation: 11, 55, 64T, 69TR, 69C, 109TL, 109TR, 109B, 124, 156L, 157B.

D. Howley: 112B.

Imperial War Museum: 3 Frontispiece, 26TL, 26B, 29B, 31T, 31B, 38, 43T, 43BL, 50, 65T, 66T, 66B, 87, 93, 94T, 94B, 95BL, 102B, 104, 112C, 113, 115B, 116B, 117T, 118, 119TR, 119TL, 127, 131, 132TR, 134T, 134B, 135T, 136T, 138, 139B, 142T, 142B, 146TL, 147TR, 147C, 147B, 149TR, 149BR, 151T, 153, 157TL.

S. H. Ker: 139, 147TL.

Keystone Agency: 17

Squadron Leader P. G. Leggett: 96TR, 97T, 97C.

Life Magazine (Wm Vandivert): 45T.

Ministry of Information: 122T.

MOD (Air): 43CL, 91, 102T.

R. Munday: 130.

Sergeant H. Newton: 98.

Cyril Peckham, FRPS: 22.

J. Pickering: 111, 116C.

PNA Ltd: 27, 67T, 119B, 123

Public Archives of Canada: 23B, 37R, 68B, 78B, 80, 81T, 81BR, 81BL, 82TL, 85, 90T, 133B, 137, 143BR, 144BR, 145T, 146B, 148B, 149TR, 154T, 156C, 159.

M. Ross: 37L, 47B.

R. J. Ryley: 116T.

C. Smith: 132B.

F.F Smith: 114T.

6 Squadron: 101, 107.

28 Squadron: 132T.

32 Squadron: 45B.

43 Squadron: 143BL.

85 Squadron: 44

111 Squadron: 35.

Lt-Col Avi M. Terlinden, BEM: 30R.

G. T. Thomas: 136B.

Topical Agency Ltd.: 51B.

R. F. Watson: 49, 52.

R. Leask Ward: 150B.

Flight Lieutenant Whittard: 150T.

The remainder are from the Author's collection.

PART TWO

Messerschmitt Bf109 AT WAR

Messerschmitt
Bf109
AT WAR

Armand van Ishoven

PART TWO

Contents

To Elza . . .
who like hundreds of thousands
of mothers feared for her son during the
long years of the Second World War.

Glossary

Luftwaffe ranks
The following table is simply a general comparison level of rank with its contemporary Royal Air Force equivalent. Several German ranks, in fact, had no direct equivalent in the British service.

Flieger – Aircraftman 2 (AC2)
Gefreiter – Aircraftmen 1 (AC1)
Obergefreiter – Leading Aircraftman (LAC)
Hauptgefreiter – Corporal
Unteroffizier/Unterfeldwebel – Sergeant
Feldwebel – Flight Sergeant
Oberfeldwebel/Stabsfeldwebel – Warrant Officer
Leutnant – Pilot Officer
Oberleutnant – Flying Officer
Hauptmann – Flight Lieutenant
Major – Squadron Leader
Oberstleutnant – Wing Commander
Oberst – Group Captain
Generalmajor – Air Commodore
Generalleutnant – Air Vice-Marshal
General der Flieger – Air Marshal
Generaloberst/Generalfeldmarschall – Air Chief Marshal
Reichsmarschall – Marshal of the RAF

Luftwaffe formations
Rotte/Deckungsrotte – Two fighters working as a fighting pair.
Schwarm – Two *Rotte*
Kette – Unit of three or four fighters
Staffel – 10 to 12 aircraft; nearest equivalent to RAF squadron
Gruppe – Three, occasionally four *Staffeln*

Geschwader – Literally 'Squadron'; comprised of three *Gruppen* usually.
Alarmstaffel – Fighter defence Flight.
Jagdstaffel – Fighter *staffel*
Nachtjagdstaffel – Night fighter *staffel*
Kunstflugstaffel – Aerobatic team, varying in numbers.

General terms
Alarmstart – Equivalent to RAF 'scramble' take-off.
Dicke Autos – Luftwaffe slang for four-engined Allied bombers
Flak – Anti-aircraft; from *Fliegerabwehrkanone*
Fl. Kp – *Fliegerkompagnie;* 'squadron' in Swiss flying services
Flugleitung – Airfield control section
Gefechtsstand – Command post/operational HQ
Hals - und Beinbruch – Literally 'May you break your neck and legs' – a traditional 'Good Luck' greeting by German fliers prior to a take-off; dates from World War I
Kriegsberichter – War correspondents
Pauke – Night fighter's equivalent of RAF's 'Tally Ho', signifying 'Attack!'
Prüfleiter – Head Technical Inspector
Rottenflieger – Wing man; also *Rottenkamerad/Kaczmarek;* same as RAF's 'No. 2'.
Viktor – Equivalent of RAF's 'Roger'; radio code for 'Yes, OK, understood' et al.
Wachtmeister – Technical Sergeant
Wart – General nickname for ground crew man; equivalent to RAF 'Erk'; also 'Black Man' from black overalls usually worn.
Werkstattszüge – Mobile workshops

Introduction

Schwarm. How a fighting foursome of Bf 109s looked to a potential opponent . . .

During 1939 to 1945 many thousands of the world's youth fought each other in small, fast, agile single-engined aircraft which offered only minimal protection against an enemy's fire, for they were encased in thin aluminium sheeting incapable of stopping a bullet. Carrying large amounts of highly inflammable fuel, such aircraft were apt to burst into searing flames or simply explode if hit. One such aircraft was the Messerschmitt Bf 109.

This book is in no way an attempt to record the full history of the Bf 109's technical development or its operational use. Very fine volumes of this nature have already been published, and this book is designed to complement them. Some of the accounts herein first appeared in German publications during the war, hence the reader should be warned that some of them may have been coloured for propaganda and/or ideological reasons. Nevertheless, it was considered useful to include a few such accounts as they were written by first-hand witnesses shortly after the action described.

Naturally, one cannot disassociate the aircraft from its designer, Professor Willy Messerschmitt. The world has yet to see

another engineer-designer produce an aircraft of which no less than 33,000 were actually built, and many of them in his own factory. Yet Messerschmitt's path to success was no bed of roses, anymore than was the career of his design, the Bf 109.

The first-ever design by young Willy Messerschmitt – he was 22 years old then – was a failure. A tail-less glider, the S9, it made its first flight on 7 May, 1921 and proved to be dangerously unstable. Considerable modification failed to make it safe to fly. When he entered two powered gliders of his own design in his first contest – the annual Rhön gliding competition, 15 to 31 August, 1924 – he met further setbacks. One of these, the S16a 'Bubi', was a total write-off after its propeller flew apart in flight; while the other, the S16b 'Betti', had to make an emergency landing when a drive chain broke. His first sports machine, the two-seat, high-wing M17, he entered in another contest, the Zugspitzflug of 31 January, 1925, carrying competition number 3. It was the only one of 13 contestants which failed to leave Schleissheim airfield, as heavy turbulence caused by the Föhn pushed it back on the ground just after take-

off, tipping it on its nose! When, on 16 May, 1925, Messerschmitt flew for the first time in his life in one of his own designs, as a passenger in an M17, the aircraft hit some high tension wires on 'finals' at Bamberg airfield and crashed, sending Messerschmitt and his pilot, Seywald, to hospital.

The most important sports flying event in Germany in 1927 was the Sachsenflug, held at the Leipzig-Mockau airfield from 30 August till 5 September. Messerschmitt designed his M19 especially for this contest and two examples were built. When the round flight of over 450km came on Sunday, 4 September the M19, D-1221, flown by Theo Croneiss, had to make an emergency landing near Warchau, Borna, having run out of fuel. The second machine, D-1206, flown by Eberhard von Conta, was written off when it had to 'land' in a forest near Bautzen, as its Bristol Cherub II engine was malfunctioning. Yet both aircraft won the Sachsenflug and brought home some 60,000 Reichmarks in prize money! Messerschmitt had so cleverly tailored the M19 – his first-ever low wing design – to the rules of the competition that it had received the handicap 'Infinite' and had thereby become the winner before even participating! Less than three weeks later, on 22 September, D-1177, one of the earliest examples of his successful four-seater airliner, the M18a, crashed at Schwarza in Germany, killing its pilot Hellmuth Schnabel of the

Deutsche Verkehrsflug AG and two passengers, although through no fault of the aircraft. The first prototype of the M20 airliner – the first Messerschmitt design to be ordered by the Deutsche Lufthansa – crashed on its first flight from Augsburg airfield on 26 February, 1928, killing its pilot Dipl Ing Hans Hackmack, a test pilot on temporary leave from Lufthansa, when he tried to jump from the aircraft after some fabric on the left wing's upper surface came loose. Hackmack had previously reached a height – then a record – of 303metres in August 1923, at the Rhön contest, flying a Harth-Messerschmitt S14 glider.

On behalf of the engine manufacturers Siemens and Halske AG, two pilots, Dr Georg Pasewaldt and Dipl Ing J von Berg, undertook a two-months demonstration tour through southern Europe with D-1229, a BFW U-12 'Flamingo', a type which was then BFW's bread-and-butter machine. Starting on 1 July, 1929, the tour successfully demonstrated the aircraft at Vienna-Aspern, Graz-Thalerhof, Budapest, Belgrade, Bucharest, Gorno, Sofia, Thessaloniki, Athens, Brindisi, Naples, Rome, Pisa, Milan, St Raphael and Marseilles, but then the plane crashed at Barcelona. On 14 October, 1930 the first military aircraft produced by Messerschmitt's firm BFW (Bayerische Flugzeugwerke) – the M22 twin-engined biplane bomber, disguised as a 'mail carrier' -

crashed while on a test flight; killing its pilot Eberhardt Mohnike, a WWI fighter pilot who had served with Jasta II and had obtained nine victories. The cause was again failure of one of the three-blade propellers, which flew apart in mid-air. On 6 October that year, D-1930, one of the Lufthansa's M20b aircraft, crashed on a Reichswehr firing range while about to land at Dresden airfield during the regular service between Berlin-Dresden-Prague-Vienna. All aboard – pilot Erich Pust, wireless operator Hermann Lange, five male passengers and the wife of Lufthansa's representative in Sofia – were killed. To add to the dismal chain of events, D-1928, another Lufthansa M20, crashed at Rietschen, in Silesia, on 14 April, 1931 while on a charter flight, killing its pilot Adolf Schirmer and flight mechanic Ulrich Bischoff, though only slightly bruising some of the passengers, all of whom were Reichswehr officers. The effective result of all these crashes was that Lufthansa refused to accept any more M20s. Nothing now could prevent Messerschmitt's company, BFW, going bankrupt on 1 June, 1931.

Hardly three months later came the news that D-1812, an M18d owned by the Deutsche Verkehrsflug AG but operated by the Munich Photogrammetrie GmbH firm, had crashed on 16 September near Ljungbyhed, Sweden during some photo survey work. The machine had shed a wing when the pilot, Johann Wirtz, had attempted to dive through

Far left: Friedrich Harth airborne in the S8 glider in August 1921. On 13 September that year Harth succeeded in remaining airborne for 21 minutes – a record for the period. The S8 was financed, designed and built by Willy Messerschmitt and Harth.

Below left: During the 1928-29 winter the Nordbayerische Verkehrsflug GmbH had some of its M-18bs fitted with ski-undercarriages in an attempt to maintain normal services. The chubby but efficient four-passenger air liner proved to be much more economic to operate than the contemporary motley collection of aircraft used by Lufthansa.

Below: D-1812, an M-18b (Wk Nr 469), owned by Nordbayerische Verkehrsflug GmbH but chartered by Photogrammetrie GmbH of Munich; seen here at Ljungbyhed airfield, Sweden shortly before its fatal crash on 17 September, 1931. Behind it a line-up of some Svenska 'Jaktfalk' of the Swedish Air Force.

Left: Lufthansa mechanics servicing the 700hp BMW VIu engine of D-2005, 'Odenwald' (Wk Nr 549, later re-registered as D-UNAH); one of the M-20bs which served Lufthansa faithfully for many years. Note how a cowling panel served as a servicing platform. During WW2, six M-20bs and two M-20as continued to be flown by Lufthansa, and the last remaining pair – a M-20a and a M-20b – were destroyed in 1943 while on charter to the Luftwaffe./ *Lufthansa*

Below: D-2307, the M-29 in which Fritz Morzik intended to participate in the 3rd Challenge de Tourisme International, after landing at Brunswick on 8 August, 1932 to learn that his friend Kreutzkamp had crashed in another M-29. The type was immediately grounded by the DVL. Morzik became a 'Generalmajor' during the war, and was the Luftwaffe's last Chief of Wehrmacht Air Transport./ *F Morzik*

a hole in the overcast. The man sent to investigate the accident was Dipl Ing Heinrich Hertel of the Adlershof Research Facility (DVL) for Aviation; he was later to become Ernst Heinkel's chief of development and as such responsible for the Heinkel He 112b, the Messerschmitt Bf 109's most serious competitor. In 1932 Messerschmitt developed an aircraft especially for the Challenge de Tourisme International, the European aircraft rally. D-2308, one of four racing M29 low-wing two-seaters that were to take part, crashed on 8 August, a few days before the contest, killing its pilot Fridolin Kreutzkamp, a flying instructor. The following day another M29 failed in the air, killing its flight mechanic Starchinsky, though the pilot Reinhold Poss parachuted to safety. Immediately the M29 was banned from flying by the DVL and therefore from participating in the event for which it had been particularly designed. In 1934 Messerschmitt again designed a machine for this same international rally, the M37, later to become famous as the Bf 108 'Taifun'. Ill-luck continued to dog his efforts, and a few days before the contest, on 27 July, 1934 the first prototype, D-IBUM, crashed near Augsburg, killing its pilot Freiherr Wolf von Dungern, an official with the German Ministry of Aviation. Only feverishly executed

Below: How Ernst Udet saw the rivalry between Willy Messerschmitt (l) and Ernst Heinkel (r). On 6 June, 1938, Udet flew the Heinkel He 100V-2 to better the 100km closed circuit landplane speed record of 634.73 km hr; after which both designers tried to capture the absolute world speed record.

Bottom: Presentation of D-IONO, a Bf 108 'Taifun', on the airfield at Campo dos Affonsos, near Rio de Janeiro, Brazil on 29 May, 1936. It crossed the Atlantic aboard the Zeppelin LZ 129 – the ill-fated 'Hindenburg'./ *Dipl Ing Fuchs*

modifications permitted the other Bf 108 aircraft to take part in the rally. Ultimately it became one of Messerschmitt's most outstanding designs.

Even when the Bf 109 finally appeared, the dispiriting saga of accidents and setbacks did not cease. In the summer of 1935, D-IABI, the first Bf 109 prototype, was flown from the Augsburg factory to the E-Stelle (Erprobungs-Stelle – testing centre) at Rechlin to be tested by Luftwaffe experts, but its undercarriage gave way during landing. This was a bad start for a fighter which already appeared to stand little chance of being ordered in quantity for the Luftwaffe, though ultimately it was put into series production. The first of the three prototypes – Bf 109 V3 D-IOQY, WN 760 – to be sent to Spain for operational evaluation by the Legion Condor crashed on take-off for its first flight in Spain, from Seville airfield on 10 December 1936. The normal teething troubles associated with any new type of aircraft taken into service, combined with the Bf 109's novel flying characteristics, began to take their toll. The second of the three prototypes sent to Spain – Bf 109 V4, D-IALY, *Werke – Nummer 878* – was damaged when landing at Villa del Prado from its first operational mission on 20 January 1937. Its tailwheel failed to extend and the rudder was damaged in the ensuing landing. Leutnant Hannes Trautloft, the pilot of this first-ever combat sortie for a Bf 109, decided to have the tail wheel locked down.

The first Bf 109B-2 to be licence-built by the Gerhard Fieseler Werke GmbH at Kassel (*WN* 3001) made a belly-landing on 21 January, 1937; the accident report stated that the undercarriage would not lower. A month later, on 26 February, the first Bf 109 of the B-series, D-IPSA, *WN* 1001, crashed near

Augsburg after being side-slipped too steeply, killing its pilot. On 7 April, D-IIBA (*WN* 808) of the E'Stelle, Rechlin, belly-landed with a jammed undercarriage; on 5 August *WN* 325 of Lehrgeschwader II, Barth, collided with another aircraft during combat formation training, though its pilot baled out safely; and on 8 September *WN* 1034 crashed at Felgentreu. The pilot of *WN* 1034, Oberleutnant Pantke, had never flown a Bf 109 at altitude and was unfamiliar with the oxygen equipment; he lost consciousness, crashed, and was killed.

When in February 1937 the first Bf 109 B-1s were delivered to II./JG 132 'Richthofen' at Jüterbog-Damm, there was a spate of unexplained fatalities. It was only when on 29 May, 1938, Dr Ing Hermann Wurster was performing terminal-velocity dives that the reason for these accidents became clear. While he was recovering from a dive one half of the stabiliser suddenly flew off. He managed to bring back the crippled 109 to base where

Top: At the official opening of the new Budapest-Budaörs airfield in Hungary on 20 June, 1937, eight Bf 109Bs gave the new fighter its debut to non-German audiences.

Above: Bf 109E of Lt Miessfeldt, of 9./JG 2, which hit some birch trees on take-off from Signy-le-Petit, near Sedan, 1940. Note how the cockpit section survived virtually intact./*R Rothenfelder*

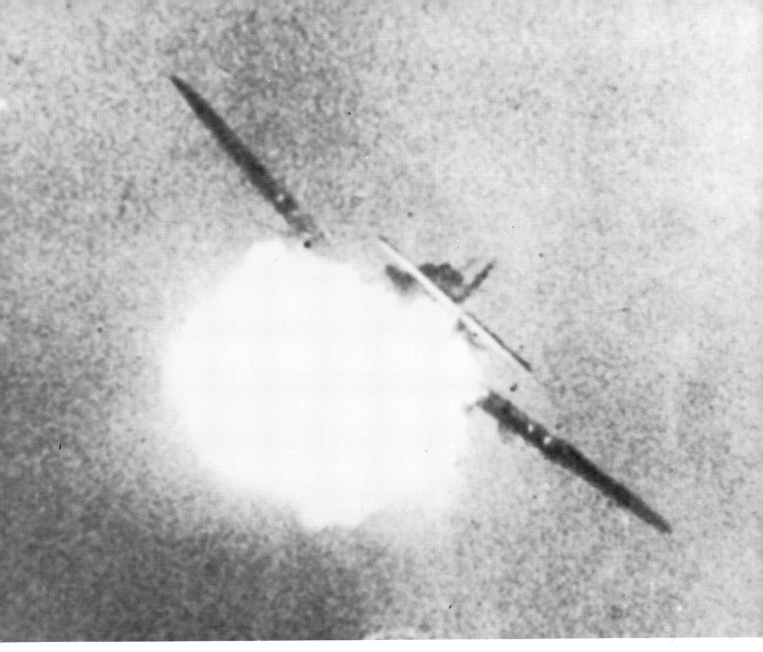

it was found that the front attachment fitting of the stabiliser had given way. Several other machines then revealed cracks at the same spot.

The pilot of *WN* 1038 of II/JG 132, Jüterbog-Damm, inadvertently feathered its propeller after take-off on 3 March, 1938, thereby cutting the engine. Trying to regain the airfield, he stalled, crashed and was killed. Three weeks later, on 31 March, the pilot of *WN* 539 of I/JG 234 Köln tried a steep turn after taking off from Göttingen airfield for a ferry flight to Köln-Ostheim; the Bf 109 stalled and killed him.

The Bf 109's debut outside Germany was equally chequered. For the official opening of the new Budapest-Budaörs airfield in Hungary a large aviation display was organised on 20 June, 1937. The Luftwaffe decided to send a *Kunstflugstaffel* (aerobatics team) of nine Bf 109s. Pilots from various fighter units were selected and ordered to Bad Aibling for training. The team leader was Major von

Janson from the RLM; leader of the left *Kette*, or sub-Flight, was Oberleutnant Hannes Trautloft; and leader of the right *Kette* was Oberleutnant Strümpel. Preliminary training proved impossible because of bad weather conditions, and when the nine Bf 109s took off at Budapest for their unrehearsed display Strümpel's aircraft lost its canopy, leaving eight machines to perform, in asymmetrical formation. Because of his inexperience in formation aerobatics, Major von Janson forgot to allow for the very strong wind that day, and the flying display was flown practically out of sight of the spectators. A final loop, started with too little speed, then scattered the eight Messerschmitts all over the sky. That evening the pilots, without their *Staffelkapitän*, tried to drown their sorrows in a Budapest bar where the speciality of the *Bardamen*, or bar ladies, was distributing false beards to customers. Next day eight of the nine Bf 109s were flown from Budapest to Bad Aibling by bearded pilots.

BALL OF FIRE – a Bf 109F in its death throes, captured on cine film by its victor, Lt Mendenhall of the US 8th Air Force./*USAF*

Below: FIRST TO SPAIN.
D-IOQY, Bf 109 V3 (Wk Nr
760), the first example to fly
in Spain, in late 1936, was
damaged on its first landing
there on 11 December, 1936.
Seen here over the Wertach,
a tributary of the River Lech,
west of Augsburg airfield.

Bottom right: Inside the
Projektbüro, where such
famous aircraft as the Bf
108, Bf 109 and Bf 110 were
'born'. Far left is Dipl Ing
Robert Lusser, and next to
him Dipl Ing Woldemar
Voigt of Me 262 fame.
Photograph taken in 1939.

Born in Bavaria

Augsburg dates from 15 BC, when a settlement was founded in that part of Bavaria by the Romans, who bestowed upon it the name Augusta Vindelicorum, in honour of Emperor Augustus. It was well situated. Many roads coming from the Alpine passes converged there and crossed an important east-west road. In the days of Tacitus the settlement had already become an important trading centre, and during Augsburg's most splendid period of history – the 15th, 16th and early 17th centuries – the names of some of its most prominent merchants, like Fugger and Welser, became world-famous. Alongside the road leading to Landsberg in the south, near Haunstetten, lay the site of the airfield where the Bayerische Rumpler Werke AG built Rumpler machines during the 1914-18 war. And it was there that the Bf 109 story started. Indeed, it was in Augsburg that, on 30 July, 1926, the Bayerische Flugzeugwerke AG (BFW) was incorporated and established itself in the factory of the former Rumperwerke on Augsburg-Haunstetten airfield, using the machinery of the Udet-Flugzeugbau GmbH. At the head of BFW was Willy Messerschmitt. Bankruptcy proceedings had been started against the concern at the Augsburg court on 1 June, 1931, but an

agreement had been reached between all creditors at a meeting in December 1932, and on 1 May, 1933 the BFW AG was able to start a new career.

On 1 November, 1933 Dipl Ing Robert Lusser joined BFW as head of the project office that took care of aero-dynamics and configuration design of new projects. His salary was 800 Reichmarks per month, augmented by RM 0.50 per horsepower of every aircraft delivered to a customer! During the first post-World War I Deutschlandflug (an air rally around Germany) in 1925 Lusser became acquainted with Hans Klemm, chief designer in the aircraft building department

of the Daimler Motor company at Sindelfingen. He immediately persuaded Klemm to take him into his employ and to teach him the intricacies of aircraft design. When Klemm founded his own firm, Klemm Flugzeugbau GmbH, at Böblingen in the following year, Lusser remained with him, becoming a director of the company and taking part in various design projects. The first such design was the L25 low-wing, two-seater sports aircraft, and later Lusser was involved in most other Klemm machines, including the Klemm Kl-31 and Kl 32, low-wing, three- and four-seater tourers. In 1932 he left Klemm to join the Ernst Heinkel Flugzeugwerke GmbH at Warnemünde, where he became chief of the design department for sports aircraft. In this capacity he designed the Heinkel He 71, a single-seat development of the fast He 64 which had been designed by the twin brothers, Siegfried and Walter Günter.

On 20 October, 1933, just nine months after Adolf Hitler came to power in Germany, Hermann Göring, who had been Minister of the Reich for Aviation since 1 May that year, expressed the hope that BFW would design a fast fighter. He did so in a highly confidential letter to Theo Croneiss, another ex-World War I fighter pilot, whom Göring had ordered to liquidate his Deutsche Verkehrflug AG, Lufthansa's only competitor, after which Göring asked him to join Messerschmitt in reorganising and rebuilding the BFW company.

'I dare expect of your energy', wrote Göring, 'that you will immediately and passionately build up an aircraft firm which, I hope, will soon bring out a first-class airliner. Equally important, however, is the development of a lightning-fast courier aircraft (*blitzschnelles Kurierflugzeug*) which needs only to be a single seater . . . Furthermore, I ask you to destroy this letter after reading, for reasons that are clear to you.

With Heil Hitler and best wishes.'

GÖRING

Naturally, Göring could not specifically say, even in a 'to be destroyed' confidential letter, that he expected Messerschmitt to design a military fighter. Nevertheless, both Croneiss and Messerschmitt were in no doubt as to what was meant by a *blitzschnelles Kurierflugzeug*.

A few weeks later, early in 1934, the C-Amt (Technical Office) of Göring's Ministry issued a requirement for a single-seat, all-metal monoplane fighter, based on a concept of the staff of the still-secret Luftwaffe, to supersede the Luftwaffe's first-generation biplane fighters. This requirement was issued to selected aircraft manufacturers, including Focke-Wulf, Ernst Heinkel and Arado – but *not* to BFW.

The omission was directly attributable to Göring's deputy, Erhard Milch, one of Lufthansa's directors and, since the various M20 accidents, Messerschmitt's chief detractor. After prolonged arguments the requirement for a new fighter was finally, if reluctantly, issued to BFW, though it was made clear to Messerschmitt that any development contract was not likely to be followed by a series production order. Messerschmitt lost no time in starting the design of a fighter as specified.

Various writers in the past have claimed that the Bf 109 was designed by Willy Messerschmitt and Oberingenieur Walter Rethel. In late 1975, from Bad Wörishofen, Rethel himself wrote to the author that, the types Bf 108 and Bf 109 originated in 1934. 'I came from the Arado works and joined Messerschmitt AG as chief of the design department that drew the blueprints needed actually to build the aircraft in March 1938.' In fact, when the design of the Bf 109 was initiated in March 1934, it drew heavily on the experience gained from designing the all-metal four-seater M37 (later titled Bf 108), design of which had started some seven months earlier, and the first flight of which was only three months away. Much of the

work was done by Robert Lusser and his office.

Also working on the Bf 109 project was Richard Bauer, chief design engineer. Responsible for actual construction of the first prototype was Hubert Bauer, workshop manager and head of the experimental construction department. Born 20 March, 1902, Bauer had joined the Junkers Works at Dessau in 1925 as a jig designer, before going to work for Messerschmitt in 1929. He was later to become a specialist in the series production of aircraft and was still with Messerschmitt when, after World War 2, licence-construction of F-104G Starfighters was taken in hand.

Collaboration between Messerschmitt and Lusser was not always easy, as witness this note sent by Lusser to Messerschmitt when the former returned from his winter vacation in early 1935:

'After returning from my vacation I was told that you have raised extremely grave reproaches against Herr von Chlingensperg and against the Projektbüro (Lusser's department) I take this opportunity to note down also those items that have, since the Europarundflug, sometimes caused grave altercations between yourself and the Projektbüro.

Below: 'Gefolgschaftsabend' – an evening reunion of BFW staff at Augsburg in 1937. Bottom left, wearing spectacles, is Robert Lusser; to his right Kurt Tank of Fw 190 fame. At top is Hubert Bauer, next to Willy Stör, holding paper. Just behind Lusser is Erwin Aichele, famed for his sport-flying exploits with BFW or Messerschmitt aircraft.

Bottom: Willy Messerschmitt (left) with the manager of the experimental workshop Hubert Bauer, admiring models of BFW-designed aircraft in the professor's office.

1 *Performance calculations Me 109*
In mid-November 1934 you announced
that according to your calculations the
climbing performance of the Me 109 had
been given as some two minutes (= 25%)
too favourable, and that you had requested
Herr Urban to check the calculations
independently of the Projektbüro. After a
day and a half you came to me, very excited,
and declared that your fears had been
proved true, and that the firm has been
much harmed through our mistake. However, it became clear that Herr Urban had
yet to finish his calculations; when these
were completed, a climbing time was
determined which was even better than
that calculated and guaranteed by us. . . .

2 *Diving speed:*
At the end of October the diving speed of
the Me 109 had to be calculated. The result
of our calculation seemed to be impossibly
high to you, and you ordered Herr Kraus
to check our calculations again. The result
was that Herr Kraus indicated our calculations though novel in method were correct.

3 *The profile problem:*
In mid-November you reproached us on
the occasion of the choice of a wing profile
for the Me 109, saying we had not taken
into consideration the profile of the M29.
As in previous cases, I explained to you
that the M29 profile was not only not better,
but even markedly worse than the American
profile that is used by us. Yet, to date, you
have not acknowledged this clear proof,
and continue to think of using the M29
profile again.

4 *Me 109 drag measurements. Interference.*
In early December thorough drag measurements and calculations were made for the
Me 109. Due to measuring differences
between the two wind tunnels at Göttingen
there was some uncertainty in the results,
which could, however, have been cleared
up had we limited our measurements to the
one wind tunnel. During these (last) 14
days you have, you say, not slept for nights
on end! My constant efforts to calm you
down . . . were totally without result. On
the other hand you have reproached me
daily that I treated these questions much
too lightly, and that I resisted your efforts
to reach the ultimate in speed. The final
calculations and considerations proved that
all your calculations were wrong!'

Lusser also touched on other subjects, such
as the weight of the Bf 110's wing spar, the
length of the Bf 110's fuselage, and impossible deadlines. He ended the note by saying:

'Nobody would be happier than I if the
candid airing of these various items leads to
clearing the (present) atmosphere, which is in
the interests chiefly of yourself and the BFW.'

At the end of May 1935 – not September, as widely stated – and barely 15 months after Messerschmitt had initiated its design, the all-silver D-IABI, the first-ever Bf 109, stood ready for its first flight on Augsburg-Haunstetten airfield. *Flugkapitän* Hans Knoetzsch, a 27-years old test pilot, was standing by. Nicknamed 'Bubi' by all, Knoetzsch had only joined BFW the previous year. After a spell as a bank clerk in Berlin, he had been selected for a free course of flying tuition by the Ring der Flieger in 1924 while he was still too young. Working at the Berlin-Staaken airfield office of the Sportflug until he could start learning to fly in 1925, he then obtained his seaplane, glider and blind-flying ratings. In 1929-30 he was the works-pilot with Hanns Klemm Flugzeugbau GmbH, where Robert Lusser was also working at that time. From 1930-34 he was pilot and scientific assistant at the German Aviation Research Institute at Berlin-Adlershof, then he joined Messerschmitt's BFW as chief pilot in 1934. Two years later he was to leave BFW to become Fieseler's chief pilot.

On this May day, however, he was to make the first test flight of the world's most advanced fighter. Donning the white gloves without which he never flew, he climbed into the narrow cockpit, closed the canopy and started the Rolls-Royce Kestrel engine. After a brief check of the engine, Knoetzsch made several ground runs across the airfield. Then – the moment of truth. Positioning himself at the end of the airfield, he made a final check of the engine and took off. The prototype Bf 109 had no automatic undercarriage retraction mechanism, so he had to wind the wheels up manually. On the ground Messerschmitt and his staff anxiously followed every movement of D-IABI.

Knoetzsch stayed airborne for 20 minutes, making several circuits of the airfield, then came in to land. When he opened the canopy, his smiling face told everyone concerned that the Bf 109 possessed perfect handling qualities the Bf 109 possessed perfect handling qualities. The Bf 109 was born – six months before the first Hawker Hurricane and 10 months before the first Supermarine Spitfire.

Below: Dipl Ing Walter Rethel, the man usually credited with the design of the Bf 109, but who did not join Messerschmitt until March 1938 when the Bf 109 had already been in production for over a year. Seen here (left) with Willy Messerschmitt in 1943./ *Dipl Ing W Rethel*

Left: PROTOTYPE, D-IABI. On arrival at Rechlin after its first ferry flight from Augsberg, via Leipzig, D-IABI's undercarriage collapsed.

Below: A sight which had seemed impossible in 1934, but first became a reality in 1936 – series production at Messerschmitt's works. A wartime Bf 109G assembly line; giving an excellent 'inside' view of the much-criticised Bf 109 undercarriage attachments and assembly./MBB GmbH

The Designer Speaks

On Monday, 22 November, 1937, Adolf Hitler visited Augsburg, where the Bf 109 was demonstrated to him. From left; Betriebsführer (Works Manager) Theo Croneiss; Hitler; Rayan Kokothaki, who succeeded Croneiss when the latter died in 1942; Karl Wahl, Gauleiter of Augsburg; and Willy Messerschmitt as Hitler arrived at the works. After the Bf 109 demonstration, Messerschmitt took Hitler aside to show him the mock-up of a four-engined bomber – which nobody at the RLM had heard of – Projekt Nr P.1064, later to become the Me 261.

Top: Willy Messerschmitt with Flugkapitän Dr Hermann Wurster, who on 11 November, 1937 established an absolute world speed record for landplanes of 610.950 km/hr, in Bf 109 V13, D-IPKY.

Above: Eighteen months later, on 26 April, 1939, Flugkapitän Fritz Wendel (seen here with Messerschmitt) established the absolute speed record in D-INJR, the Bf 209 V-1 that was officially designated Me 109R, with a confirmed speed of 755.138km/hr.

'In 1932 I tried to design an aircraft to be as fast as possible: a two-seat light aircraft, but with an engine of only 150 hp and a landing speed of only 65 km/h (the M29). Through a carefully studied shape and smoothing of the external surfaces, the use of slotted wings and, for the first time, a single-legged under-carriage, it reached a horizontal speed of 260 km/h. Through this aircraft I learned very much that, later, I could use in the development of fighter aircraft. Therefore I have plenty of reasons to remember fondly the Europaflights.'
Messerschmitt during his speech to the Deutsche Akademie der Luftfahrtforschung (German Academy for Aviation Research), 26 November, 1937.

'With extremely limited means I designed and built a series of sports and transport aircraft which, through their high performance, served as first steps towards a high performance fighter. Soon after, when I received the assignment to develop a fighter, it was evident to me that it would have to derive from aircraft like the M23 and M29. I then tried to equip an aircraft as small and light as possible with a powerful engine, in order to create a fighter that could out-perform anything then known. This was proved clearly at the International Flying Meeting in Zürich in 1937. Since that time this aircraft (the Bf 109) has been developed constantly

at a hectic pace to meet the new challenges, and improved upon over and over again, so that to this day our enemies consider it the most sucessful fighter in the world. In English circles now and then one hears the assertion that they have brought out an aircraft superior to the Me 109. Nothing can better disprove this than the list of our victories. From the steadily improving per-formance of the Me 109 in the course of this war, and its lasting superiority, you can see that we are actively maintaining this superior-ity into the future as well.'
Messerschmitt in a German broadcast, 8 December, 1942.

'As an illustration of the struggle for the right shape I would like to mention that in 1934, when the Me 109 originated, the prevalent view in (German) military circles was that the biplane was the right formula for a fighter aircraft. It was not easy for me to devlop a monoplane fighter. I had first to fight for my ideas before I could transform them into reality. Only comparative flights by the fast monoplane convinced the doubters of its superiority in aerial combat. The same conclusion had been reached in every other country and the triumph of the monoplane could no longer be delayed. What was valid for fighter aircraft was also valid for all other aircraft, including airliners.'
Messerschmitt, Lisbon, November 1961.

And a footnote from another voice:
'I have been told that a Bf 109 cost approximately 150,000 Reichsmarks in 1939, though later it became somewhat more expensive. Assuming that the Reichsmark was worth double the value of the present Deutschmark, then the most modern fighter which existed then would be worth DM 300,000 today. I look wistfully upon these figures from the past. Today the price of the least expensive jet aircraft is DM 2.5 million, and can even reach DM 6 million.'
Dr Franz Josef Strauss, then the West German Defence minister speaking about the Bf 109 in 1958.

Above left: 'In 1932 I tried to design an aircraft as fast as possible . . . through this aircraft I learned much that I could later use in the development of fighter aircraft . . . ' The racing M-29 on finals displays its slender lines, with design features later inherited by the Bf 109 – slim fuselage, high tailplane, and stalky undercarriage. Strangely, it also resembled strongly the initial Spitfire design . . .

Top: GUNNER'S VIEW. A Bf 109E-4 breaks away after a simulated attack on a Junkers Ju 87.

Above: 'Father' of the Bf 109, the Bf 108 'Taifun' flew in hundreds all over the world. Here, at the July 1937 Zurich meeting, Ernst Udet is about to give General der Flieger Erhard Milch and a woman companion a ride in Udet's personal Bf 108, D-IBVQ./*Photopress*

First Blood

KETTE. Fonr Bf 109B-2s of
2.J/88 over the scorched
Spanish landscape; their
VDM Hamilton, controllable
pitch, metal airscrews
glinting in the sun./E Neumann

Late in 1936 three Bf 109 prototypes were sent for operational evaluation to Spain, where civil war had begun in July. These were: V3, *WN* 760, D-IOQY; V4, *WN* 878, D-IALY; and V5, *WN* 879, D-IIGO*. On 9 December, 1936, Oberstleutnant Wolfram von Richthofen ordered Lt Hannes Trautloft, who had arrived in Spain on 7 August, to go to Seville airfield, there to test-fly Bf 109 V3, which had just been prepared. Unable to take off from Vitoria airfield because of fog, Trautloft had to make the journey in an ancient car and arrived next day at Seville, only to be told that the day before a young *Leutnant* had crashed V3 while attempting to take off. Trautloft, therefore, had to wait until the ground staff had prepared V4. In his diary he noted:

'*12 December, 1936.* The new Bf 109 simply looks fabulous. Alongside it the good old He 51 looks like a withered maiden, and yet only with a heavy heart can I part from her, grown grey in honour.
13 December. We are still not in warpaint. I have removed the top hat we painted on our machines until now and had a green heart painted on the aircraft instead. Thuringia, my home country and the green heart of Germany, should be here too. [Trautloft later became *Kommodore* of his Jagdgeschwader 54 "*Grünherz*', or green heart".]
14 December. At last the 109 is ready. However, there is no instructor or expert to check me out. A mechanic from Junkers [the Bf 109 then had a Junkers Jumo engine] can only explain the instruments, levers, undercarriage retraction controls and so on to me. When I ask him how V3 was "pranged" he answers laconically that "apparently the machine has a tendency to swerve to the left on take-off. "The take-off certainly is unusual, but as soon as I am in the air I feel at home in the new bird. Its flight characteristics are fantastic. When I am airborne I find an Italian Fiat fighter above the airfield. So far the Fiat has been reckoned the fastest of all Franco's fighters, but I get behind it and have overtaken it in a moment, leaving it far behind.
23 December, 1936. I have been in Seville for nearly two weeks now, as the Bf 109 goes down with one teething trouble after another. They are all trifling. First the tail wheel does not work, then the water pump, then the carburettor, then the undercarriage locking mechanism. But the repairs take time and the wasted hours mount up.
2 January, 1937. Today I have yet another emergency landing. The main problem is the continued heat, which makes trouble with the cooling of the engine and carburettor adjustment.

14 January. The Bf 109 is ready for ferrying to the Madrid front. To fly the 109 is really a joy. When I had to land at Caceres because the weather worsened, the people on the ground seemed like the strangely slow-moving inhabitants of a far-away planet. I need time to get used to the earth again. Spanish mechanics jostle each other around my 109 and marvel at this new high-speed bird.'
Hannes Trautloft ended World War 2 as an *Oberst*, with 57 confirmed victories.

In April 1937, 2.J/88, one of the four *Staffeln* of Jagdgruppe 88, the Legion Condor's fighter complement, replaced its Heinkel He 51s with the first Bf 109Bs to arrive in Spain; by that time the three prototypes had been field-tested for seven weeks. Günther Lützow, one of Jagdgruppe 88's pilots who was to gain five victories in Spain and end in World War 2 with a tally of 108 victories, described his Spanish missions of July 1937 in the 1940 edition of the Luftwaffe Yearbook:
'The enemy had broken through near Brunete, endangering the important supply route Talavera – Madrid, the loss of which would have been catastrophic. One rainy night in early July I received an urgent order to move that same night and be ready for action at dawn in Avila, west of Madrid. That meant covering 350 km of country roads – what a prospect! At once I got everyone out of bed and had the officers and NCOs report to me. "Everything has to be evacuated", I told them, "trucks have to be loaded and a locomotive has to be found. The advance party must be ready to leave in half an hour at the latest, and the fuel truck must leave at once. We will take off at daybreak; by that time the train has to be in Avila." With only the light of pocket torches and headlamps the tents were taken down, spare parts packed and trucks loaded. My interpreter scooted off to the nearest railway station, roused the station-master out of his bed and mobilised a locomotive. The *Spiess* (senior NCO) was everywhere spurring the men on; he was both indestructible and indispensable.
'When I took off at first light I was not at all sure that everything would work out right. The Spaniards should have been able to help us out, but it was doubtful if they would have everything we needed to hand. But when we landed at Avila, the commander of the advance party was there to report to me. Thank God, this party at least had arrived! But where was the fuel truck, the most important item of all? Was it lying somewhere along the road with a broken axle? Had the engine broken down? Nobody knew. And the

---

*Bf 109 V5, WN 879, was indeed D-IIGO, and not as sometimes claimed D-IEKS.

187

Above: Bf 109B-2 of J/88, Legion Condor, in Spain. The first Bf 109s were hurriedly sent to Spain when it became apparent that the Heinkel He 51 biplanes were no match for the Russian, Polikarpov-designed I-15s coming into use by the Spanish Republicans. The 'Franco' markings, black cross on a white background on the tail, and colours reversed on the wings, are evident here.

Right: Two views of the Bf 109B-2 of Hauptmann Gotthardt Handrick who was 'Staffelkapitan' of 2.J/88 in Spain. Winner of the Pentathlon at the Berlin Olympic Games in 1936, Handrick appropriately marked his personal aircraft with the five Olympic rings symbol, on the propeller spinner. Note engine starting crank handle in position in latter view./ *G Handrick*

convoy with the spare parts? I was getting damnably nervous. We still had not received any orders, either, and the radio station could tell me nothing. So there was nothing to do but wait, which is most uncomfortable in such a situation.

'As if all this were not enough, the commander of Avila arrived, and since for the moment I was the ranking officer of the party, I had to report to him. He asked me if the Jus [Junkers Ju 52/3m's] could be put into action. What a question! The only thing we knew for sure was that there was AA artillery around Brunete in huge quantities. Through binoculars we had followed a mission flown by the Italians during the morning. The *flocks* [anti-aircraft bursts] that had been thrown up for a quarter of an hour on end made it look very unwise to use the good old Jus in daytime. Emphatically I advised against it. The commander listened quietly to me, but he didn't seem to understand. Well, he'll learn soon enough.

'When I got back to my *Staffel* I found that in the meantime the convoy with our living quarters had arrived. The mechanics were already working on their machines, and shortly afterwards the fuel truck also appeared. Everything was OK now. We were ready.

'Alongside us were some reconnaissance aircraft and at the other side of the airfield were the Italians with 45 Fiats – *molto bene*! Everywhere the usual protective trenches

had been dug, bomb-proof rooms built and alarm systems constructed. It amused us: why all the precautions? The enemy would surely not venture across the lines. After all, there were fighters on the airfield and AA artillery too. That should be enough! But for the first time we were quite wrong.

'The enemy played all his trumps at once. They attacked, crossing the front lines singly or in groups – yes, they even daringly attacked our airfield. We had to fly standing patrols, and be ready at all times, from 0415 till 2130 hrs. We shot down some, but time and time again fresh aircraft attacked. And we had other missions to fly too. Three or four times every day we had to accompany bombers or reconnaissance aircraft, always at 6-7,000 metres. Every time we were in contact with the enemy; and every time we met AA fire on a scale we had never before experienced. We had a very difficult time. Everybody had to give his utmost, always fighting and always confronting some new experience. There was no time for reflection: we traded experiences, then they were translated into orders and used in practice. For the rest, we just flew or slept!

'To open the assault from our side, we sent bombers or reconnaissance aircraft across the front at great height to draw the enemy AA and attack it with bombs. We accompanied these aircraft across and hung about between Brunete and Madrid to attack all aircraft that

came from the fighter airfields on the other side of the capital. Ten minutes later the Heinkel He 51s would make low-level attacks against enemy 3.7cm and 2cm batteries and keep the gunners' heads down with machine-gun fire and fragmentation bombs. Then the Jus appeared, accompanied by Fiats. When we saw them we would hold our breath. Flying very close to each other in a compact mass, awfully low, they looked such a ripe target for the AA. But nothing disastrous happened. The Jus droned on unconcerned and dropped their bombs on the positions in the narrow passes where thousands of reservists were lying up, wreaking havoc.

'Why was the AA so ineffective? It had no option as time and time again well-aimed bombs crashed down to destroy guns, injure gun crews and force other batteries to change position. Nevertheless some guns – and no small number at that – did obstinately fire at the black mass of bombers and scored hits, but in relation to the number of guns down below the results were minimal. Thus the plan of the Commander and his chief of staff effectively eliminated most of the AA during the crucial attack.

'Some 3,000 metres above the Jus about 60 fighters were swarming. A few Fiats had

Above left: 'Rottenflieger.' Bf 109B-2 of 2.J/88 formating on his 'No 1' over the Mediterranean coastline near Benicarlo, 1938./ E Neumann

Left: Another view of the same Bf 109B-2. Note exhaust 'trap door' at rear of radiator./G Handrick

Above: HARMONISATION. A Bf 109B-2 of the Legion Condor trestled into flying position for its guns to be harmonised by the 'Fluzeugrüstpersonal' – the squadron armourers./ G Handrick

come along, but mostly it was 'Ratas' and
Curtisses *versus* my small formation. Seven
against 40! There was no time to aim carefully.
It was turn, attack, aim at the red circle, press
the buttons, pull out, gain some height, turn
back, get the next one in front of one's guns,
hold it – this time too many are behind me –
dive down and break away for a moment to
get one's breath back. Now some of them
were trying to get at the Jus, smelling an easy
prey. I attacked them out of the sun and
pulled up – but too fiercely: the plane
wallowed for a bit and lost speed. Just then
a glance below found a 'Rata' climbing up
at me, four small flames flickering from his
engine. Closer and closer he came to me, but
I couldn't do anything for the moment. I was
defenceless – this was the end, I thought.
But at last I got up some speed again and
evaded him for a moment. Then I saw two
or three behind a Messerschmitt – a comrade
needed help. As fast as possible I went at
them, blazing away. On and on it went,
seconds became an eternity, but at last the
Jus were gone and the mission has been
accomplished. But there was no time to be
tired. It was back to the airfield, take aboard
fuel and ammo, then the same thing all over
again!'

On 24 April, 1945, Oberst Günther Lützow,
victor in 108 combats, was reported missing
near Donauwörth, flying a Messerschmitt
Me 262 jet fighter of JV 44.

A gold medal winner at the Berlin Olympic
Games, 1936, was Gotthard Handrick, an
Oberleutnant in the Luftwaffe. He was victor
in the pentathlon, which consisted of horse
riding, fencing, pistol shooting, swimming
and running. Later he became Kommodore
of Jagdgeschwader 26, and ended World War
2 as Kommandeur of the 8th Jagddivision in
Vienna, credited with a total of 10 victories.
Before the war he served with the Legion
Condor in Spain and when the civil war ended
he wrote in the *Buch der Spanienflieger* – the
book of those who flew in Spain:

'In the course of an aerial combat I got to
grips with a Curtiss and, as this was one of
my first air fights, I was naturally convinced
that I would shoot down the enemy in no
time. How wrong I was! Apart from the fact
that my guns did not seem to function
properly, I was none too clever in my handling
of the aircraft. I attacked the Curtiss from
behind and he turned back, but instead of
pulling up before pressing the attack, I let
go immediately. In each attack I only succeeded in firing ten rounds. The Curtiss,
though much slower than my machine, was
very manoeuvrable and an excellent climber;
moreover, he shot extremely well. Gradually
we got farther and farther from the coast,
and finally were five kilometres out at sea, in
the vicinity of Gijon, 50-60km away from
the front. It was high time to end the combat.
I got closer and closer to the Curtiss, until

eventually a terrible noise told me I had rammed him. The wing of my machine was hit close to the fuselage and the controls were jammed. I went into three or four involuntary rolls, one after the other, until at last I regained control and could fly more or less straight ahead. Ought I to jump over the sea? No, thank you! The water was too cold in October. So I flew towards the land, not daring to think what I would do should someone jump me.

'At last I came in sight of the front. At Llanes airfield I could crash the machine in peace and quiet on the airfield. But then I recalled the words of the *Gruppenkommandeur*: ''Where on earth are you going to find a replacement if you destroy an aircraft? Every bridge in the hinterland has been blown up and it could be weeks before you get a new machine.'' So I flew my unhappy aircraft on to Santander. Thank heaven, I was only 150 metres up. Cautiously I lowered the undercarriage. Whereupon a piece of the enemy Curtiss dropped off, a souvenir from one of my first aerial combats that I still keep, and now and then look at thinking that a man needs luck! After the landing I found that the right wing was done for, the fuselage full of bruises and damaged at the back, and that the tailplane needed replacement. But I was happy I had held out, because two days later the damage had been more or less repaired and she was flying again.'

Lieber Besuch
aus U.S.A.

Foreign Pilots

Left: Three of the six Bf 109s that created a great impression at the 1937 Zürich-Dubendorf meeting; from nearest, V-8, D-IPLU; V-7, D-IJHA; and V-10, in military camouflage. The other three were V-9; V-13, D-IPKY; and Udet's all-red V-15, D-ISLU.

Bottom left: 'A dear visitor from the USA' – Ernst Udet's cartoon view of 'Lucky Lindy' climbing into a Bf 109.

In all probability the first non-German pilot to fly a Bf 109 was Maggiore (Major) Aldo Remondino of the Regia Aeronautica. He was the *Comandante* of the *Squadriglia acrobatica* that performed so graciously with their Fiat CR 32s at the Zürich International Flying Meeting, 23 July to 1 August, 1937. The personal friendship between General Valle, commander of the Italian Air Force, and General der Flieger Erhard Milch made it possible to arrange – in the utmost secrecy – for Major Remondino to fly one of the six Bf 109 prototypes which had caused something of a sensation when they participated in various events at the meeting. After an introductory flight in one of the Bf 108s also on hand, the Italian was able to try out the Bf 109 just after sunrise, when Dübendorf airfield was still deserted.

Thirty-eight years later, having in the meantime become a *Generale di Squadra Aerea* and vice-President of the Italian airline Alitalia, Remondino still remembered that flight. 'The flight lasted one hour' he wrote, and I could form a clear opinion of the features of the monoplane. It was undoubtedly more advanced as far as speed and climb were concerned than our Fiat CR 32, but had remarkably inferior manoeuvrability.'

The Luftwaffe was then highly secretive about its latest fighter. Little could Milch suspect that, hardly six months after the Italians's flight, the first 'potential enemy' pilot would have already thoroughly tested a Bf 109B. A machine used by the Legion Condor in Spain had fallen into the hands of the Republicans and the Spanish Government offered the French Government an

opportunity to test the little fighter, together with a Heinkel He 111 that had been captured intact. Three French specialists arrived in Barcelona on 31 January, 1938 and were taken to the nearby airfield at Sabadell, where the two captured aircraft stood waiting.

To Capitaine Rozanoff of the French Testing Centre at Bretigny fell the task of testing the Messerschmitt, which took 10 hours' flying time. In order to make the tests as accurate as possible the air speed indicator (ASI) was calibrated by flying a measured stretch along the ruler-straight road between Tarragona and Reus. The French delegation was much impressed by the aircraft's performance and their findings were incorporated in an extensive report – which fell into German hands when France was over-run two years later in June 1940! The report stressed the negative influence exerted by the engine's torque when making a climbing turn to the right. General d'Harcourt, commander of French fighter units, was quick to signal this characteristic to his pilots when France declared war on Germany in September 1939.

The first American pilot to fly a Bf 109 was Major Al Williams, USMC, the noted US Naval flier who won the 1923 Pulitzer Trophy, and at one period held the world speed record of 266mph. Williams, a friend of General-major Ernst Udet, was touring Europe in his extremely colourful NR 1050 'Gulfhawk', a modified Grumman G22, which he used in the promotion of Gulf products. He made a private deal with Udet. The German could fly Williams' brilliant orange-painted biplane if Williams could fly a Bf 109. The temptation

Maggiore (Major) Aldo Remondino, the first non-German pilot to fly a Bf 109; seen here at Dübendorf in 1937 in the cockpit of his Fiat Cr 32 fighter. Of interest is the gun ring sight immediately in front of his windscreen./*Photopress*

was too great for Udet, and the Luftwaffe wanted to impress the world with its new fighter.

The day was 15 July, 1938. With Udet, Williams flew to the Fieseler works at Kassel, where the Bf 109D was being licence-built. Later Williams reported:

'After inspecting the local plant, we came upon the Me 109 that was waiting for me. This was my first chance really to study the gadgets and instruments in its cockpit. Each was christened with a name that ranged anywhere from an inch to an inch and a half in length. None of them meant anything to me, and I was compelled to identify their location and their uses by following the instructions of the patient chap who explained them to me . . .

'I stalled around a little bit, until I became somewhat familiarised with gadgets and controls, retractable landing gear, controllable-pitch propeller switch, auxiliary hand pumps, manually controlled flaps, and the various gauges and main and reserve gasoline cut-off valves. Standing still, the controls were light and delicate to the touch. The engine sounded like a dream, no rattling or vibrating as in the case of aircooled radials. This was a 12-cylinder in-line job, and it ran like a watch.

'Fixing my parachute in place and snugging down for the ride ahead, I taxied out into the field. There's never a moment when the pilot of a new ship is not keenly alert for the chance of learning something about that ship's performance. Many times it's only a hint, but many times, indeed, that hint is all-sufficient to keep him out of trouble. The ground control was excellent. Without using the wheel brakes, on the way out to the take-off position, I found that a propeller blast on the rudder brought a surprisingly pleasant reaction, in spite of the fact that the vertical fin and the rudder were both rather small. The take-off was normal, and I estimated that the ground run was fully one-half the distance used by the Hawker Hurricane and about one-fourth the distance used by the Supermarine Spitfire.

'I have my own little formula to be followed in flying a new ship, and I stick to it religiously. Leaving the landing gear extended, I climbed up to about a thousand feet, set the propeller blades at the required high pitch, checked the engine instruments, and then slowed the engine down. The air speed indicator, of course, was calibrated in kilometres. I slowed the ship down to about 130 kilometres, pulled the nose up, and let it fall away. Repeating the motion again by pulling the nose of the ship up this time beyond the stalling angle, I watched it sink evenly and steadily, with no hint of crankiness.

'Flying along at about 20 miles above stalling speed, the ailerons had excellent control along with a fully effective rudder and elevator. This was all I could ask. A few turns to the right and to the left at reduced speed, a couple of side slips, and I was ready to come in for my first landing. It has always been my practice, irrespective of the new type of ship I'm flying, to take off, go through such procedures to become adjusted to its flight characteristics, and then go around for the first landing within two minutes after the take-off. This is to make sure of at least one

Dipl Ing Carl Francke, a Rechlin test pilot, in his Bf 109 at Dübendorf. He won the Climb and Dive contest of this meeting.

Udet's friend, Al Williams, standing on the left float of his personally-financed Kirkham-Williams would-be entrant for the 1927 Schneider Trophy race. Had he won, the USA would have gained permanent possession of the trophy; but Williams' aircraft was not ready in time.

routine approach for a landing while the engine is still good.

'I was amazed when I brought the Messerschmitt around, tipped it over on one side, and slid toward the ground. Leveling out we got away with a three-point landing with the air-speed indicator reading about 105 kilometres per hour. The Me 109 was an easy ship to fly, and with one landing behind me, we went to work – or rather to play.

'For the first take-off, I had set the flaps at about 15 degrees to facilitate the take-off. On the way in for a landing I found that 20 degrees on the flaps was a more suitable angle of attack. The controls, sensitive ailerons, and tail group were fully effective to the time the wheels touched the ground. So much for that. This, after all, was supposed to be an outstanding single-seater fighter, and in the half hour allowed me, I was determined to find out if the Messerschmitt was or was not what it was cracked up to be.

'The supercharger boost gauge was calibrated in atmospheres instead of inches of mercury. I recall a little difficulty in remembering what my instructor had told me about

the permissible supercharge boost at low altitudes. I said this Messerschmitt was fast. The Germans had said so, too, to the tune of 350 to 360 mph, and their claims were demonstrated to be accurate. It is also interesting to note, in 1940, that the British concede the Messerschmitts to be good for 354 mph.

'The most delightful features of the Messerschmitt were, first, in spite of its remarkably sensitive reaction to the controls, the ship showed no disposition to wander or "yaw" as we call it; neither was there any tendency to "hunt". It was a ship where the touch of a pianist would be right in keeping with the fineness of the response. And, likewise, I am sure that any ham-handed pilot who handled the controls in brutal fashion would soon be made to feel ashamed of himself. Seldom do we find a single-seater that does not stiffen up on the controls as the ship is pushed to and beyond its top speed. I checked the control reaction in three stages – one as I have already mentioned, slightly above the stalling speed, and the controls worked beautifully.

'In the second stage, about cruising speed, a movement of the control stick brought just exactly the reaction to be expected. And at high speed, wide open, the control sensitivity checked most satisfactorily.

'Then I wanted one more check and that was at the bottom of the dive where the speed would be in excess of that ship's straightaway performance. So down we went about 2,000 feet with the air speed indicator amusing itself by adding a lot of big numbers – to a little over 400 mph. A gentle draw back on the control effected recovery from the dive; then up the other side of the hill. It was at that point that I subjected the ailerons to a critical test. I had pulled out of the dive around 400 mph and had started in a left-hand climbing turn. The ship was banked to about 40 degrees with the left wing low. I touched the right rudder, pressed forward on it slowly but steadily, moving the control stick to the right, and that Messerschmitt actually snapped out of the left-hand climbing turn into a right-handed climbing turn. That satisfied me. From there on, I tried every aerobatic maneuver I had ever executed in any other single-seater fighter with the exception of the outside loop and the inverted loop.

'The guns on this ship – five of them, all hunched on the fuselage – certainly made me feel as if I were aiming guns and not flying an airplane. In addition, I was particularly intrigued to find the control stick equipped with a tiny flap which was hinged to lie on top of the stick when not in use and to be swung forward and down – parallel with the front edge of the control stick handle. This little flap was the electric trigger which completed the circuit, when pressed by the forefinger, to operate all five machine guns. I found this trigger sensitive to the touch and extremely light, later ascertaining that a pressure of 3 milligrams was required to close the circuit and actuate the guns.

'The trigger arrangement was the final little detail which brought me the impression that instead of actually flying an airplane upon which guns were mounted, I was actually aiming a delicately balanced rifle.

'When you see a man take off in a type of airplane he hasn't flown before, you can tell before that chap returns to the ground whether he likes the ship or not. If the ship is tricky and cranky or he is not satisfied with it, he'll probably make some big figure eights and maybe a few little dives, or a couple of loops. But if he really flies the ship and rides the sky with it, amusing himself with all sorts of aerobatic maneuvers, you can walk up to that chap as soon as he completes his landing and tell him you are glad he liked the ship. And that is exactly what Ernst Udet said to me after I had zoomed the field a half dozen times and overstayed my specified time in the air. As I taxied into the line, Udet, keen as a whip, and never missing a trick, walked toward me saying, "Al, you like that ship huh?"

'The longer one is at the flying business, the more firmly convinced he becomes that he knows very little about it. I must say, however, the Messerschmitt Me 109 is the finest airplane I have ever flown. It was a very happy day for me thus to enjoy the opportunity of flying and studying one of Germany's first-line single-seater fighters. I was told, of course, that the performance of the Heinkel 112 was about the same as the Messerschmitt, and I have been assured on this point, repeatedly. As far as I know, I'm the only pilot outside the members of the air force who has ever flown a first-line Messerschmitt Me 109.

'Along with its delightful flight characteristics, the visibility in this Messerschmitt is all that a fighter pilot could reasonably ask. There are a great many single-seater fighters in the world that I have not flown, but I had formed my opinion of the flight characteristics of the Messerschmitt after studying it on the ground and before flying it. And those estimates were confirmed in flight. I had made my own estimates of the performance and maneuverability characteristics of a lot of other single-seater fighters, and I'd be willing to wager that none of them represent the general, all-around flight and fighting characteristics possessed by the Me 109.

'There was only one critical question I had about the Messerschmitt that I flew, and that concerned the retractable landing gear. The wheels were hinged to fold outwards, toward the wing tips, retracted. This placed additional weight in the wings several feet from the fuselage.

'I asked Udet about this and he informed me that this would be changed. According to the new plan, the wheels would fold inward, toward the center of the wing, and in retracted position would be neatly tucked directly under the fuselage, a desirable feature in regard to balance and maneuverability. However, photographs I saw at a much later date did not show the change, but I still think this would be a definite improvement. Before dismissing my flight in the Me 109, it is necessary to include a comment on that already offered concerning the accessibility of the engine for maintenance service. I will give it to you point blank and let you estimate its value. The engine of the Messerschmitt can be removed, replaced with another – ready to go – inside of 12 minutes.

'You can imagine the uproar of doubt and incredulity in official circles when I returned to the States and spread that word around. The reason for the uproar was quite obvious, in that in very many instances, between 24 and 36 hours were required to remove one engine and replace it with another in many of our standard types of fighting planes. But, when other Americans returned home from an inspection of the German Air Force and told the same story, great impetus was given to the development of a quick motor replacement in service ships. . . . The Germans had developed the technique and trained the ground crews to effect this change of engines in the specified length of time on the open airdrome – given, of course, decent weather conditions.

'It was explained to me that, from a tactical standpoint, this ultra-rapid change of motors was of utmost importance. For instance, a pilot returning from an active front to his own airdrome could radio ahead and notify the field force that ne needed a new engine. By the time he landed, they could be ready for him.

'Ordinary service to an aircraft, such as filling the gasoline tank, checking and replenishing the oil supply, and reloading ammunition belts, requires between ten and fifteen minutes. The new development, therefore, enables the Germans to change an engine while the rest of the service is going on. It's startling performance – namely, yanking one engine and replacing it with another, and turning it over to the pilot inside of 12 minutes'.

The next American to pilot the Bf 109 was

Trans-Atlantic hero Charles Lindbergh visits the Augsburg works. From left: Lindbergh, Willy Messerschmitt, Fritz Wendel, Lilly Stromeyer (Messerschmitt's future wife), Herman Wurster, and Willy Stör.

no less a personality than Charles Lindbergh, the internationally famed trans-Atlantic solo flier. On Wednesday, 19 October, 1938, Lindbergh was flown from Staaken, Berlin to Augsburg in a Junkers Ju 52/3m. In his diary he noted: 'After inspecting the factory we walked to the flying field, where demonstration flights of the 109 and 110 were made for us. The speed and manoeuvrability of the 109 was, of course, most impressive. A small plane always looks much faster than a larger one and is quicker in manoeuvres. On the other hand it was amazing to see a two-engine plane (the 110) do acrobatic flying almost as well as the smaller type. After watching the demonstrations I made two flights in the

Messerschmitt 108, a small, four-place, all-metal, low-wing monoplane with slots, flaps, and retracting gear. Both the 109 and 110 have slots and flaps. It was originally planned that I fly a 109, but the Germans did not want Détroyat [a French military pilot] to fly this plane, and did not want to let me fly it without asking him to do so. They had no objection to him flying the 108. Consequently, I will fly the 109 at Rechlin after this trip. Détroyat told us – including the Germans with us – that some of these French pilots had tested a captured 109 in Spain. It had a 211 Junkers engine and made 465 km/h. Everyone laughed. This incident is well known to both French and German aviators. The French were apparently much impressed with the characteristics of the 109.'

Two days later, 21 October, Lindbergh finally had the opportunity to fly a Bf 109 at the Luftwaffe Test Centre at Rechlin (E'Stelle Rechlin). Laconically he noted down: 'We next inspected the Messerschmitt 110, then passed on to the 109 I was to fly. I got in the cockpit while one of the officers described the instruments and controls. The greatest complication lay in the necessity of adjusting the propeller pitch for take-off, cruising, and diving. Then there were the controls for the flaps, the retracting gear, for flying above 2,000 metres, for locking and unlocking the tail wheel, and for the other usual devices on a modern pursuit plane. After studying the cockpit I got out and put on a parachute, while a mechanic started the engine. Then, after taxying slowly down to the starting point, I took off.

'The plane handled beautifully. I spent a quarter of an hour familiarising myself with the instruments and controls, then spent 15 minutes more doing manoeuvres of various types – rolls, dives, Immelmanns, etc. After half an hour I landed, took off again, circled the field, and landed a second time. Then I taxied back to the line. The 109 takes off and lands as easily as it flies.'

What the Americans probably did not know was that an American pilot had already shot down a Bf 109, and on the same day another American pilot had been shot down by one. In Spain, Frank G Tinker, flying a 'Rata' in a squadron manned mainly by Russians, and operating from Manzanares de la Sierra, shot down the Bf 109 flown by Höness on 13 July, 1937; while Harold 'Whitey' Dahl, flying a 'Chato', also in a unit manned mainly by Russian pilots that operated from Campo Soto, was brought down by a Bf 109 and taken prisoner. For their 'services' the American pilots were paid more than handsomely, earning some 18,000 pesetas per month. The ordinary Spanish workman then averaged 120 pesetas monthly.

Hermann Wurster briefing Lindbergh in a Bf 108 four-seater, prior to Lindbergh's first flight in a Bf 109.

First 'Tommy'

Above: The first Luftwaffe pilot to shoot down an RAF aircraft in WW2. Feldwebel Alfred Held joined Infantry Regiment 20 in April 1932, started gliding and then joined the Luftwaffe. Serving first with JG Richthofen, he next joined JG Horst Wessel. He also served in Spain with the Legion Condor, and was severely injured in a crash on 30 June, 1938.

Top right: Vickers Wellington bombers of 149 Squadron RAF, from Mildenhall, pictured at Le Bourget aerodrome, Paris on 10 July, 1939 in their pre-war codings. Less than two months later some were wrecks in the Jade Bight . . .

Bottom right: The 'Gneisenau', probably the target for the Wellington shot down by Held, seen here mounting an Arado Ar 196 of 10. (See)/ LG 2, based at Travemünde. Like many other German warships, the 'Gneisenau' replaced its Heinkel He 60s with Arado Ar 196's of Bordfliegerstaffeln 1./196 and 5./196, based at Wilhelmshaven and Kiel-Holtenau, only a few weeks before war came in 1939.

One hour after the war between England and Germany started, at 1200hrs on 3 September, 1939, Flying Officer Andrew McPherson of 139 Squadron RAF took off from RAF Wyton in a Blenheim IV, N6215. His orders were to reconnoitre the German Fleet bases. At 1650hrs he landed back at Wyton with the news that, notwithstanding the misty weather, he and his crew had observed a number of warships in the Schillig Roads, off Wilhelmshaven. Next morning McPherson was again over Wilhelmshaven and Brunsbüttel, and as a direct result of his findings the first RAF bombing raid of the war was ordered. Here was an opportunity to deal a heavy blow to the enemy Kriegsmarine; the battleship *Admiral Scheer* was riding at anchor in the Schillig Roads, together with an armada of cruisers and destroyers, while the *Scharnhorst* and *Gneisenau* battlecruisers were moored in the Elbe off Brunsbüttel.

The ships were attacked by five Blenheims of 107 Squadron from Wattisham, of which four failed to return, and five Blenheims of 110 Squadron, also from Wattisham, of which one was lost. The attack, executed with great courage and determination, failed completely in its objective, due mainly to the old-pattern bombs used, all of which either missed the targets or failed to explode on impact. A further force comprising five Blenheims of 139 Squadron, six Hampdens of 49 Squadron and six Hampdens from 83 Squadron – both latter units based at Scampton – failed to find any targets because of the weather. Later in the day, 4 September, after the weather had improved slightly, six Wellingtons from 9 Squadron (Honington) and eight more from 149 Squadron (Mildenhall) attempted to attack the *Scharnhorst* and *Gneisenau* off Brunsbüttel. One of the 9 Squadron bombers was to become the first RAF aircraft to be shot down in WW2 by a Luftwaffe pilot.

Long before the Wellingtons approached their targets the German fighters had been alerted, and Bf 109Es of II./JG 77 lay waiting at Nordholz airfield, 12km south of Cuxhaven, and only 45km north-east of Wilhelmshaven. This *Gruppe* had its origin in the Flieger-staffel (J) Kiel-Holtenau which had been inaugurated on 1 October, 1934. In 1937 it was retitled I.(1) JG 136; in 1938, II./JG 333; and finally in May 1939 it became II./JG77. Its commander was Oberstleutnant Schumacher, who held this appointment until succeeded by Major Harry von Bülow-Bothkamp at the end of 1939. One of the unit's pilots, Feldwebel Alfred Held (*Held* means 'hero' in German, incidentally) was responsible for the Luftwaffe's first victory over the RAF. The 26-years old pilot, who hailed from Weissenburg, near Nürnberg, reported his victory to the *PK-Kompanies* (similar to war correspondents) in the following terms:

'We were alerted around six in the afternoon. In the shortest time possible we were off towards the enemy. Now at last things were getting started! Our formation soon reached Wilhelmshaven but nothing was to be seen over the harbour. So we turned away to the Jade Bight, where we could hear AA guns booming even above the noise of our engines. But while we were turning away I spotted three unidentified aircraft, with AA shells exploding among and behind them. We raced towards them, gratefully noticing that the AA guns were holding their fire. But the enemy aircraft had disappeared. They had been engaged by the AA guns of a German warship that we were then flying over and when I glanced down I could see two English aircraft lying in the water – twin-engined bombers, one of them still burning. So the first Tommies had met their fate.

'But while we were circling above this memorable spot I suddenly observed, very far away, another twin-engined aircraft which I recognised as English. Our formation curved towards it. The *Leutnant* leading our formation positioned himself above the Tommy in order to attack, but unfortunately he was still too far away to shoot at him with any chance of success. I was much nearer to the Englishman and did not hesitate to engage him.

'With my *Staffel* comrades still relatively far behind me, I already had the Englishman in my sights. Calmly and confidently I fired the first bullets into his aircraft, feeling as hardened to combat as if I had already shot

down a dozen Englishmen. However, the bomber's rear gunner wasn't going to allow me any complacence. As I streaked he fired one burst after another at me. Despite fiercely concentrating all my senses on the job, I managed to make out clearly every single detail of the Wellington bomber, even its various crew members. Whether that rear gunner was a good shot and had hit me I could not see for the moment. So, unperturbed, every time I had a free field of fire I shot at the enemy aircraft. Was I a better shot than the Englishman? Time and again we rushed past each other, machine guns hammering away and engines howling like maddened beasts, and thus twisting about we strayed far out over the Jade Bight.

'As if the Englishman sensed the death-blow coming he dived his bomber to get more speed and escape from my fire. Lower and lower I forced the Tommy, but still he defended himself desperately. Then – I could hardly believe my eyes – a long flame shot from the left side of the bomber. Was this the finale? Already the aircraft seemed to be out of control and wallowing about. A last burst of fire from my guns – and that

was enough. The aircraft dropped its nose and fell. I throttled down and circled to follow the Englishman's descent, but already there was just a burning pile in the water, and that lasted only a few seconds. Then the waves closed the grave and foaming wavetops glided above it as before.

'My first victory! I realised this as I was flying home and was extremely happy. When I proudly landed my fighter after rocking my wings, my comrades ran wildly towards me from all sides. They knew about my victory already and all wanted to shake hands heartily with me. I had trouble fending off their congratulations and eager questioning. 'The Victor of the Jade', I heard one of them cry. But first I had to examine my aircraft, which brought me back safely. How lucky I had been! The Tommy had only hit me once.'

A short time later Feldwebel Troitsch of the same *Gruppe* shot down a second bomber. He reported to the PK-men:

'We were flying above the German Bight off the Elbe estuary. I noticed the Englishmen far below us, very low over the water. As my comrades had apparently not yet spotted the enemy formation, I told them. I was flying in the front of our formation so I was the first to fire. When we got nearer I recognised the Englishmen as Wellington bombers, twin-engined aircraft with a rear gunner at the end of their fuselages.

'Two of the aircraft immediately turned towards the low-hanging clouds and disappeared. The third one was right in front of my guns and I closed to 100 metres to be sure of hitting him. At 50 metres the Englishman's left wing broke off and a flame shot from the fuselage. Shortly before the Englishman had returned my fire, though without hitting my machine, I found out later. By the time the bomber was engulfed in flames I was only 20 metres behind him. The burning tail fell off and streaked past, just above my machine, so that I had to dive to avoid being swallowed by the flames. I dived away to the right and followed the bomber, which dropped from some 400 metres into the water, where it quickly disappeared, leaving just an oil slick. I then attacked a second bomber which appeared among the ragged clouds. At full revs I raced after him and again his rear gunner tried to rake me, but this Tommy had no success either. Unfortunately I lost the Englishman, as we were soon into cloud. But as I curved away I found myself fired on by the Englishman's front gunner. I dived immediately to follow the bomber, but then realised we were too far out to sea.'

This day's operations, with its disastrous results for the RAF, was described thus in the *Adler von Friesland*, Luftflotte 2's own newspaper:

Left: Though practice with a 12-bore against clay pigeons (as here at the RAF's Central Gunnery School) was valuable training, the Wellingtons' air gunners were severely hampered by fixed, ie, non-revolving, gun turrets during the combats over the Jade Bight, giving Held and his comrades a relatively easy task.

Right: Alfred Held on 9 October, 1939, just over three weeks before his death in an air collision on 2 November. His decorations include the Silver Spanish Cross (on right pocket); Iron Cross, 2nd Class, awarded for his victory on September 4; Badge of the Spanish Military Order of Merit, 1st Class; and the Spanien Feldzugmedaille (Spanish campaign medal).

Below: When war started in September 1939, all Bf 109Bs had been replaced by Bf 109Ds and Es in the various fighter units. Here, a Bf 109B-1 and its pilot, Keil, pose at Döberitz in 1938./
W Schäfer

'The attack against German naval bases along the North Sea by some 20 English longe-range bombers of the newest type was a total failure. The bombs dropped caused no damage. Fighters and AA artillery brought down, with certainty, 10 English aircraft in the area of the Coastal Commander, East Frisia alone. Four of them were brought down by a man-of-war of the Kriegsmarine.'

The corresponding entry in the Operational Record Book (Form 540) of 9 Squadron RAF was terse:

'Nos 2 and 3 of A Flight did not return to base and were reported missing. First squadron to draw blood.'

Feldwebel Alfred Held received the Iron Cross, Second Class for his first victory. It was also to be his last. One month later his elder brother, Wachtmeister Friedrich Held died on the Western Front. On 2 November, 1939 Alfred Held's aircraft was accidentally rammed by another German aircraft and he crashed to his death.

At the time Held's 'first' victory was widely proclaimed in the German Press. In April 1963, however, Generalmajor a. D. Carl Schumacher, who in 1939 had been Kommandeur of II./JG 77 said that he had always believed that Feldwebel Troitsch was actually the first to shoot down an RAF aircraft.

Erster Luftsieg

Left: 'Jagdflieger'. Major Helmuth Wick, commander of JG Richthofen, in his Bf 109E-3, autumn 1940, checking instruments prior to an 'Einsatz' (war sortie). By this time Wick was the most successful Luftwaffe fighter pilot, apart from Werner Mölders and Adolf Galland./*Bundesarchiv*

Below: The 'Pik As' (Ace of Spades) insigne of JG 53 being spray-stencilled onto Leutnant Wick's Bf 109E.

Helmut Wick was born in Mannheim on 5 August, 1919. On the outbreak of war he was serving as a fighter pilot with JG 53, which left its base at Wiesbaden-Erbenheim for airfields behind the Siegfried Line and was entrusted with guarding the German border in the Eiffel mountains and Saarbrücken region. On 22 November, 1939, as a *Leutnant* with I./JG 53 flying a Bf 109E, Wick obtained his first victory (*erster Luftsieg*) when near Phalsbourg he shot down a French Curtiss H75A, No 95 of GC II/4, from Xaffévillers. Wick later became commander of JG2, 'Richthofen', and wrote a series of articles for *Der Adler*, entitled *Hetzjagd am Himmel* (Drag-hunt in the sky). This was how he described his first victory:

'It was in November 1939. We were stationed at an airfield behind the Siegfried Line and kept ourselves busy with a very necessary, if not exactly stimulating task; border-surveillance flights. Whenever an old fighter pilot hears those words he backs away; nobody wants to know about border-surveillance, which offers nothing but hour-long boring flights without contact with the enemy. It was 22 November when I first saw the roundels of an enemy aircraft. As the French did not fly over the German border, for once, we decided to get nearer and visit them at home. The wind from the east quickly took us towards France. Suddenly I saw a whole gaggle of aircraft flying at some 6,000metres near Nancy, and realised at once that they were not German. We started flying in a circle, but immediately two aircraft separated from the gaggle and hurtled down at us.

'Now I recognised them – Curtisses. We dived to get away (I was flying with just my *Rottenkamerad*) and as we anticipated, the two unsuspecting Frenchmen dived after us. When I started a climbing turn one of the Frenchmen was sitting right behind me. I can still remember perfectly how I could see his roundels when I looked behind. It was one of the most memorable moments of my life and I confess that seeing those red-white-blue roundels was rather exciting – all the more so because the Frenchman was firing away with all his guns. Realising that somebody is behind you, shooting at you, is very unpleasant; after all, it was my first aerial combat. However, I remembered the lesson given to me by Mölders, my instructor – 'In a critical situation, first get away, then watch for developments.'. I pushed the nose of my bird down and, being much faster than the Frenchman, shook him loose rapidly. When I could no longer see him I thought that the others must be above me to my left. But nothing was to be seen there. Could they be to the right? When I looked in that direction I could hardly believe my eyes. I was looking straight at four radial engines sprouting small red flames. As usual in such cases, a ridiculous thought crossed my mind: are they allowed to shoot at me like that? Just as quickly I was deliberating; shall I try to get away again? No! Now I'll get at them. One *has* to go down. I clenched my teeth and pushed stick and rudder to the right.

'When I completed my turn the first one already shot past. The second followed right behind him and I attacked this one frontally. Looking right into his guns firing was nasty. We were too near each other to get any results. He jumped over me, and now the third one was there, as near as the second. I shifted my machine to get him nicely lined up and aimed just as I had learned at school.

Left: Luftwaffe fighters along the French border in the early days of the war only occasionally met the French 'Ballons de protection' . . .

Below: . . . More frequent were encounters with Curtiss 75s of the French Armee de l'Air, which, after some initial successes, proved to be no match for the Bf 109E.

Right: Another 'opponent' was the French 75-mm anti-aircraft (AA) gun. These existed in several versions but basically dated from WW1-vintage designs, and were sorely inadequate for their purpose by 1939.

Far right: Backing the AA defences, the French used location and listening devices such as this cumbersome machine.

At my first shots I saw some metal pieces coming off the Frenchman; then both his wings gave way. Closely behind him came the fourth Curtiss, also firing at me, as I could see by the fire from his gun barrels. I was not hit, however; everything just passed me by. The first two climbed again, but I did likewise so that they could not catch me. It was now time for me to go home as I was getting low on fuel. My *Rottenkamerad*, whom I later found safe and sound at base, had lost me during the diving and twisting.

'On the way back I did not meet any more Frenchmen – though I wasn't sorry about that! The first aerial victory of my life was enough for one day. But after I had shaken off the other Frenchmen and was flying alone towards Germany at high altitude, I suddenly got the 'hunting fever' and relived the various phases of the tense combat that I had fought against four times superior forces. My first aerial victory! Never have I sat more happily in my faithful bird than on that unforgettable 22 November.

'I was so confident of being victorious in any future combat – and I hoped it would be soon – and so engrossed in my happiness, that I lost my way. I simply flew in a general easterly direction and was soon completely

lost. This was not too serious: as soon as any large recognition feature showed up I could get orientated again. Very soon I saw far below the autobahn winding through the landscape. I was back over Germany already and when, soon after, a wide river that could only be the Rhine showed up, followed by an airfield, nothing could go wrong – even if it wasn't my home field. I landed with the last drop of my fuel. It was Mannheim. I think I gave the good refuelling people a raspberry because they did not work fast enough for my liking, but I was in a hurry to get home again and waggle my wings. On the very short trip to my base airfield I was happy as a schoolboy that I too could fly over our command post waggling my wings. And I did it thoroughly. My mechanics were over the moon too. I realised how excited I was when I kept trying to get out of my cockpit without noticing that my seat harness was still fastened.

'The most remarkable thing about my first victory was that I had wanted to turn back on the outward flight. My machine had been washed down shortly before take-off, and at altitude ice had formed, which was annoying. For some time I vacillated between a desire to turn back and remove the ice, and the hope that something might turn up. This hope triumphed over the wish to return, and even today I'm happy about that.'

On 28 November, 1940, almost exactly a year later, Wick was himself shot down south of the Isle of Wight and parachuted into the English Channel. He was never found. In that year he had become one of the Luftwaffe's most successful fighter pilots, with a credited score of 56 victories. His conqueror was Flight Lieutenant John C Dundas, DFC, flying a Spitfire of 609 Squadron RAF. Wick was Dundas's 13th victim but seconds later Dundas was himself killed by Wick's *Rottenkamerad*.

Far left: LUFTSIEGE. 21 victory symbols on the rudder of Wick's Bf 109, with Wick (3rd from left) receiving the congratulations of his pilots. His 20th 'Luftsiege' (victory) brought him his Ritterkreuz (Knight's Cross to the Iron Cross) award. Of interest are the Luftwaffe kapok-filled lifejackets being worn by Wick and several of the pilots, plus the signal flare cartridges strapped around the thighs of the two pilots at right of photo.

Far left, below: As one of the Luftwaffe's most successful fighter pilots in the summer of 1940, Helmuth Wick was promoted to command the elite JG 2 Richthofen. He is seen here shortly after, being interviewed by official war correspondents from the German Rundfunk (Radio).

Left: The Old and New – Hermann Göring, commander of the Richthofen Geschwader in 1918, congratulates Helmuth Wick in 1940. Between them is General Hans Jeschonnek, then Chief of Staff of the Luftwaffe, who committed suicide in August 1943. Note the Geschwader Richthofen band on Göring's greatcoat sleeve.

Below: '. . . He was seen to parachute into the Channel but has been missing since . . .' – 28 November, 1940.

Battle over England

Bf 109Es operated against England from British soil! After Germany seized the Channel Islands in 1940, some Bf 109s were based there during the Battle of Britain. Here a Bf 109E-4 of JG 53 'Pik As' is being refuelled at La Villiaze airfield, Guernsey with the aid of a locally commandeered lorry (J H Miller went out of business several years ago). On 9 August, 1940, a Bf 109E-1 of I./JG 53 collided with a flak-tower on Guernsey, killing the gun crew.

'While we are climbing our engines drone away evenly. To my left and right fly the other machines of my *Staffel*. The morning mists above the French west coast slowly recede behind us. The altimeter indicates 4,000 metres . . . 5,000 metres. We put on our oxygen; we go for altitude. Direction – London. Our mission is *Freie Jagd* (Free Hunt). We cross the Channel. From our height it looks like a broad river. Small clouds cover the white coast of Old England. We are on 'the other side.' The clouds that form a layer over southern England at an altitude of between 2,000 and 3,000 metres become denser and denser. Every opening is watched closely. It is through these that 'the others' will come at us. A *Deckungsrotte* (two fighters working together) watch the sky above and behind to counter any surprises from those directions. Visibility is perfect – one can clearly make out Canterbury. Soon the flak will start; this area is already well known to us for that.

This Bf 109E-4 carried the personal emblem of Helmuth Wick, in front of the air intake, and an unusual form of Balkenkreuz on its fuselage. *E Obermaier*

'Suddenly something crackles in our headsets. '*Achtung*! Six to eight aircraft below us in the cloud gap.' One hears this often and usually they are our own aircraft on their way back, but this time we know for sure that they are not ours. In addition their line-formation is suspect. So beware! They climb higher. The dark silhouettes of Spitfires stand out clearly against the white cloud cover. I reckon they are 1,000 metres below us. But dammit, why doesn't our *Staffelführer* attack now? When they spot us our chance will be gone. We continue flying a sharp left turn but our leader, an old hand, knows why. And suddenly I understand. Of course, the attack has to come from out of the sun.

The uncertain moment before any combat has now gone – now we can start. I am flying the third machine behind our *Staffelführer*. We attack while diving and rapidly get nearer. A smoke trail curves downwards, falls into the clouds – our leader has got the first one. The next Spitfire now looms large in front of me. Its cockades shine provokingly. Flip the safety catch – push the buttons – dammit! He has spotted me and turns steeply away. At the same moment I have another in front of me, flying in the same direction. I am near enough to ram him, so clear are the sharp

Top left: Adolf Galland rose rapidly to fame as a fighter pilot and leader during 1940. Here he is wearing an immaculate white flying overall, and a strictly non-issue polka-dot neck scarf./ *A Weise*

Bottom left: Adolf Galland's aircraft when commander of III./JG 26 in the later stages of the Battle of Britain, at Caffiers, France. On the rudder are 22 Luftsiege symbols – by the end of the war there were to be 104./*A Weise*

Top and above: Two views of Feldwebel Beese's 'Yellow 11' of 9./JG 26 – a Bf 109E-3 – after a crash-landing in the coastal dunes near Calais, August 1940. The bullet which ripped into the aircraft from behind, indicated, was stopped by the pilot's armoured head-rest./ *A Weise (both)*

215

wing-tips, the cooler, the cockades. Guns and cannon hammer away and the Spitfire explodes in a ball of fire. I watch the Tommy go down trailing black smoke. He is the fourth of his tribe to get acquainted with the guns of my loyal '5'.

'What is that – smoke trail very close to my machine? All is tension again. But suddenly they are gone. I can just see a Tommy upside down behind me disappearing downwards, burning. Bits and pieces trail behind him. A 109 passes me, flying faster, than I and I recognise a comrade of my *Staffel*. So it was he who shot down the Tommy behind my back.

'In a few seconds everything is over. A quick glance at my instruments – everything is still all right . . .'

This account by Leutnant Erwin Leykauf of JG 54 was written after a combat on 11 November, 1940. He ended the war as an Oberleutnant, credited with 33 victories.

Top left: 'Schwarze' 4 – Black 4. A Bf 109 belonging to 8./JG 54, based at Le Mans, March 1941./*A Weise*

Centre left: WAITING. A scene to be found on practically any fighter station of the Luftwaffe – and the RAF – during the hot summer of 1940. Members of 7./JG 54 at Soesterberg, July 1940; from left, Feldwebel Michel; Leutnants Behrens and E Leykauf. Note the Staffelwagen just behind the pilots' row of deckchairs./*E Leykauf*

Below left: Pilots of 9./JG 2 Richthofen at Octeville, Le Havre in 1940, discussing the next mission. From left: Uffz Neumann (killed October 1940); Staffelkapitän Oberleutnant Röders (killed Spring 1941); Uffz Rudi Rothenfelder; Feldwebel Maier (later killed in action); Oberfeldwebel Brunkhorst, nicknamed 'Ghandi'; and Gefreiter Schaaf (later killed in action)./*R Rothenfelder*

Bottom left: Bf 109Es of 8./JG 54 at dispersal on Guines airfield, France, (near Calais), 1940. Schwarze Drei (Black Three) was flown by Leutnant E. Leykauf./*E Leykauf*

WREN ODDENTIFICATION

When Willy produced his one-seater,
And began building castles in Spain,
They believed he had got a World-beater,
Till it met Sydney Camm's Hurricane.

Willy's gone and made another,   *Unbraced tailplane ends its figure.*
Something like its elder brother—   *One-O-nine F is its name—*
Wing-tips rounded, spinner's bigger.   *F for futile, not for fame.*

Above: World-famous were the brilliant Wren 'Oddentification' series of aircraft recognition cartoons published during the war by the artist, E A 'Chris' Wren – an original approach to the serious subject of teaching aircraft recognition. This is how Wren 'saw' the Bf 109E and Bf 109F versions./*Chris Wren*

Below: In the same vein were the cartoon series 'Salient Characteristics' by Cummings, which appeared in the official British publication 'Aircraft Recognition'. This panel illustrated the principal recognition features of the Bf 109G in the journal issued April 1944./*Crown copyright*

Approaching, the projecting intake for the super-charger is very prominent on the port side. Notice that the radiators under the wings are wide but very shallow in contrast to those of the Spitfire which are narrow and deep.

The nose shows an almost even curve above and below to a very large spinner. In fact, the spinner may be said to form the nose of the aeroplane and is a distinctive feature.

The fin and rudder is noticeably small. In spite of its straight leading-edge the general appearance is rounded and there is a characteristic " heel " to the rudder.

The abnormal length of fuselage from wing to tailplane becomes visible in any plan view. Notable are the almost pointed wing tips and the small size of the tailplane.

In rear views a useful check point is the high mounting of the tailplane. In this view the fuse-lage, because of the inverted-Vee engine, has the appearance of squatting close on the wing.

Bottom right: During the French campaign the idea of using the Bf 109 as a 'Jagdbomber' – 'Jabo' (fighter-bomber) had already been considered – to the dismay of the fighter pilots. Illustrated is one such 'Jabo', Bf 109E-4/B of II (Schlacht) /LG 2 at Calais-Marck in October 1940. The SC 250 bomb is chalk-inscribed 'Hals und Beinbruch' (literally, 'Neck and Leg Break' – a traditional 'Good Luck' greeting by German airmen prior to any mission, dating from WWI) – and signed 'Uncle Hugo'./*A Weise*

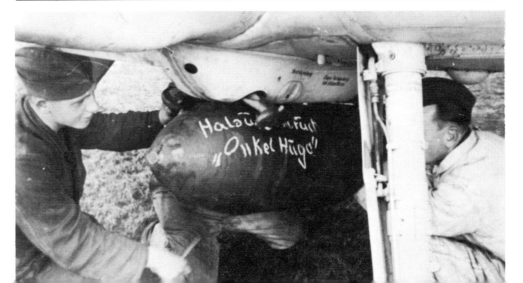

Fighting the Spitfire

ERWIN LEYKAUF

Hauptmann Friedrich Geisshardt, 'Kommandeur' of III./JG 25, seated in the cockpit of Spitfire VB RF-E (AA 940) in 1943. The Spitfire that belonged to No 303 (Polish) Squadron landed undamaged in France. Geisshardt was shot down shortly after this photograph was taken while attacking 8th US Air Force bombers attacking the Erla VII Repair Depot near Antwerp on 4 April, 1943, *A. Weise*

During what was later called the 'Battle of Britain', we flew the Messerschmitt Bf109E. The essential difference from the Spitfire Mark I flown at that time by the RAF was that the Spitfire was less manoeuvrable in the rolling plane. With its shorter wings (2 metres less wingspan) and its square-tipped wings, the Bf 109 was more manoeuvrable and slightly faster. (It is of interest that the English later on clipped the wings of the Spitfire.) The Bf 109s also had leading edge slots. When the 109 was flown, advertently or inadvertently, too slow, the slots shot forward out of the wing, sometimes with a loud bang which could be heard above the noise of the engine. Many times the slots coming out frightenened young pilots when they flew the Bf 109 for the first time in aerial combat. One often flew near the stalling speed in combat, not only when flying straight and level but especially when turning and climbing. Sometimes the slots would suddenly fly out with a bang as if one had been hit, especially when one had throttled back

to bank steeply. Indeed many fresh young pilots thought they were pulling very tight turns even when the slots were still closed against the wing. For us, the more experienced pilots, real manoeuvring only started when the slots were out. For this reason it is possible to find pilots from that period (1940) who will tell you that the Spitfire turned better than the Bf 109. That is not true. I myself had many dogfights with Spitfires and I could always out-turn them.

One had to enter the turn correctly, then open up the engine. It was a matter of feel. When one noticed the speed becoming critical – the aircraft vibrated – one had to ease up a bit, then pull back again, so that in plan the best turn would have looked like an egg or a horizontal ellipse rather than a circle. In this way one could out-turn the Spitfire – and I shot down six of them doing it. This advantage to the Bf 109 soon changed when improved Spitfires were delivered.

When, many years later, I got to see the Spitfire 'Pilots' Notes' it became clear to me why on many occasions we were able to surprise Spitfire pilots – at least in the beginning. Many times we wondered how it was possible. Today it seems to me that simply flying the Spitfire was a full time job judging by the contents of the 'Pilot's Notes'. The Bf 109 was much simpler, technically speaking. For example we had the *Propellorautomatik*, automatic propellor pitch setting. When one gunned the engine, the pitch was automatically reduced. But we could also alter the pitch setting by hand, and this could be used to get a higher rate of fire from our nose guns which were synchronised with the propellor. Flying level and wanting a higher rate of fire, like for instance when attacking a bomber, one had only to set the pitch setting at 11 o'clock (12 o'clock being the maximum). This very low pitch resulted in a very high rpm and thus a high rate of fire.

Late in 1940 or early in 1941 I had an interesting encounter with a Spitfire, a combat 'in reverse' in effect. I was flying at 4000 metres (13,000 feet) above Maidstone, a noted fighter airfield, on my way home. We had been in a dogfight, our formation had been scattered and I was alone. Many times after an aerial combat we were short of fuel and the red lamp frequently came on when we were halfway across the Channel. This time the red lamp flickered on and off while I was still over England.

By radio I tried to find out if any of the others were in the vicinity. 'Igel Fünf' confirmed that he was. I called, 'This is Igel Einz, come nearer', and gave him my position south of Maidstone.

I asked 'Hanni?' (altitude)

'Hanni four thousand.'

'Good, my Hanni is also four thousand, come nearer'. I looked around but didn't see anything, wondering where he was. At last I spotted him, coming up from behind getting nearer and nearer until I called.

'Mensch, tuck in close, my red lamp is already flickering'.

He answered 'Viktor, Viktor, I'm coming'.

At last he came closer and I started looking at my map. I reflected that even if my engine was to stop, I still could get across the Channel. (From 4000 metres above Dover one could just reach the French coast in a glide and we were over the coast near Dover.)

I called, 'Stay to my left'.

'Viktor, Viktor'.

Then I looked behind me and thought what a strange aircraft it was! I couldn't see the two radiators below the wings but quickly noticed the red spinner (which, incidentally, none of us had – contrary to what has been claimed later). I had never seen a Bf 109 with a red spinner – and suddenly it dawned on me – it was a Spitfire!

He was already perhaps only two or three hundred metres, flying very fast and eventually he came alongside. I could only think that his guns had jammed. I was so frightened that I opened up the throttle and there we were, suddenly flying in formation! And now something funny happened. I thought: '*Donnerwetter*, if I keep on flying like this I'll get in front of him and he'll have me cold. To make it worse I am low on fuel!'

Probably he was thinking at that same moment: 'Dammit, when I dive away, he'll get behind me and that will be my lot!'

'What do *we* do now?'

At that moment I saw him throttle back. So I said to myself 'there is only one thing to do, to throttle back', so I throttled back.

And there we were flying very slowly in formation with me thinking: 'If I stall and fall away I will have him on my tail but if he stalls then I am behind *him*!'

I watched him hanging there, very near, perhaps two wingspans away, and it made a formidable impression upon me. Probably he was also thinking that if he were to make a wrong move he would be lost. I knew, too, that there was little hope for me as I had very little fuel left; but this was something he didn't know!

There was nothing else he could do but keep on flying as slowly as possible.

Then he opened his canopy. I can still see him today. He wore a leather flying helmet and had pushed his goggles up. Then I thought about flaps and I lowered them. I looked at him and saw that he had also his flaps down. The seemingly huge roundels on his fuselage dazzled me. Now we were at minimum flying speed, neither wanting to advance on the other. But then he could no longer hold on. He had to open his throttle... I could see black smoke coming from his exhaust stubs. He advanced a bit and I thought: 'Now I'll get you'. I kept on flying as slowly as possible but he receded again and once more we were flying alongside. Then . . . with our left hands we waved to each other . . . a unique occurrence!

For quite some time we kept on flying side by side, always in the direction of France. The unspoken question for us both was: How do we lose each other? There was only one possibility: to get away as suddenly as possible'. Then all at once, I could no longer see him and I thought 'Now he has got you after all'. I pushed the stick forward but then saw his blue belly, falling away far below me; he disappeared.

We had by now arrived halfway across the Channel and he had probably had to turn back because his fuel was getting low. Of course he was not to know that by coincidence my own fuel warning light was on.

Oberleutnant Erwin Leykauf, photographed in Russia in 1943.

Above Tundra, Ice and Steppe

Above: SNOW DISPERSAL. A Bf 109F of III./JG 53, 'Pik As' being prepared for a mission during the bitter cold of the 1941-42 winter campaign./W Schäfer

Right: The first Luftwaffe pilot to shoot down a Russian aircraft after the start of the war with Russia. Oberleutnant Robert Olejnik with his 'Wart' (mechanic) Uffz Mackert, standing by the tail of Olejnik's Bf 109F-2 (Wk Nr 6743), and the rudder victory tally of 21 'Luftsiege'./R Olejnik

The first German pilot to shoot down a Russian aircraft in World War 2 was Robert Olejnik, now living in retirement in Oberschleissheim where, before the war, he was an instructor at the Fighter Pilot's School. He recalls:

'From the middle of February 1941 I was *Staffelkapitän* of 4./JG3, as an *Oberleutnant*. On 1 June we moved from St Pol airfield in northern France to Breslau-Gandau, by way of Strasbourg and Regensburg. All members of the *Geschwader* had to be on duty from dawn to dusk; letters were censored and all leave cancelled. We were totally in the dark about our future activities or eventual missions. On 19 June the complete II./JG3 left with all its Bf 109F-2s for the airstrip at Dub, some 8km from the Polish town of Zamosc, which lay 80km south-east of Lublin, and about 50km from the nearest Russian soil. On the occasion of the Midsummer Night celebrations we lit a huge bonfire and had the usual cold drinks. Then around midnight there came a telephone call from the *Geschwader*: 'All unit commanders immediately to the command post'. There each received an envelope with a mission order, but it was only to be opened when the code word 'Barbarossa' was given .It was impossible to think about sleep; though we all lay down in our tents to rest, we were excited and full of tension. On 22 June, 1941, at about 0230hrs, the password came through. I opened my envelope and found that an attack against the Soviet Union was about to begin.

'Everybody in the *Geschwader* knew that I was an early riser and that I liked to fly the first missions at dawn, so I made the first take-off. About 0330 hours I took off with my *Rottenflieger* to reconnoitre Russian airfields near the border, watching for enemy fighters. In doing so I discovered that on every enemy airfield two or three Russian fighters were stood at the ready. After flying over several airfields, and on the way back, I again flew over the first airfield I'd seen. As I got nearer I saw that two aircraft were already manned by pilots. At a height of 7-800metres I flew a wide turn round the airfield and watched closely. After one and a half circuits, I saw the Russians start their engines and taxi out, then take off immediately. As they were obviously looking for a fight, I attacked the first 'Rata' with a height advantage of 3-400metres, and succeeded in shooting it down with only a few rounds in my first attack. Comparing times with my *Rottenflieger* later, this happened at 0358hrs on 22 June, 1941. The second fighter was probably shocked by seeing one of his unit going down burning and flew away, because I could no longer find him. Returning over our own airfield, I waggled my wings three times. Unbelieving, my comrades shook their heads – most of them had only just woken and were peering sleepily from their tents.'

Olejnik had already obtained eight victories in the West and later rose to *Major*. In November 1943 he went to Erprobungs-Kommando 16, which took a part in developing the Messerschmitt Me163 rocket fighter, where he suffered a severe accident.

Murmansk was the gateway through which much of the war material being sent by England and America entered the Soviet Union. Month after month the German and Finnish armies tried to capture this vital harbour, or at least to interrupt the rail link to Leningrad, more than 1,000km to the south. They never succeeded. On various airfields west of Murmansk, mostly on Finnish territory, were stationed the Bf109s of Jagdgeschwader 5, 'Eismeer Jäger' (Hunters of the Arctic Sea). This unit, which had been organised in January 1942 from sections of I./JG77 and IV./JG1, constantly operated over the lonely, endless tundra in very bitter weather conditions. In the spring of 1943 some war correspondents visited 6./JG5 to gather first-hand stories for 'those back home'. *Staffelkapitän* from June 1942 was Oberleutnant Heinrich Ehrler who, at the time of the following interview, was credited with 77 aerial victories and the destruction of 11 locomotives. On Saturday, 27 March, 1943 he shot down five Russian aircraft in one mission:

'We had taken off with six machines (109Fs) to do some 'free hunting' and went to look for the enemy over his own airfields. This time we were lucky and bounced a gaggle of Airacobras, Kittyhawks and IL.2 attack aircraft west of Schonguij, about 20km south of Murmansk. Altogether there were some 30 aircraft, which had apparently just taken off, intending a surprise raid on one of our bases. The surprise was to be for the Russians, however. The enemy formation flew on a westerly heading, very low over the tundra – first a close formation of 15 aircraft, with the rest following in pairs. Four of us attacked the main formation. Such an attack always moves fast. That day it lasted hardly four minutes before I had sent down numbers one to five. Two hit the ground east of Tuloma, the third on the west bank. I got the fourth and fifth in a wide right turn. The next candidate was now flying to my left, slightly in front of me, and I was at a height of only 150metres. Below me to the left three Kittyhawks and an Airacobra were twisting around.

At the moment I was about to open fire at the enemy flying in front of me, there was a

loud bang in the cockpit and I was immediately surrounded by heavy smoke. What had happened? A heavy machine gun bullet had hit right behind the engine in my ammunition feed and exploded one of my own cannon shells. After I had dived away I tried to ascertain the extent of the damage. The engine was still running perfectly. But I had been hit in the left leg and hand by some very small splinters, a very large hole had appeared in my left wing, and the tip of the right wing had been blown off. The wounds hardly hurt, but after several minutes of debating whether I should resume fighting or fly home, I decided, reluctantly, to go back. It turned out later that I had been hit twice and the machine was only held together by a very thin metal strip. Another fight and it would surely have given way.'

Eventually, facing a courtmartial following the sinking of the *Tirpitz*, and then holding the rank of *Major*, Heinrich Ehrler was killed on 4 April, 1945 while flying with the *Geschwaderschwarm* of JG7. It was just a few weeks before the war ended.

The next day, 28 March, 1943, also saw some heavy fighting in the air. Leutnant Theo Weissenberger, one of 6./JG5's most successful pilots and, before the war, a former glider pilot and NSFK *Sturmführer*, explained how he obtained his 69th, 70th and 71st victories:

Top: GREEN-HEART. Bf 109G-5/R3 of II./JG 54 'Grünherz' returning from a sortie over the Eastern front. Clearly visible is the 'Beule' – hump – covering the breeches and ammunition magazine of the Rheinmetall-Borsig MG 131 guns. Note too the fuel drop-tank's minimal clearance with the ground – an added hazard to take-off and landing for Bf 109 pilots./*Bundesarchiv*

Above: Pilots of Jagdgruppe z b V. Petsamo – later, in May 1942, incorporated in JG 5, 'Eismeer' – on arrival at Kirkenes airfield in Norway on 1 June, 1941. This photo was taken at 2330 hours, by the light of the 'midnight sun' . . ./*M Villing*

Above: Bf 109G-4s of II./JG 3. While based at airfields in the Wiesbaden-Mannheim area for a rest period, the whole 'Geschwader' was titled 'Udet' in late 1941, after Ernst Udet's suicide./ *Bundesarchiv*

Right: Line-up of Bf 109G-4s of II./JG 3. Aircraft nearest camera was flown by the 'Gruppe' adjutant; while the third machine was that of the 'Geschwader' adjutant. Note speckled camouflage applied to the engine sections, contrasting with the remaining overall markings./*Bundesarchiv*

'We had taken off to protect some fast bombers and met about 20 Kittyhawks and Airacobras. Within two minutes I shot down two Airacobras, and three minutes later a Kittyhawk, my 71st victory. Then I got mixed up with a lone Kittyhawk but simply could not get him in front of my guns during the twisting combat that followed. It was a real merry-go-round. At last, after what seemed an eternity, I got behind him so that I could fire a burst at him. The Curtiss flew right through it, turned upside down without catching fire, and crashed vertically. I saw it hit the ground beside a lake and explode.'

Weissenberger eventually chalked up a total of 208 victories and survived the war. On 10 June, 1950, he died in a racing car accident at the Nürburgring.

Feldwebel Hans Döbrich shot down two Hawker Hurricanes on 22 September, 1942, his 15th and 16th victories:

'We were on escort for a bomber formation and met about 40 Hurricanes and Curtiss Tomahawks over the enemy airfield at Murmaschi. Eight of us attacked and completely surprised the enemy formation. I saw three Russians get out of their aircraft and take to their parachutes as soon as they were shot at! Out of the two Hurricanes I shot down two black specks also jumped, sinking to the ground below their white parachutes. During this combat I counted a total of 12 who jumped by parachute; all the time one or two slowly sinking white spots could be seen. At the end we counted 12 white spots on the ground round the airfield – 12 parachutes – and 16 smoking and burning wrecks.'

Oberfeldwebel Albert Brunner, a flying instructor before joining 6./JG5, described his 39th, 40th, 41st and 42nd victories:

'We took off when the alarm sounded. Low-flying enemy aircraft were attacking a neighbouring airfield. During the approach to the airfield I shot down a Tomahawk, and then suddenly there was a gaggle of Airacobras. I engaged four of them and had soon shot down two. My fourth opponent I attacked frontally. Suddenly there were all kinds of noises in my plane; the engine stopped, pieces flew off my wings and tail. Nothing else to do but out and down. I was lucky to spot a frozen lake nearby and succeeded in performing a belly-landing on its frozen surface. After setting my machine afire, I simply waited because I knew my comrades would search and find me. Sure enough, two 109s appeared overhead and spotted my emergency landing field. Shortly after a Fieseler Storch landed right beside me – to the surprise of some mountain troops nearby. I went home.'

On 7 May, 1943, Brunner had to abandon his aircraft, but was too low for his parachute to open fully. His friends recovered his body.

Just before his death, he told another war correspondent of an eerie experience when he shot down his 14th and 15th opponents in the late summer of 1942.

'We were standing by at readiness on our airfield at Petsamo. A formation of Junkers 88s was going to attack a Russian airfield near Murmansk and we fighter pilots were to accompany them as protection. We hadn't flown for four days and our fingers were itching. The bombers took off and we followed suit. You know how things are when you are flying. Details of the earth vanish rapidly, and the land below changes from moment to moment. Here along the Arctic Sea front it is full of variation. Many reefs are to be seen, and many small islands lie like stranded wrecks in the surf. But we who had flown this route before, over and over again, hardly noticed it all. I still remember perfectly the tune I was humming: "If I were a little bird and had two wings, I would fly to you . . . "

'We had gained a high altitude and it was time to put on our oxygen masks, but I waited some time before doing so. I kept on humming my little song. Suddenly, I heard the voice of the *Staffelführer* over my radio: "Hey! Who do you think you are singing like that, Father Christmas? Have you gone nuts?" He was right: only a madman would be singing. The rebuke called me back to my senses "God"! I thought, 'have I been dreaming?" Now it was time to put on my

Above: HERALDRY. The standard outside of the 'Gefechtsstand' (Command Post) of JG 54, 'Grünherz' at Siwerskaya; displaying the individual insignia of I., II., and III Gruppen. Throughout 1942 this 'Geschwader' was constantly on the move, from one 'hot spot' to another./A Weise

Right: Deadly enemies since the Spanish civil war; a Bf 109F-2 of II./JG 54, flown by the 'Geschwader' adjutant, standing cheek by jowl with a captured Russian 'Rata' (Polikarpov I-16) on the Eastern front in the spring of 1942./Bundesarchiv

Centre right: Muscle-power is used to shove this Bf 109F-2 – the personal aircraft of the 'Gruppe' commander of II./JG 54 – into a makeshift dispersal bay./Bundesarchiv

Bottom right: 'General Winter', Germany's most implacable opponent throughout the Russian campaign, provided a daily chore for the ground crews during the winter of 1941-42. The markings on this Bf 109 indicate it was usually flown by the 'Gruppe's' Technical Officer.

oxygen mask, because we were climbing higher and higher. It became imperative to keep one's eyes open because enemy fighters were about. Hurricane and Tomahawk – the names told you where they came from – and those agile, fast-as-lightning Airacobras carrying a cannon and four machine guns. In front of us were some small clouds, coloured like mother-of-pearl. I heard the urgent voice of my *Kaczmarek*, a *Leutnant*. "Look out! Enemy above to the left!" Now I too could see three silver specks in the direction of the sea, about the same height as ourselves. They were still a long way off. Then, while I was deciding what we should do I heard in the radio – very clearly and distinctly – a female voice!

'None of us understood what was happening. This female voice out of the blue surprised us so much that at first nobody noticed that she was speaking in Russian. She sounded shrill and sharp. Nobody understood what she was saying. Still

recovering from my amazement I heard someone mutter: "Shut up, you silly bitch." Then – I don't know who it was – somebody said: "Nitschewo, Madka, nitschewo". I've never forgotten what follows. An insolent, brutal laugh, so shocking that I still hear it in my mind. Certainly it wasn't one of us, but whether it was the laughter of a woman I cannot say. Again the laughter rang out over the air. Suddenly I got mad. Any misgivings were dispelled: the hunting fever gripped me. We were just three against three – a fair fight: the three of us and the three silver specks that apparently did not want to see us. I started a turn – again I heard that hideous laughter, even more repulsive and I shot the first one down from the turn. Then I had to let the *Leutnant* have a go, because he had only recently joined us and needed his first victory. However, nobody should think an aerial combat is that easy. It takes a lot of nerve to cope with the thousand unforeseen events and imponder-

Above: 'General Mud' was the second enemy of any invader of Russia; as illustrated by this Bf 109G-2 of 4./JG 54, 'Grunherz' on its return to Siwerskaya after a sortie./*Bundesarchiv*

Right: The extreme climatic conditions on the Russian front called for unorthodox solutions to some problems of maintenance. Here a home-made wooden 'hangar' has been erected around this Bf 109F of JG 54. Note absence of swastika marking on tail./*W Schäfer*

ables; often one is astonished that things have turned out all right.

'I saw the *Leutnant* shoot down his first enemy while I covered him from the rear. I watched how neatly he got closer, saw his burst of fire, and then his opponent going down burning. But I kept wondering about that laughter. Somewhere there had to be somebody on our frequency who could actually see us, because right after the *Leutnant* shot down his man, the laughter sounded again – shrill, as if coming from Hell. 'God!. Shut up', I cried. I shot down number three – now I had my 14th and 15th victories – yet the sneering laughter peeled out again. Were they trying to frighten us?

Since hearing that laughter, the *Staffel* has scored over 500 kills. Where did the female voice come from? The answer proved to be simple. Somehow it had got on to the same frequency by chance or on purpose – who knows? We heard later that the woman had been giving a lecture – on cooking!'

229

Hungarian Escape

One of the many air forces to use Bf109s was the Royal Hungarian Air Force (*Magyar Kiralyi Legiero*), which first operated the type against the Russian Air Force and later against the USAAF. In the spring of 1943 the first Bf 109s were delivered to Hungary and Daniel Holeczy – then a *Leutnant* in the RHAF, but in 1975 a BAC 111 Series 500 captain with the German Bavaria airline – well remembers his first flight in a Bf109:

'At that time I considered myself an experienced pilot, with some 300hours on the Fiat CR32, Fiat CR42, and the Heja (Hungarian-built version of the Italian Reggiane Re 2000.) The controls of the 109 were not as light as those of the Italian machines. An Italian fighter moved like a pencil – you had an immediate reaction. In the 109 you had to use some force – the reaction was there but it was heavy. The German aircraft were hard, heavy, coarse, more difficult to fly, but they were much faster. The 109 had a very narrow track and during take-off and landing you had to work hard to keep it straight, as opposed to the Heja whose undercarriage was very wide and therefore easy to keep straight. Suddenly we jumped from around 800 to 1,200hp – that was a lot of horsepower in those days.'

One of the first Hungarian pilots to score a 'victory' while flying a Bf 109 was Sergeant Dezsö Szentgyörgyi, at the end of 1942. Unhappily for him his first 'victory' proved to be a Luftwaffe Heinkel He 111, which was forced to crash-land! Though there were no casualties, congratulations were hardly forthcoming. This episode did not prevent him becoming the RHAF's leading ace, with 34 victories accredited to him by the end of the war.

On 18 June, 1942 two young Hungarian fighter pilots graduated from the RHAF Academy as second Lieutenants. As Hungarian ranks are placed behind the name, these were Debrödy György hadnagy and Kenyeres Miklos hadnagy, and both were mighty proud to be then assigned to 5/2 v.szd (vadasz szazad – fighter squadron.) The unit operated with Heja's, soon to be replaced by Messerschmitt Bf 109Gs, and together with

5/1 v.szd, made up 5/1 v.oszt (*vadasz osztaly* – fighter group). It was better known as the 'Puma Group' from the group's insignia, a blood-red puma head, designed by the group's commander Aladar de Heppes von Belenyes alesredes (*alesredes* – wing commander), a professional soldier of noble birth. Debrödy was to end the war with 26 confirmed victories, Kenyeres with 18 and de Heppes with eight. The Puma Group's motto translated as 'Our leader is courage, luck is our wingman' – a curiously appropriate one in the context of the subsequent adventures of the two freshly-graduated fighter pilots. Debrödy recalls the story thus:

'Uman airfield at the end of January 1944. East of Uman, a Russian town about half-way between Kiev and Odessa, units of the German Wehrmacht are surrounded by the Red Army, and the Luftwaffe has undertaken to supply the pocket with food and ammunition. Junkers Ju 52/3m are to be used for the job. There are two airfields within the pocket, but as these are under enemy fire the supply aircraft are using two emergency fields. The Ju 52/3ms have to fly across 40 to 50km of enemy-held territory bristling with AA guns and intensive Russian fighter activity. Escort for the unarmed, lumbering "*Tante Ju*" is provided by 10/JG 51, whose *Staffelkapitän* is Oberleutnant Günther von Fassong, and the Hungarian 5/2.v.szd, commanded by Josef Kovacs szazados (*szazados* – captain). Because of the short range of the Bf 109s used, a second sortie is necessary when the Ju aircraft fly back carrying wounded and sick soldiers.

'On 1 February, as on most other days, I drive to the airfield early, together with Miklos Kenyeres, expecting another sortie. I already have 15 victories to my credit and the air activity holds promise of more. Heavy clouds hang very low, yet we soon receive the order for another escort mission. Quickly we contact the Jus and escort them safely to the

Above: General Magyarossy inspecting the 'Puma' Group on the Eastern Front, 1943. At left, Major A de Heppes, Group Commander; Captain Gyula Horväth; the General, talking to Lt Kalman; Lt George Pavay-Vaina; and far right, Lt Debrödy György./*G Debrödy*

Top right: Second Lieutenant Debrödy climbing out of his Bf 109G-4, Summer, 1943./ *G Debrödy*

Centre right: Two Luftwaffe officers (far left) talking with Lts S. Paszthy, G. Debrödy, L. Molnar, and Bejczy of the 'Puma' Group, 1943./ *G Debrödy*

Bottom right: An emergency landing by an Hungarian Bf 109G at Umany airfield Russia, in mid-1943./*G Debrödy*

meadow within gliding distance. Ploughing up the ground poses little difficulty, but I have to admit that I am quite shaky as the result of this unexpected development. Being well drilled in emergency procedures, my first reaction is to destroy my radio equipment. Luckily uninjured, I jump from my crippled aircraft and start to run, at the same time looking at my surroundings. Some 600 to 700metres away I see khaki-clad soldiers emerging from the edge of the surrounding woods. And at the same moment – I hardly dare believe my eyes – a 109 turning sharply, lowering its landing gear and flaps, and landing almost parallel to the path taken by my own 109. Then I remember how, a few months ago, Kenyeres and I tried out the possibility of seating two in a 109, and how we had agreed that two normal-sized pilots in summer clothing, wearing no parachutes, would be able to fly a 109 if the canopy was left off. In an Olympic spurt I start running towards the other 109. As soon as it stops the canopy flies open, then off, and I recognise Kenyeres dumping his parachute and flying jacket, all the while waving and shouting at me. When I get to the 109 I have already thrown away my jacket and Kenyeres is sitting deep in the seat pan. At the same time the Russians, probably realising they have little chance of capturing me alive, start using their weapons. Above the noise of the 109's engine ticking over I can hear the whine of bullets and, I vaguely remember, explosions – possibly from mortar fire.

'I jump on Kenyeres' back, riding him piggy-back style and trying to reach the rudder pedals, as he asks me: he will operate the stick and throttle lever. My head is completely exposed over the windshield and I am gripping desperately the two handgrips in the corner of the windscreen as we attempt to take off. The first blast of the revved-up propeller blows away my goggles and flying helmet, so I cannot see a thing. Kenyeres

beleaguered pocket. As we are flying back under the clouds, looking for possible strafing targets so that we will not have used all this fuel for nothing, a Yak 9 suddenly drops out of the clouds right in front of me, though just a little out of range. This unexpected gift diverts my attention so much that I completely forget to look for his comrade. (As it turned out, he came out of the clouds behind me, in front of Kenyeres.) Unfortunately our radio is not working today, so Kenyeres tries to divert the attention of the second Yak by firing at him, even though he has little chance of hitting him. Meanwhile I am busy trying to get within range and aim for a certain kill, when suddenly there is a loud crashing sound. Heat and black smoke blown in my face makes me realise that my engine is on fire and that for me the mission is over. Meanwhile Kenyeres has succeeded getting into range and shoots down the victorious Yak – Kenyeres' 18th victory. The bullets stop flying around my 109.

'I jettison my canopy, but my low altitude forces me to abandon any hope of taking to my parachute. I am over a dense forest area, but am lucky to spot a reasonably-sized

231

frantically shouts for rudder control, but it doesn't help. He has to stop again. We try to sort out our handling problems, then start again. We gather speed and suddenly – I don't know how – the bumping stops and we are airborne! But though we have solved one problem, we soon have plenty of others. With the undercarriage and flaps retracted, the 109 picks up speed, and then I feel the increasing pull of the slipstream. Its suction strives to separate me from Kenyeres and the aircraft. The only holds I have are the two hand grips and my knees jammed on Kenyeres' waist. The combination of icy wind, tremendous suction and – probably – near exhaustion soon brings me to the point where I am willing to give up. In desperation I start to bite on Kenyeres flying helmet – my only possible means of communication with him. He gets the message and, not needing much visibility now anyway, crouches even lower and to one side so that I can find a little shelter behind the windscreen.

'It is pointless to wonder what would happen if a Russian fighter should drop out of the clouds now, so we both concentrate on flying the aircraft and fighting the wind and cold. Getting near to Uman, Kenyeres starts his preparations for the landing, and as the undercarriage and flaps come down, our speed is reduced and so is the slipstream and suction. The lessened strain on my hands and knees signal the approaching end of our nightmarish journey. With reduced speed we are able to exchange a few words about the landing, but I am reluctant to stick my head out again, even by an inch, to give him the minimum visibility needed for a safe landing. I do so only when he brings the speed down

Top right: COMRADES.
Miklos Kenyeres (left),
Kalman (centre), and
György Debrödy, at Umany
airfield, April 1943. Before
long Kenyeres was to rescue
Debrödy from certain
capture behind the Russian
lines; and shortly afterwards
become a prisoner himself./
G Debrödy

Centre right: Hungarian
armourers servicing and
re-arming the engine-
mounted 20-mm Mauser MG
151/20 cannon and the
30-mm Rheinmetall-Borsig
MK 108 gun./*G Debrödy*

Right: Another view of some
Hungarian armourers
checking over the guns of a
'Puma' Group Bf 109G. The
magazines of the two 13-mm
Rheinmetall-Borsig MG 131
fuselage-installed machine
guns held 300 rounds for
each gun./*G Debrödy*

232

and we are floating just above the ground. Down below, the ground crew recognise the markings on Kenyeres' 109 as it comes in to land, but at the same time realise that it has a strange profile. After a surprisingly good landing on Uman airfield, and once the propeller is still, we crawl out of the good old 109 with deep gratitude in our hearts. We start hugging each other and I am close to tears with emotion. Only now does the reason for the strange profile become clear to the ground crews. Needless to say, the shouting, celebration, hugging and eager questioning is endless.

'Nervous reaction works differently in different people. For the remainder of that day Kenyeres walks around, all alone, not wanting to speak about the sortie any more. In contrast, I have the urge to prove to myself that the adventure has left no mark on me, so I make another sortie in the afternoon – though, I confess, with a pounding heart.

'Two days later, on 3 February, we both get the same assignment again. The ceiling is only 200metres. On returning we run into heavy AA fire, and I see Kenyeres' 109 hit and start to burn. His body catapults from the aircraft and when his parachute opens I see an object fall away; he has lost one of his boots. I watch him landing in the trees. But he is moving as he hangs from the straps, and waves at me as if to say "So long". Circling the spot where he landed, I notice Russian soldiers already approaching. There is just nothing I can do for my friend, who so valiantly risked his life and freedom for me at almost the same spot. I circle once more and bid him goodbye with my wings. Shortly after I have to make a forced landing, wheels down, in a meadow, having run out of fuel. But I am on our side of the lines.'

Thirty two years later Kenyeres was living in Spain, and Debrödy in the USA. But they never miss a chance to visit each other and are occasionally joined by their former commander, Aladar de Heppes – the 'Old Puma'.

Top left: Scene at Veszprem airfield, summer 1944. A Bf 109G-5 of the 'Puma' Home Defence Regiment./
A de Heppes

Centre left: One of the 'Puma's' Bf 109Gs being manhandled to dispersal at Veszprem airfield, summer 1944./*A de Heppes*

Left: Aladar de Heppes von Belenyes, Group Commander of 5./1 v.oszt (Fighter Group) on 30 May, 1943, after obtaining his first two victories with his Bf 109, VO+39./*A de Heppes*

233

Repairing the Bf109

Top and above: Two aspects of a trial installation tested at Deurne airfield. Liquid oxygen was injected into the engine's air intake to increase its ceiling. On the first test flight of this Bf 109F on 11 March 1943, Erla VII's chief test pilot Hans Fay reached a height of 13,000 metres (41,000 feet) but had to jettison the canopy before landing as it was still completely covered with ice after descending to 1000 metres (3,000 feet).

During the Polish campaign various German manufacturers had to organise, at only eight days notice, convoys consisting of three trucks equipped as mobile workshops, complete with lathe, welding gear and the like – the *Werkstattszüge* – to repair Luftwaffe aircraft immediately behind the front lines. These were manned by specialists from various departments of each works. When the Wehrmacht swept through Belgium, Holland and France, these *Werkstattszüge* followed close on the heels of the armoured divisions. More effort was soon asked of the German aviation industry. On 8 June 1940, after Belgium's capitulation and during the last throes of French resistance, Feldmarschall Göring ordered Generalmajor Thomas to Göring's command train 'Asia' at Givet, France, near the Belgian border. Thomas was then Head of the Department for War Economy and Armament within the German forces' supreme headquarters, and was duly ordered by Göring to make a number of provisions, including the establishment of large-scale repair depots – *Reparaturbetriebe* – for German forces in the various occupied countries. Thomas lost no time and only days later several firms within Germany's aviation industry were 'invited' to set up such repair

depots, among them the Erla Maschinenwerk GmbH of Leipzig. This firm, founded on 18 July, 1934, had been licence-building Messerschmitt Bf 109s since 1937.

Ingenieur Fritz Bartsch, a long-serving staff member, was selected to organise a *Reparturbetrieb* in Belgium, where in the meantime the Department for War Economy and Armament had found a suitable location. This was the former Minerva Works at Mortsel, a suburb south of Antwerp, conveniently situated near the Deurne-Antwerp airfield and close to a railway siding. It had been the place where – until halted by bankruptcy – Minerva cars had been built, rivals in quality and price to the famed Rolls-Royce. By 20 June Bartsch was in Antwerp, but soon left for Dunkirk to acquire as necessary transport for the repair depot, five lorries abandoned by the British Expeditionary Force. As soon as he returned he hired some 50 local craftsmen and sought contact with various local contractors and suppliers who would be willing to work for the Germans. The Minerva works buildings were cleaned up, a modern office building constructed (which still stands today) and, near the end of June, the first damaged Bf 109s began to arrive by lorry. During October 1940 some Junkers 87s were also repaired as well as the Bf 109s, but this was stopped when Junkers themselves set up a repair depot at Courcelles, north of Charleroi in Belgium. In December Bartsch, now works manager, or *Betriebsleiter*, was seconded by Peter von Schalscha-Ehrenfeld, another long-serving member of the staff. Necessary tools and machinery were bought in various parts of occupied Belgium and France, many of them in Paris, and by the new year, 1941, Frontreparturbetrieb GL Erla VII was a going concern.

Trainloads of damaged Bf 109s arrived at the depot and were swiftly stripped down completely. Damaged items were either discarded or repaired and placed in storage racks alongside undamaged and overhauled

Below: Civilian Belgian workers repairing Bf 109 fins at the Erla VII repair depot at Mortsel, near Antwerp.

Bottom: Works Manager F Bartsch (dark suit, centre) conducting some German official visitors around the depot.

assemblies. Fuselages and wings were put into calibration cradles and, where necessary, re-adjusted, then stored. From the stock of stored items, completely overhauled Bf 109s were then assembled; to all intents and purposes an assembly line was eventually set up. Serviced engines were delivered from the depot operated by Daimler-Benz in adjoining buildings. Great care was taken to ensure that the latest modifications were incorporated during overhaul, including the installation of the most recent factory conversion sets – *Umrüst Bausätze* – so that some repaired Bf 109s from Erla VII were more up to date than those produced by the aircraft industry itself. As a final step, the repaired Bf 109s were carefully cleaned and polished and then taken by lorry to the nearby Deurne-Antwerp airfield, 3Km away by road and the location of Erla VII's rigging and test-flying department. At the airfield the former Stampe-Vertongen factory, where prior to the war the delightful SV.4b trainers had been built, was taken into use.

Once assembled, repaired Bf 109s were thoroughly inspected and then test-flown by Erla's works-pilots. Then, after acceptance by the RLM controllers, the aircraft were flown to assigned units by Luftwaffe pilots. One of the first pair of Bf 109s to be repaired at Erla VII, a Bf 109E-1, was test-flown on 16 July, 1940. As a finale to the test, a high-speed dive was started, but the pilot was apparently unable to pull out. The Messerschmitt dived straight into the ground, killing its pilot before the eyes of the men of II./KG3, then operating Dornier Do 17z aircraft from the airfield during the Battle of Britain. Soon between five and seven Bf 109s were being test-flown every day and, after a spell of bad weather, 50 or more could often be seen standing ready to take to the air. When it was being test-flown the aircraft bore no normal identification markings, simply the first letter of the individual pilot's name, chalked in white on the fuselage: F stood for Fay, G for Göhringer, Hi for Heyne, M for Matschurek, and W for Weichelt, etc. Luftwaffe pilots detached to fetch a Bf 109 often indulged in extremely low flying, perhaps to impress an 'acquaintance' from the previous evening. Many a red-faced pilot had to land back at Deurne with his propeller – costing RM 9,500 – bent backwards after touching the water of the river Scheldt. On one occasion even the cover for the underwing radiator was missing after a similar 'test flight.'

In order to ensure an adequate supply of skilled workers, a special school was created at Kortrijk, in Flanders, where woodworking craftsmen and by then unemployed diamond workers could be retrained as skilled metal craftsmen. Indeed, the need for skilled workers grew steadily as an increasing number of Bf

Top left: Repaired aircraft were taken by lorry to Antwerp-Deurne airfield from Erla VII.

Bottom left: As in every air force's maintenance depots, defects and remedial results were usually chalked temporarily on some prominent part of an aircraft; in this case the propeller blade. Inscription here reads – 'Motor schüttelt – läuft hoch' – Engine vibrates, idles too fast.

109s were brought in for repair and as the German aircraft industry began ordering sub-assemblies for their own production lines, such as bomb racks for the Focke-Wulf Fw 190 – an item designed by German Erla VII engineers at Mortsel. Another repair depot, Erla VI, was at the same time repairing Messerschmitt Bf 110s and Me 210s, Heinkel He 111s and Dornier Do 217s at Evere airfield, north of Brussels. In May 1942 the first set of plans for the Messerschmitt Me 262 twin-jet arrived at Erla VII, together with an order to prepare for series repair of this revolutionary new aircraft! By early 1943 Erla VII was employed about 3,000 workers at Mortsel, augmented by 400 more at Deurne airfield, and 200 in a workshop set up in a former diamond-cutting establishment in Antwerp's Lamorinière Street, for the diamond-cutting trade had been stopped by the war. From every front wagon-loads of Bf 109s were brought to Mortsel – from within

Above: Most of the Bf 109s were test-flown painted in a light grey (Hellgrau 76) finish, and carrying the first letter of the particular test pilot's surname chalked on the fuselage. The Balkenkreuz and swastika markings were already painted on. Note the pre-war Citroen 'towing tractor'.

Germany, from Russia, even from North Africa with desert sand still lodged in various parts. In addition, arrangements were already in hand to commence similar complete overhaul maintenance for Focke-Wulf Fw 190s, the first of which arrived at Erla VII in the summer of 1943.

By this time Erla VII had become so vital to the German war effort that the decision was made to work day and night continuously, with the work force divided into three shifts. None of this activity went unnoticed by the Allies. Several intelligence rings operating inside Belgium sent regular reports to London on various subjects, including the economic situation, military movements and among other specifications, Erla VII and its activities. Some of the rings conveyed weekly reports, via couriers, by way of neutral Spain. In 1941 the 'Tegal' intelligence ring had been reporting on Erla VII, but when this ring was virtually liquidated by numerous arrests by the Germans, the task of informing London of the activities at Mortsel became the responsibility of the 'Boucle' ring. Two of 'Boucle's' men, known by their code names as 'Ulysse' and 'Le Sage', lived in the immediate vicinity of the Erla works, and with their report of 30 March 1943 they even succeeded in sending plans of the repair depot to London. By then however the Allies had decided to do something about Erla VII and the US 8th Air Force was tasked with the job. Since 17 August 1942, when 12 B-17 'Flying Fortresses' had stepped lightly on the little finger of the German war machine by dropping 18 tons of bombs on the Rouen marshalling yards in France, the 'Mighty Eighth' had gone from strength to strength. As a direct outcome of the Casablanca Conference (14 to 26 January,

1943), Germany's aircraft industry was second on the Allied bombing priority list; only attacks on U-boat yards were deemed more important.

On 4 April 1943, during the daily operations conference at headquarters of the 8th Bomber Command at Daws Hill Lodge, near High Wycombe, Buckinghamshire, the meteorological officer 'promised' only one-tenth cloud over Antwerp for the following day. Texas-born Lieutenant-General Ira Eaker, after staring at the wall map with its many red-ribboned routes to and from various targets, ordered the attack on Erla VII for next day. Field Order No.140, dated 4 April, 1943, supplemented by 1st Wing FO No 126 and 2nd Wing FO No 88, specified the target and ordered the attack for 15.31 hours on 5 April by all available B-17s of 1st Wing and all available B-24s of 2nd Wing. The familiar multi-colour perspective maps were taken from their their secret files and distributed to pilots, navigators and bombardiers; these showed Antwerp as it would look when approached from 26,000 feet. Shortly after 3 pm on 5 April air raid sirens wailed across Antwerp. Streetcars and all other traffic halted; some people went to the air-raid shelters; others simply continued as normal. Reserve Flak-Abteilung 295 (an AA unit), whose six batteries were located around Antwerp, were ordered to 'Alarm' status and their 9cm Flak M39 anti-aircraft guns – captured from the French – were swung towards the west.

At 15.24hrs Flakuntergruppe Antwerpen reported the first enemy aeroplane in sight. Escorted by RAF fighters, 83 Fortress IIs and Liberators belonging to the 44th, 91st, 93rd, 303rd, 305th and 306th Bomb Groups were rapidly nearing the target, spread out in tight

Below: A pair of Bf 109s prior to test-flying. At left can be seen the offices of the pre-1939 Stampe-Vertongen aircraft firm.

Top, right and far right: Erla VII buildings being repaired after the US 8th AF's bombing raid of 5 April, 1943.

Centre, right and far right: Two views of the assembly line at the Rivierenhof plant, where a completely overhauled and repaired Bf 109 was rolled out every hour.

boxes between 23,000 and 26,000ft. Two minutes later the armada was over its IP (Initial Point) at Lokeren, between Ghent and Antwerp, and set a direct course for its objective. In the meantime Fock-Wulf Fw 190s from various *Geschwader* stationed in France and Flanders had been vectored towards the bombers. At the IP a first B-17 was shot down by Oberleutnant Glunz of JG26, though by then Hauptmann Fritz Geisshardt, commander of III./JG26 had already been shot down too.

When the first bombs hit the Erla and Daimler works and fires broke out panic spread among the workers, but thereafter the sticks all fell clear of the works. The results of the raid were disastrous – but not for the Erla works, which was only moderately damaged and even less for the Daimler depot, which was hardly touched. The chief sufferers were the civilian Belgian population in the neighbourhood. Most of the 491,000lb of bombs dropped fell east of the target, towards the built-up centre of Mortsel suburb. Photographs taken during the raid from the bombers showed bombs exploding 5 miles away from the designated target. As the last bombers droned westwards hundreds of civilians lay dead beneath the ruins of their homes, including nearly 100 schoolchildren whose school had been destroyed by direct hits.

The German propaganda machine swung into immediate action. On 11 April Josef Goebbels wrote in his diary: 'An imposing funeral has been arranged by the local authorities for the victims of an American bomb attack on Antwerp. The English and Americans have not yet taken any notice of our propaganda about Antwerp. That is proof of their bad conscience. It supports our idea of making first-class propaganda material of the Antwerp incident.' Of the 79 Fortresses and 25 Liberators that had been despatched, no fewer than 21 had aborted the mission. Three other B-17s were shot down, one each by Oberlautnant Stammberger and Major 'Pips' Priller, and the third by 1./Res. Flak-Abteilung 295. They all belonged to the 306th Bomb Group. After the raid Allied aircraft made several sorties to photograph the damage for assessment. The resulting interpretation reports, drawn up at RAF Medmenham, proved that clearance of the damaged sections of Erla VII was rapidly taken in hand, and much reconstruction had been completed by July that year. On 20 April the 'Boucle' ring reported on the raid. The homes of two of its agents, 'Ulysse' and 'Le Sage', were in ruins, though neither agent was hurt. The report gave the number of civilian casualties as 802 killed and ended by requesting that any future attacks on Erla VII be undertaken by low-flying Mosquito bombers, 'The raid seems to have been performed from too high,' they complained. Only a few weeks after the bombing production was back to normal. Deurne airfield, where at the time of the raid about 50 repaired Bf 109s had been standing, awaiting testing, had not even been scratched by the bombing.

For the remainder of the war Erla VII was unmolested, except for a few sporadic strafings by Allied fighters against Deurne airfield – as on 28 May 1944, when Lieutenant-Colonel

Below: More Bf 109s awaiting flight testing at Deurne airfield, near Antwerp. The hangar was built in the 1920s, and camouflaged by the Germans to look like a row of houses.

Bottom: Some of the civil test pilots of the Erla VII repair depot. The chalked letter F here denoted test pilot Hans Fay, second from left in this quartet./H Fay

Robert L Coffey, flying a P-47D Thunderbolt of the 388th Fighter-bomber Squadron, set two parked Bf 109 afire. Many times Erla VII received visitors like Feldmarschall Sperrle, who was furious to discover over 100 Bf 109s parked in the open on Deurne airfield.

From late 1942 all test-flying at Deurne was undertaken with fully armed aircraft, but nevertheless during 1943 an *Alarmstaffel* was created to defend Erla VII in the event of any further raids against the works. Several Bf 109s were always available on the airfield, either waiting for test flights or collection by the Luftwaffe. Now three or four Bf 109s were always kept fully armed and fuelled, dispersed around the field, ready to be manned by the test pilots. To make cold starts easier, the engines' oil was diluted with petrol and during the winter engines were kept constantly warm. On the sound of the alarm the German civilian test pilots immediately became members of the Luftwaffe with military rank, and had to defend the airfield and Erla VII. At first Belgian civilian personnel had been ordered to start the engines when the alarm sounded, but when they protested this order was rescinded.

A few Allied aircraft were shot down by Bf 109s flown by Erla test pilots from Deurne airfield. One was Flight Lieutenant M. Lipinsky of No 315 (Polish) Squadron, who was brought down by Hans Fay on 4 May 1943. Lipinsky was on that occasion flying his Spitfire IX EN131, on a 'Ramrod' mission protecting 8th Air Force bombers attacking the General Motors plant north of Antwerp. He was badly wounded in the leg and had died by the time his parachute reached the ground. On 5 November, 1943, Generalfeldmarschall Erhard Milch sent a letter to Erla VII congratulating the pilots of the Erla-Industrie-Jagerschwarm – Leutnant Göhringer and test pilots Fay and Mörtel – for their victories to date, which comprised one Spitfire and two four-engined bombers.

Even before the bombing raid it had been decided to disperse production at Erla VII. Three quayside hangars from the port of Antwerp were commandeered and, notwithstanding acts of sabotage by members of the Belgian underground, these were erected in the Rivierenhof public park 4km east of the city centre. They were skilfully camouflaged and housed an assembly line that accommodated 54 Bf 109s and produced a totally repaired and overhauled Bf 109 every hour. From that point on test flying was also carried on from Brasschaat airfield, 15km north-east of Antwerp, and occasionally from St Truiden airfield, 70km east-south-east of Antwerp, where Erla VII ran a small repair shop. At the end of May 1943, Betriebsführer (Works Manager) Bartsch could report that no less than 2,000 aircraft had been repaired by Erla. Telegrams of congratulations poured in, signed by – among others – General Sperrle, Generalingenieur Scheuermann, and General der Flieger Wimmer. Nine months later Bartsch reported to Milch that on 24 February 1944 the 3,000th machine had been repaired since July 1940. Apart from the ever-growing volume of repair work, an increasing number of small sub-assemblies were ordered by German aircraft manufacturers. One example at the end of 1943 was the start of production of a *Rüstsatz* (modification kit) which brought the cockpit ventilation of older variants of Bf 109 to the standard of the Bf 109G-5. The prototype *Rüstsatz* was initially tried and tested by JG 300.

On 6 June 1944 the Allies landed in Normandy, but this did not seem to have unduly alarmed Germans in occupied Belgium. Years later, Bartsch remembered that when he celebrated his birthday on 7 August 1944, there was still no serious thought of leaving Antwerp. Nevertheless, the speed of the Allies' advance through France soon changed this complacent outlook and at the end of August about two-thirds of all machinery at Erla VII was loaded aboard five barges for transport to Germany. Only two barges eventually arrived at Münster, where the firm of L. Hansen was also engaged in repairing Bf 109s. By this time Erla VII was employing nearly 10,000 workers, supervised by a staff of 100 Germans, including men of the *Werkschütz* – a military unit for protection of the installations. Now that liberation was in sight, trouble was experienced with local workers who refused further work and an escalating amount of sabotage was reported. The last remaining Germans only got away in the nick of time when Canadian troops unexpectedly entered Antwerp on 4 September 1944. At Deurne airfield the last two Bf 109s took off as Canadian armoured vehicles rolled on to the airfield. Many 109s had to be abandoned as they were either not fit to fly, or no pilots were available to fly them away. One of the Bf 109s remaining was 'liberated' by some RAF personnel, who occupied the airfield after the Germans had gone, and Squadron Leader Guy Plamondon of 193 Squadron planned to fly it. However, to the dismay of the squadron personnel who had put in many off-duty hours in servicing the aircraft, it was taken away before any flight could be made. Meanwhile the remaining staff of Erla VII had re-assembled at Münster. Near the end of the war Herr Bartsch and others of Erla VII gathered at Leipzig, and on 14 April 1945 were ordered to form a special unit, with some 160 military personnel, to help build Messerschmitt Me 262s. Nothing came of the plan, for the end of the war was only days away.

Defending Neutrality

The Messerschmitt Bf 109s debut in the service of the Swiss Air Force was – to say the least – painful. Wanting to replace its ageing fighters with up-to-date machines, in 1938 the Swiss government ordered the best fighter available at the time – the Bf 109. A series of 10 Jumo 210-engined Bf 109D-1s was available and ready for delivery in November 1938. The first was ferried from Augsburg to Dübendorf by Mani Moser, former chief pilot of the KTA (Kriegstechnische Abteilung). At Dübendorf the *Bise* (local wind) was blowing and when attempting a cross-wind landing the Bf 109 ground looped after touch-down and broke its undercarriage. It took about 100hr (one

working week) to repair the aircraft at Dübendorf. In December one of the next Bf 109s to be ferried was flown by Ernst Wyss, Moser's successor as KTA's chief pilot. Due to heavy snowstorms he was forced to land at Friedrichshafen and continue his flight to Dübendorf next day. A failing engine necessitated a forced landing, with wheels retracted, in the neighbourhood of Frauenfeld. The aircraft was returned to Augsburg by rail for repair, and was ready again in January 1939. On 7 May, 1939, J 314 was ferried from Regensburg to Altenrhein where the A.G. für Dornier-Flugzeuge installed the armament. During the first trial flight on 7 June, flown by

Swiss Bf 109E-3s practising war formations – the necessary 'price' of defending neutrality . . ./ *H Thurnheer (both)*

KTA pilot Oblt Gottfried Suter, loss of engine power caused the aircraft to stall and it crashed into the Bodensee (Lake Constance), killing its pilot. On 24 June, J 322 was delivered but the aircarft crashed near Mollis on 14 July, 1939 after engine failure caused by a broken valve spring. The pilot Lt Wannenmacher was badly injured.

All these accidents gave rise to comments in the Swiss Press, so that in early August 1939, the Eigenössisches Militärdepartment (Swiss Ministry of Defence) saw itself obliged to issue a statement denying assertions published in the press to the effect that the Messerschmitt was a failure and had to be taken out of service. The statement assured that the fighter was up to expectations. Notwithstanding the ominous beginnings, few problems were actually encountered when the Bf 109 was finally introduced into service. Hauptmann Albert Fisher, commander of Fliegerkompanie 8, later to become a director of Swiss Airline, Swissair, remembers:

'The conversion course of my unit at Geneva lasted some two weeks. We first flew the Taifun (Bf 108) to learn the new landing technique. There were very few accidents. The

Morane MS 406 was much more delicate. With the Morane people sometimes bounced hugely on landing, whereas the main risk with the 109 was ground-looping, as the undercarriage track was so narrow. One had to watch it closely when landing. It wasn't difficult – just too new. You had the closed cabin, flaps, retractable undercarriage, different visibility – things like that. The other

Above: Bf 109E-3, J-313 of
Cp Av 6, taxying./*H Thurnheer*

Left: Under temporary
shelter, this Bf 109E-3 of Cp
Av 6 displays the unit
insigne, a flying witch on a
broomstick./*H Thurnheer*

difficulty was that one had to change the
propeller's pitch by hand and its control was
similar to a clock. At 12 o'clock you had pitch
for take-off; cruising was at 10.30; and when
one needed speed, the setting was towards 10.
When one forgot to change the pitch setting
before landing, one simply didn't touch the
ground – one just kept floating. I remember
once while landing at Geneva I forgot to
change the pitch setting back, and floated the
whole length of the airfield. When one realised
what was happening one had to open up to full
rpm, and with this wrong setting the machine
rolled very badly to one side, very low above
the ground. Such things did happen, but they
were always due to carelessness. One officer in

my Fl. Kp once took off from Interlaken – this
was even more stupid – with his propeller at
coarse pitch. Like that one simply did not
leave the ground. We immediately saw what
had happened; but he didn't. Finally he rolled
through some undergrowth and fell into the
River Lütsche. There were few accidents due
to technical faults, but things changed when,
in May 1944, we got the Bf 109F. They
were a complete failure – very poorly built
and clearly sabotaged, probably by non-
German labour. We found deliberate faults,
foreign bodies here and there, and so on. We
had to make one emergency landing after
another! The aircraft were even sent for
complete overhaul, but it was hopeless as we
couldn't get any spare parts.'

Walo Hörning, who from 1938 to 1941 was
commander of Fl. Kp 21, and later of Flieger
Abteilung 7, recalled one of the rare accidents
caused by a technical fault:

'Oberleutnant Victor Streiff, deputy commander of Fl. Kp 21, had an unusual accident
during a patrol on 2 January, 1940. He was
flying J 312 with his Sohn ('son' – wing-man)
and they were chasing a Luftwaffe Bf 110 from
Dübendorf towards Winterthur below a layer
of high fog. They were flying only some
100metres above the ground and 100metres
below the fog layer at a speed of about 320
km/h. Suddenly Streiff's Bf 109 became
grossly tail-heavy and could not be kept level
by pushing the stick forward. As a result it
started looping and entered the cloud layer.
Streiff quickly threw off the canopy and baled
out while the aircraft was on its back. Hanging
below his parachute, he heard the 109 complete

GRIM BEAUTY. Bf 109D-1, J-305 of Fl. Kp 21 silhouetted against the rugged Alps – often described as the Roof of Europe./*A Fischer*

its loop – he could not see it in the clouds – and immediately afterwards crash into the ground. Streiff got down safely, though his parachute only opened fully a few metres above the earth, and he landed about 500-metres away from his crashed aircraft. It was later found that the screw for trimming the tailplane had come loose from its support and at the high speed they were flying, the elevator had taken its fully negative position and forced the nose of the aircraft upwards.'

One of the first Swiss service pilots to fly a Bf 109 was Capitaine Hans Thurnheer of Compagnie d'Aviation 6, a squadron manned by personnel of the French-speaking region of Switzerland (though at one period 60 per cent of its personnel were German-speaking). His carefully preserved *Carnet de Vol* (log-book) records that he first flew a Bf 109 at Dübendorf on 7 January 1940; this was J-301, the lowest-serialled of the first batch of Jumo 210-engined Bf 109D-1s – or 'Jumos', as the Swiss pilots called them. His first flight in a 'Daimler' (Bf 109E-3) took place on 6 July, 1939, after some flights in a Bf 108. Thurnheer recalled:

'We were of course very impressed when we heard that we were to fly the 109. It was during January 1939 that we converted at Dübendorf. We had only one Taifun (Bf 108) and that was not enough, so Messerschmitt's chief 108 pilot, Brindlinger, came to Dübendorf with another Taifun with German registration and wearing a swastika on its tail. On 4 January, 1939 I flew in HB-HEB (Bf 108B-1, c/n 1988, registered on 27 December, 1938). Then came my first take-off in a Jumo. I still remember how, when I had at last retracted the undercarriage, set the propeller at its proper setting and glanced outside, I was already over Rapperswil (about 20km southeast of Dübendorf airfield.) One pilot after another was converted to the new type and we were mighty proud to be flying such an aircraft – a giant step from our Dewoitine D-27s.

'When we saw contrails for the first time we were rather alarmed, as at that time we didn't know what they were. We were frightened when suddenly the leading aircraft started to "steam". We didn't know where the "steam-clouds" came from, but then we did really crazy things like climbing without pressurised cabins to a height of nearly 11,000 metres (36,000 feet). Making contrails soon became a sport for us and we made various figures in the sky. We even had two specialists who tried to write "CPA 6" (our unit abbreviation) in the sky above Zürich. What they "wrote" was unreadable, of course, but the strange sign in the air prompted a local Swiss newspaper to write that St Niklaus von der Flueh, a Swiss saint who had once lived at Sachseln and still revered by pilgrims, had put his "protective hand above the sinful city of Zürich!"

'The Bf 109Es were delivered by Messerschmitt without armament or radio and only with basic instruments, and when war broke out not all our aircraft had full armament. We regretted that the Oerlikon 20-mm MG FF cannon was installed, as we considered the cannon made by the Schweizerische Waffenfabrik to be better. This had a high initial velocity and its trajectory was much flatter, but it was impossible to instal this type of cannon in the 109. When Germany invaded France on 10 May, 1940 Swiss air space was repeatedly violated by Luftwaffe aircraft, mostly bombers returning from raids on France. On the very first day I engaged a Junkers Ju 88 while flying J-316. I fired some warning shots across its nose, then attacked in earnest when the Junkers' gunners answered my first shots. It disappeared into cloud.

'On 1 June a dozen Heinkel He 111s of KG 55 penetrated Swiss air space and I was one of four 109 pilots who engaged tham above the Jura mountains, flying J-315. When we tried to make them land they fired at us, so we attacked and shot down two without loss to ourselves. This action brought me in front of a court martial, because Germany claimed that we had attacked the bombers over French territory. This was not really the case, but Germany put such heavy pressure on the Swiss Government that it was forced to have the matter investigated by a court martial. It was all very depressing for us, as we honestly believed we had only done our duty.

'But the worst fight was yet to come – on 8 June, 1940. The first losses sustained by the Luftwaffe at the hands of Swiss 109s had already infuriated Göring. Just imagine: German-built fighters from a small, neutral country, flown for the most part by German-speaking pilots – it was too much! Göing ordered sharp measures to be taken: he would teach those Swiss a thing or two. As threats from the German hierarchy had not met with much result, he decided to take steps himself and ordered several formations of Heinkel He 111 bombers to fly intentionally over Switzerland on 4 June, accompanied for the first time by Messerschmitt Bf 110s. The result was that two Bf 110s and one He 111 were shot down, for the loss of one Swiss Bf 109C, J-310.

'Göring's temper rose, and for 8 June he ordered the Swiss to be challenged by a complete *Zerstorergruppe* of Bf 110s operating from Freiburg, only 45km from the Swiss border. At 3.30 in the morning Fl. Kps 6, 15 and 21 were at a state of readiness. A few minutes before noon we were ordered to take off from Thun. Less than 20 minutes later we were over the Jura mountains where we soon spotted the Bf 110s – 32 of them! It

was a spine-chilling sight and even today when I hear the number 110 or see a picture of a 110, I become uneasy. Before we arrived on the scene two 109s of Fl. Kp 15 had engaged the Germans and one 109 had been shot down. This mass of aircraft was flying around in huge circles at three different height levels. We were in no way prepared to attack such a mass of aircraft at that time, and that is why all 12 of us each attacked separately. That was a mistake, because the Germans were well prepared and when we attacked they immediately tried to encircle us. All we could do was try get a 110 in a favourable position for a quick attack – fire, then try to escape as fast as possible. There were various methods of getting away, such as very tight loop – which the 110 could not follow – or half a loop followed by a roll. Anyway it was a rather dangerous situation, as we were alone when we attacked. If we had then had the battle experience we later accumulated, we would have shot down more than the three we managed to get. We had no losses. Hauptmann Homberger was shot through the lungs, but managed to land at Biel. He was also shot in the buttocks, but a good luck charm he was carrying in his purse saved him from further harm!'

Not all Luftwaffe aircraft came over Switzerland with belligerent intentions, however; some simply lost their way. Feldwebel Martin Villing, who in mid-1942 instructed future Luftwaffe fighter pilots in southern France, was one:

'On 12 June, 1942 we were ordered to ferry seven Bf 109s, destined for Africa, from Le Bourget, Paris, where they had been overhauled, to Munich-Riem airfield. Freiburg was to be our first stop. We wanted to paint the town red and each of us had a bottle of cognac aboard to show off, as this was unobtainable in Germany at that time. Obergefreiter Heinrich Scharf and I took off at 5.30 in the afternoon towards Freiburg. Beforehand I had obtained information from the Met Office and calculated our bearings. We climbed to 2,500metres as visibility was good. Everything went according to plan until we arrived in the neighbourhood of Freiburg. We looked for the Rhine without success as there was a thunder storm above the Rhine valley and everything looked black. We could not see the town of Freiburg and gradually our situation became critical as our fuel would only last for another 10minutes. I searched and searched, becoming more nervous all the time. The red warning light started to flicker: it was high time to land. Far away to the right I spotted a large town which I took to be Freiburg. We turned towards it, flying very low over the railway station twice but unable to read which town it was. Then I suddenly saw gliders flying very near. Think-

Right: As in any military service, muscle-power is a constant necessity. Ground crews manhandling a Swiss Bf 109E-3 into its parking area.

Below right: ENFORCED 'GUEST'. Heinkel He 111P (Wk Nr 1905) of the Luftwaffe's KG 55, which was shot down by Bf 109Es of Fl. Kp 15, near Ursins, in May 1940./*J P Thevoz*

ing that these were German, and reasoning that where there were gliders there must be an airfield, we flew in their direction, soon spotted the airfield and let down our undercarriages to land.

'I was actually landing when I noticed white crosses on the parked aircraft – and suddenly it dawned on me that I was in Switzerland! We had arrived at Bern-Belpmoos airfield. With the last drops of fuel I rolled out after landing, then my engine stopped. Before I had even opened my canopy two Swiss guards motioned me out of the aircraft; they probably feared that I would destroy the machine. My *Rottenflieger* saw it all from above and wanted to fly away, but then his engine started spluttering and he only just managed to land. While he was still rolling the Swiss fired a shot through the aircraft fuselage half a metre behind the cockpit. They later declared that they thought he wanted to take off again.'

A few weeks later the two Germans received company: Alfredo, an Italian pilot who had also lost his bearings. The two Luftwaffe pilots were released on 21 December, 1942 in exchange for Flight Lieutenant Wooll, RAF, who had landed his Mosquito PR IV, DK310, GL-Y at Bern-Belpmoos on 24 August, 1942. The two German aircraft, Bf 109F-4/Zs. remained in their hangar at Bern for the duration of the war. In the summer of 1946 they were given Swiss registrations J-715 and J-716, made one test flight each and were then flown to Emmen, where they were scrapped early in 1947.

Obergefreiter Martin Scharf died when his aircraft crashed at Verneuil, France on 20 June, 1944. Martin Villing ended the war as an *Offiziersanwärter* – officer-candidate – serving with III./JG 5, having obtained 21 accredited victories. When he was finally released as a prisoner of war on 17 June, 1947, one of the first things he did was to meet in Konstanz with one of his former Swiss guards to thank him for his excellent treatment while an internee. Villing then resumed his original trade as a machine mechanic in his birthplace, Stockach, where 33 years later he recalled his adventures.

Far left: UNINVITED. Oberfeldwebel Martin Villing, one of the two Luftwaffe pilots who landed at Bern, Switzerland on 25 July, 1942, in his Bf 109F-4/Z./*M Villing*

Left: 'Enjoying' captivity in Switzerland; from left, Oberfeldwebel Martin Villing; an Italian fighter pilot; and Obergefreiter Scharf, 1942./*M Villing*

251

Away from War

During WW2, Sweden, like Switzerland, was a haven of neutrality, and occasionally a Bf 109 would 'get lost' and wind up in this neutral country. The months April and May 1945 saw a number of Luftwaffe pilots who did not cherish the idea of becoming prisoners of war, and accordingly sought refuge in Sweden. In all, 13 Bf 109s came down on Swedish soil throughout the war. Any foreign aircraft coming down in Sweden was given an official landing code identity, and it is this code which is mentioned in the first column of the following of the 'lucky 13' Bf 109s.

Left: 'VISITORS' TO SWEDEN. Bf 109s T 75 (nearest) and T 79, both of which landed at Rinkaby; the first on 12 April, 1945, and the second on 24 April, 1945./*B Widfeldt*

Centre, far left and left: T 90 being evaluated by the Swedish Air Force (Flyg Vapnet) at Bromma. It crashed before it could be handed over to the USSR./ *B Widfeldt*

Below: T 90, a Bf 109G (Wk Nr 130297) immediately after landing at Bulltofta on 4 May, 1945./*B Widfeldt*

Above: T 99, a Bf 109G-8, the last to land in Sweden. Balkenkreuz and swastika have been over-painted here; it was handed over to Russia on 8 November, 1945./ *B Widfeldt*

Code	Date	Place	Type	Werke Nr	Remarks
T 17	24 Oct 1940	Karlstadt	E-4	0820	Uffz Ludwig Fröba, 4./JG77; lost way in flight from Trondheim to Oslo. Aircraft brought to SAAB/L for technical survey.
T 25	24 Feb '42	Dorotea	E-4B(?)	?	Radio code KB+LS; pilot deserted; belly-landing. Aircraft possibly returned to Germany.
T 34	24 Aug '43	Glimakra	G-4	?	Pilot lost, baled out, aircraft crashed. Parts sold or scrapped; to Blecker and Co. AB, Malmö, 4 Feb 1944.
T 36	9 Oct '43	Kristianstad	F-2	6741	Landed after navigation error. Radio code DJ+JW. Test flownby SAAB and Fc(SAF test centre.) One cannon taken to Bofors.
T 37	9 Oct '43	Dansjö gard	G	9542	Belly-landed after navigation error. Still in Sweden 1946 at F 12.
T 56	15 Nov '44	Stordalen	G	?	Pilot lost during flight from one base to another in N. Norway; baled out and saved. Aircraft crashed, parts still remain at crash site, 1975. Built by Wiener Neustädter Fluzeugwerke / Avions Caudron.
	17 Nov '44	Kutjaure	G	?	Hgfr Ecke lost during flight from N. Norway to Bodö. Pilot baled and saved; aircraft never salvaged.
T 74	12 Apr' 45	Rinkaby	G-10	77 0261	Landed with fugitive from Berlin area. Aircraft test-flown by Fc.
T 75	12 Apr '45	Rinkaby	G-10	77 0293	Landed with T74, from Berlin area. (C/n also recorded as 77 0093 . . .?)
T 79	24 Apr '45	Rinkaby	G-14	49 0137	Landed with fugitive from Usedom, Baltic area. Testflown in Sweden. (C/n also recorded as 40 9137 . . .?)
T 90	4 May '45	Bulltofta	G	13 0297	Landed after navigation error during flight from Weichsel area. Crashed during test at Bromma Airport, prior to handing over to USSR.
T 98	8 May '45	Bredakra	G-8	?	Landed with fugitive from Kurland. Handed over to USSR on 27 August 1945.
T 99	8 May '45	Bredakra	G-8	?	Landed with fugitive from Kurland. Handed over to USSR on 8 November 1945.

Stalling Speeds and C_L Max.
$W = 5{,}580$ lb. $S = 174$ sq. f.

		Pilot's A.S.I.		Indicated airspeed V_1 (from trailing static).		C_L	
Condition		Speed at which Slots open. m.p.h.	Stalling Speed. m.p.h.	Speed at which Slots open. m.p.h.	Stalling Speed. m.p.h.	C_L at which Slots open.	C_L max.
Flaps and Ailerons	Undercarriage.						
Up	Up	111	75	120.5	95.5	0.865	1.4
Down { Flaps 42.5°	Up	90	61	100.5	81	1.2	1.9
,, { Ailerons 10° ,,	Down	90	61	100.5	81	1.2	1.9

And not only Pilots

Engine maintenance on a Bf 109G-4 of IV./JG 54 at Siwerskaya, Russia./ *Bundesarchiv*

SPIT AND POLISH. Ground crews cleaning up the Bf 109F of Oberfeldwebel Johann Pichler of III./JG 77, in Russia./*W Schäfer*

'I first got acquainted with the 109 as a trainee engine inspector, but the episode unfortunately ended with a court-martial. During 1940, II./KG 30, equipped with Junkers Ju A-5s, was stationed at Perleberg, and a Bf 109C-2 from the Werneuchen fighter pilots' school had been sent to Perleberg to be used in air fighting exercises. Its pilot was Oberfeldwebel Gessner. After a few flights shortly before Christmas 1940, the pilot reported the engine as running rough at an approximate height of 300metres. The *Prüfleiter* (head of section) ordered me to find the fault and remedy it. After re-adjusting the carburettor – the Jumo 210 did not have fuel injection – I ordered a test flight and asked the pilot to make a low pass over the airfield so that I could see if the engine still left any smoke trail. He did so, and the engine ran faultlessly. The result, however, was that the head of flying control, a *Major* without flying experience, had the pilot arrested right out of the cockpit for violation of flying discipline! Even when I told him that I had ordered the flight, the well-fed *Major* would not change his mind. The pilot remained detailed over Christmas and the New Year in spite of protests from the civilian personnel in the repair shop, pilots of II./KG 30 and myself – and despite the fact, too, that the pilot was an instructor at Werneuchen. Then events in the west took the pilot to France, where he scored 16 victories in a short time.

'The *Major* still insisted on a court-martial however, and the pilot was brought back from

Left, top to bottom: 'Warte'. 'Warts', or 'Black Men' (from the black overalls usually worn) – the indispensable, hard-working ground crews who provided the essential foundation for all operational flying. These particular airmen served with III./JG 26./*A Weise*

SWEAT AND MUSCLE. The two essential ingredients of good servicing; exemplified here by two 'Warts' of JG 3, 'Udet', working on a Bf 109G-6/E2/Trop 'Pulk-Zerstörer'. Note the Wfr.Gr. 21 mortars under the wings, and spiral nose marking, in black and white./*Bundesarchiv*

Calibrating the engine fuel consumption at Deurne airfield on a Bf 109 repaired at the Erla VII depot (see text).

Left: Three views in sequence showing Bf 109E-4, (Wk Nr 1623) of JG 77, which made a belly-landing on a frozen lake at Haugesund, Norway in 1941. While local children act as a counterweight, the aircraft is raised by means of inflatable bags. Later support jacks are put under the machine, and the undercarriage lowered./ *O Rumler (all three)*

Above: Hauptmann Günther Schack, commander of I./JG 51, explains to his ground crew some defect found during his recent mission./*G Schack*

Top centre: 'Waffenwarte' – The armourers check over belts of ammunition prior to filling the guns' tanks.

Top, far right: HARMONISATION. Another essential task for the armourers; aligning and adjusting the gun barrels and mountings to ensure all are correctly synchronised in firing. In this case use is being made of a prepared plywood harmonisation disc.

Above right: 'White 9' of III./JG 26 has a change of motor at Caffiers, France in late 1940./*A Weise*

the front, and myself from the technical school Perleberg. The trial took place in May 1941, but thanks to a sensible judge, to Werner Baumbach as a witness and defendant, and my own technical explanation, the pilot was acquitted. As a civilian I could speak more freely. The Chief Engineer of the RLM kept nodding his approval all the time I spoke at the trial, and this gave me courage to speak out, especially against the *Major* who wanted a conviction at all costs. From then on the *Major* was ignored and despised by all personnel at the airfield. The pilot, later, often forwarded to us a case of French wine, whenever a Junkers Ju 52/3m flew over from France.

'After I had obtained my engine inspector's licence, I was sent to a large Front Repair Shop (*Feldwerft*) at Banak in Norway, to look after KG 26 and KG 30. For a while I had nothing to do with the 109 as no fighters were stationed there. In June 1942 three Russian DB-3 bombers attacked our airfield for the first time. All bombs fell in the water at the edge of the field, but nevertheless three Bf 109E-3s of III./JG 5, stationed at Kirkenes, were then detached to Banak. The Russians did not know of this and attacked next day

with 16 bombers of the DB-3 and Pe-2 types. Most of them were shot down or crashed against the mountains surrounding Porsanger Fjord during the ensuing combat. Only one Russian survived, a snow-white haired major who saved himself by parachute. We treated him decently. He had wrapped his possessions – a family picture and some roubles – in a *Pravda* newspaper. He was shivering with cold – the Arctic ocean is not exactly a sauna – and kept wondering why he was being treated so well. Next day he was taken by Ju 52/3m to General der Flieger Stumpf, commander of Luftflotte 5, whose territory included Norway and Finland.

'One of the 109s had received a hit in the cylinder head cover, but this could be welded on the spot. After this action the 109s were recalled to Kirkenes. During take-off from our *Knüppelstartbahn* (runway of wooden logs) one of the 109s swung off the runway, left the ground, stalled out of the turn and crashed to complete destruction. Yet the pilot was unhurt thanks to the robust construction of the central section of the 109s fuselage and cabin. We engine inspectors had little trouble with the 109 because it was a tough aircraft. Only

the airframe inspectors suffered, by reason of the machine's narrow undercarriage.

'I then had to work on Bf 109G-6s, at the Stavanger-Sola airfield in west Norway. Engine cooling during fuel consumption tests always presented a problem. Due to the position of the cooling radiators outside the slipstream, cooling was poor during stationary running of the engine. We solved this by asking the airfield fire brigade to spray water on the cooling radiators so that we could measure fuel consumption accurately. How tough the 109 was can be illustrated by one which crashed after an *alarm* take-off. In his haste the pilot forgot to set the tail trim at its usual position of plus 1 degree. After unsticking, the Bf 109G-6 climbed sharply, stalled and crashed, breaking into three parts. The wings came off, the engine broke loose and the fuselage finished up on its back right next to our repair shop. We lifted the fuselage and from underneath it the pilot, Feldwebel Schulte, crawled from the cabin with only a superficial scratch on his hand. We found the tail trim was still set at minus 6-degrees, thus acting as a full-up elevator.

'A delicate job, and sometimes a problem, was the adjustment of the automatic propeller-pitch setting mechanism. This mechanism was situated on top of the DB 605A (and AS) engine, in front of the double Bosch ZM2 magneto. Any incorrect adjustment could mean an accident, because rpm, boost pressure, propeller pitch and ignition timing all had to be set in harmony. At the front, this adjustment, as well as fuel consumption measurement and adjustment of the Bosch fuel-infection pump, could only be undertaken under the supervision of an engine inspection master (*Triebwerkprüfmeister*). When measuring fuel consumption the exact rpm was found by using a hand-held tachoscope. (I still remember that the tool kit we used for this job carried the number FL Nr 18605.) Mechanics and inspectors in the Luftwaffe then had to have a lot of knowledge about mechanical things, had to be capable of making parts themselves, and had to be able to 'organise' parts – in other words, of scrounging from the *Luftzeugamt*. At Stavanger I had no less than eight reserve DB 605 engines and VDM propellers. The technical officers of the *Staffel* also needed to be very knowledgeable – more so than nowaday when parts are simply replaced.'

Oskar Rumler was private mechanic to Willy Stör, German aerobatics champion of 1935 and 1936, who flew a BFW M35 on those occasions. Apart from working on Bf 109s, Rumler worked on various other aircraft types, including Messerschmitt Me 262 jets. He is now retired, living close to the large Luftwaffe base at Fürstenfeldbruck, near Munich.

Facing page, top left: 'Yellow 4' (Wk Nr 1552) under temporary shelter during routine servicing. JG 26, Caffiers, 1940./*A Weise*

Facing page, top right: Open air servicing on a DB 601 engine – the 'Werft' (repair section) of III./JG 26, Caffiers, 1940./*A Weise*

Facing page, centre left: RE-FUELLING. Adolf Galland's Bf 109E of III./JG 26 has just had its tanks replenished. Caffiers, 1940./ *A Weise*

Facing page, centre right: 'Yellow 9' of III./JG 26 undergoing daily engine servicing at Caffiers, 1940. In background is Klemm Kl 35, NR+NN, the unit 'hack' transport aircraft./ *A Weise*

Top: An airframe fitter effects a small skin repair on a Bf 109E of III./JG 26 at Caffiers, 1940./*A Weise*

Above: WOMEN AT WORK. The 'fair sex' also helped. Two German civilian helpers working on the DB 605A-1 engine of a Bf 109G-6 at the Messerschmitt Works at Regensburg-Prüfening. As was the custom, defects have been noted, in chalk, on the propeller blade./ *Messerschmitt-Archiv*

Left: WAITING, WAITING... Ground crews taking advantage of a brief pause in their round-the-clock duties to enjoy the sun, next to their 'charge', a Bf 109G-5./*Bundesarchiv*

In African Skies

On 8 November, 1942, four days after Rommel started retreating from El Alamein, British and American forces landed in French North Africa. In order to protect the rear of the Afrika Korps, Generalfeldmarschall Kesselring started flying troops to Tunisia the next day. The skies over Tunisia became yet another battlefield for the Luftwaffe. The first Bf 109s to arrive in Tunisia to fight there were those of JG 53, the famous 'Pik As' (Ace of Spades) *geschwader*. With them came the war correspondents, and one of these, Dr Erhardt Eckert, interviewed some JG 53 pilots for *Der Adler*. He started with the *Kommodore*, Oberstleutnant Günther Freiherr von Maltzahn:

'A large formation of enemy bombers attacked our airfield. When I took off the AA was already firing. I flew in the direction of the American bombers and reached its rear formation over the Gulf of Bizerta. In all there were 36 four-engined Boeing Fortress II bombers, flying in three waves. I attacked frontally the bomber flying left of the right-hand wave. Soon two of its engines stopped and, after my attack, the Boeing started to leave a smoke trail. It turned out of its formation and dived, trying to secape. After we had descended from 6,000 to 400metres, a man jumped from the aircraft and floated down with his parachute. I made one attack after another, firing with all guns. Until the end the American returned my fire. After 15 minutes' fighting the bomber crashed northwest of Medjez-el-Bab and burned out immediately.'

And here is Hauptmann Friedrich-Karl Müller, commander of I./JG 53:

'I did an *alarm* take-off when some 40 American fighters were coming in our direc-

COMRADES-IN-ARMS. Bf 109E-7 of 7./JG 26 taxiing past a Fiat CR 42 of the Regia Aeronautica; the latter trestled into flying position, presumably for a gun harmonisation check./*Bundesarchiv*

Top right: Retraction test, the hard way! Ground check on the undercarriage of a Bf 109F-2/Trop of I./JG 27 in North Africa. Wing-tips have been removed, and ground crews serve as a counterweight on the tail./*Bundesarchiv*

Centre, right and far right: 'ROTTE'. A fighting pair of Bf 109E-4/N Trop from I./JG 27 scouring the Western Desert. An otherwise effective upper camouflage scheme is nullified by reflections and shadow./*Bundesarchiv* (both)

Right: Bf 109E-7/Trop of I./JG 27, flown by the 'Gruppe' adjutant. Note 300-litre drop tank for extra range under its fuselage./*E Neumann*

Far right: START. Bf 109F-2/Trop of JG 27 revs up before taxiing away. The 'Wart' (mechanic) takes away the engine starting handle, though this item was often parked in the cockpit, behind the pilot's seat./*Bundesarchiv*

Retouching the paintwork
on a Bf 109 F-2/Trop of JG 27.
Note engine starting handle
in position, and aileron
mass-balance under far
wing./*Bundesarchiv*

tion. First I fought six Spitfires, one of which I shot down. While flying home I saw a gaggle of 40 enemy fighters some 2-3,000 metres away. The Americans didn't spot me. I climbed almost vertically, attacked the first Lightning, and it fell burning after a short burst. I dived to get away from the fire of the other fighters, but they did not react to the loss, so I could get away without further fighting. I had to land quickly as I had no more fuel left. The Lightnings mostly avoid combat. When it comes to it, however, we are always holding a winning hand.'

Oberleutnant Julius Meimberg, Staffel-kapitän of I. and II./JG 2 recalled:

'During the afternoon [of 4 December, 1942] a formation of 12 Boston bombers was reported flying over Mateur. Shortly after we spotted them and chased the gaggle which tried to get home by flying very low. Immediately, a *Schwarm* reached the Americans. One Boston had already been shot down and its smoke was mushrooming when I arrived. The other Bostons now flew even closer together and therefore constituted a considerable fire-power. I soon found myself in a firing position. The Boston's right engine at once started burning, it lost height and crashed into the ground. Next I attacked a Boston flying to my left. While turning I found that five Americans had already been shot down. As more Me's had now arrived, a real bunch gathered behind the Yankees. However, I got another one, my third Boston. It crashed down burning. I could only fire a short burst at a fourth machine as all my ammunition was spent. While flying back I spotted one of the Spitfires. Shooting down the 12 Bostons took only five minutes.'

[In fact, the Allied bombers were British – eleven Bristol Bisley aircraft from 18 Squadron RAF. Their leader, Wing Commander Hugh Gordon Malcolm, DFC, was killed, and later awarded his country's highest honour, a posthumous Victoria Cross. This massacre – some 50-60 Messerschmitts were involved in all – saw the demise of the Bisley as a day bomber, while 18 Squadron was temporarily disbanded and re-equipped to recommence operations on 27 December.]

Oberleutnant Jürgen Harder, *Gruppen-kommandeur* remembered:

'Our infantry reported than an American attack was expected along an important road. At once I started a low-level attack with the *Gruppe*. When we reached the road in question, I gave the order: "To the left – attack!". A wild hunt developed for everything that moved down below – tanks, reconnaissance vehicles, cars, trucks, motor cycles, infantry columns. One *Schwarm* attacked a train on the railway near the road. Without braking, the engineer jumped from

Above: Splendid close-up view as a Bf 109G-6/R2/Trop 'Pulk Zerstörer' of JG 3, Udet, revs its engine prior to take-off. Note Wfr Gr 21 mortar under wing./ *Bundesarchiv*

Left: Armourers rolling a 21-cm Nebelwerfer 42, air-to-air rocket, used by the Bf 109G-6/R2/Trop./ *Bundesarchiv*

Below left: An unusual camouflage pattern on a Bf 109 of 2./JG 77 at Gabes, Tunisia, 1943./*A Kohler*

Right: One way of keeping the cockpit cool was the use of a beach umbrella, as on this Bf 109F-2/Trop . . ./ *Bundesarchiv*

the locomotive and ran away across the fields. Soon, however, the train stopped as it was badly hit, and the rail line began to climb. Shortly before the end of the road I zoomed upwards to 200metres to see if I had hit a particular vehicle, when there was a loud bang in my cockpit. There was a large hole in the left side window through which the airstream entered. The left side of my face was covered with blood and blood was also flowing from my left hand. The instrument panel was completely destroyed. I called the *Gruppe* by radio: 'Am slightly wounded – flying home.' I flew back without any engine control, but performed a good landing. Shortly after the rest of the *Gruppe* arrived. We had no losses.'

Oberleutnant Fritz Dinger, *Staffelkapitän* recalls:

'My mission was to protect a large freighter that was nearing the Tunisian coast near Bizerta. While circling over the steamship I suddenly noticed a long oil streak on the water that approached in a zig-zag from the enemy side I watched the sky and the suspect oil streak at the same time. Suddenly I recognised the long, dark shape of a submarine that now set course directly towards the freighter and fired two torpedoes. Their wake could be seen clearly. I dived at once and fired at the two torpedoes to warn the ship's crew of their danger. The ship made a rapid turn and got out of the torpedoes' path. I then made three attacks against the enemy submarine which dived quickly. My *Rottenkamerad* and I saw a large oil slick on the water, so the submarine must have been at least badly damaged.'

Von Maltzahn survived the war as an *Oberst* with 68 victories, Müller crashed to his death while landing at Salzwedel on 29 May, 1944, having obtained 140 victories; Meimberg also survived the war as a *Major* with 53 accredited kills. Harder, having become *Kommodore* of JG 11, crashed to his death near Berlin on 17 February, 1945, probably due to lack of oxygen. He had obtained 64 victories, and was one of three Harder brothers – all Luftwaffe fighter pilots – to be killed in action. Dinger was killed on the ground during an air raid in Italy on 27 July 1943. He had scored 67 victories.

A Chronology of early Bf 109 development, drawn up by Dipl Ing Lusser, head
of BFW's Project Bureau, on 20 October,
1934.

DiplIng-, Fl-Stabs Ing Christensen was
an official of the Technisches Amt of the
RLM.

Main Data of the Chronology of the VJ

1. First briefing discussion in Berlin (Christensen – Lusser) *8.3.34*
2. Second discussion in Augsburg (Lucht – Christensen) *21.3.34*
   Detailed definition of task, invitation for submission of tenders.
   Start of the preliminary project.
3. First visual mock-up inspection *11.5.34*
4. Discussion of radiotelegraphy installations (Schwarz II) *12.5.34*
5. Second visual mock-up inspection
   29.5.34
   During this the following items were found missing:

   (1) Dummy engine BMW 15/115
   (2) Automatic system MGC 30
   (3) MG 17
   (4) All radio data
   (5) All Vemag documents
   (6) Reflex sight
   (7) Rolls-Royce data
   (8) Arrangement of instruments requirements
   We were commissioned to test the installation of three machine-guns.
   We were further informed that, for the time being, only water coolers could be used for JUMO 210 and BMW 115.
6. BFW is requesting the following equipment:

   (1) Complete radio apparatus
   (2) Automatic system MGC 30
   (3) Generator and transformer
   (4) MG 17
   (5) Data on high-temperature liquid cooling.
7. Third mock-up inspection. *21., 22.6.34*
   Attended by seven officials from RLM. The following new requirements are made:

   (1) View panel in the floor
   (2) Installation of BMW 116 (no dummies or data available at all)
   (3) Cartridge case collecting box
   (4) Installation of Revie 3 (no data)

   (5) Fundamental alteration of cabin
   (6) Installation of radio apparatus (no data)
   (7) Investigation of different engine mountings
   (8) Accurate mock-up construction of fuel and lubricant system (no data)
   (9) Complete table of accessories
8. Engine mock-up BMW 116 received on *1.7.34*
9. Discussion between Christensen and Lusser concerning the engine.
   17.7.34
10. Discussion between Christensen, Todtleben, Dettinger, Cornelius.
    24., 25.7.34

    (1) MGC 30
    (2) MG 17
    (3) Vemag
    (4) Arrangement of pedals
    (5) Instrument panel
    (6) Radio equipment
    (7) Variable-pitch propellers
11. Discussion between Christensen and Lusser. *24.8.34*

    (1) Submission of our designs for three MG 17
    (2) Controllable airscrew still unresolved, solution possible only in one or two months' time
    (3) Flexible engine suspension has not been decided on by the client
    (4) Radiator questions
    (5) Design of pilot's seat
    (6) Design of balance of controls
12. Mock-up MGC 30 for JUMO received on *2.10.34*
13. Commissioned Göttingen to test horizontal stabilizers and elevators. *6.10.34*
14. Start of the design and construction of a completely new, detailed engineering mock-up VJ in place of the provisional mock-up ordered by Herr Messerschmitt.
    –.10.34
15. Inspection of the engineering mock-up (16 specialists, 16 page report).
    16., 17.10.34

A letter by Udet to Messerschmitt on 4 April, 1941, concerning 25 faults of the Bf 109F which had been mentioned in a telegram from Generalfeldmarschall Kesselring, Commander of Luftflotte II.

Dear Messerschmitt,

Attached to this letter I am sending you a copy of an urgent telegram from General-feldmarschall Kesselring.

I am very surprised that the chief engineer there has waited until today to present these extensive complaints comprising 25 items and I would be very grateful to you – especially in view of the need to fight against pessimism concerning any new model – if you could send me, by return, a telegram with your comments to be forwarded to the front line.

Some of the points raised in the telegram by Kesselring, enclosed by Udet, are:

"In connection with model Bf 109F the following main complaints have been reported to me:

1. On one aircraft the tail-plane complete with tail section was torn off at the fuselage disconnecting point (panel 9). The fuselage disconnecting point was found to be too weak.

2. The external elevator bearing is breaking away and must be reinforced.

3. The bearing flange for the elevator bearing must also be reinforced.

4. The parking brake is completely inadequate. A mere reinforcement of the spring would hardly be sufficient.

5. The pilot's seat is too far to the front. It must also be pointed out that, due to the present position of the seat, a pilot in full flying kit will be unable to move the control column fully backwards and one result of this is that only wheel landings are possible.

6. The breathing tube is too short for pilots of average and above average height.

7. The breathing equipment for high-altitude flying is also inadequate. An additional pressure-oxygen unit is urgently required.

8. Do away with the engine's pannier.

9. The front and rear bolts holding the wing-tip edges deflect and rattle.

10. The ammunition boxes fitted in the wings are loose and have jammed. This was temporarily remedied in the unit by means of wooden blocks fitted underneath, but this does not present a permanent solution.

11. The oil radiator is inadequately secured.

12. A solution of the wing surface deformation problem which since the unit reported adverse flying qualities with a deformed aircraft has also been observed on the right-hand wing.

13. Securing of plating on landing gear, oil radiator and water cooler.

14. Thermostat must be secured more firmly.

15. The welding of aileron horns on aircraft supplied is to be subjected to a test by the unit based on instructions to be issued by the *Generalluftzeugmeister*.

16. The distance between the ribs of the aileron is larger on the model F than on the model E. Due to poor quality stitching the fabric tends to pull out of shape.

17. Tyre wear is extremely high due to the pronounced toe-in, this is particularly noticeable among aircraft using concrete runways where a tyre change is necessary after 20 sorties.

18. The fuel consumption varies considerably for different aircraft, e.g. the aircraft produced by Arado require 70 litres per hour more than others. It is assumed that the aircraft companies will carry out, belatedly, a more thorough tuning of engines.

19. The red fuel warning lamp shows inaccurate readings. It was found that in one case the lamp did not light up until the fuel had dropped to 10 litres, whereas in another case the lamp was observed to light up with 60 litres in the tank.

20. Complaints regarding the automatic propeller system.

21. Cable securing screws on the valve body are too long, so that the cylinder wall is pierced when the screws are tightened. Result: oil running through.

22. Since the 15mm bush and the deep-groove-type radial ball-bearing at the supercharger are frequently being deflected, an order must be given to have the end clearance checked, if possible, after five hours operating time. Within one quarter, 30 superchargers out of 400 have shown such faults and had to be replaced.

23. One unit proposes a higher basic setting of the supercharger to improve high altitude performance.

24. Due to leaking valves there is a relatively high wear of N-engines (which have a life of about 40 hours). This leads to an increased demand for spare engines.

25. Reduced altitude performance was observed with repaired engines. It is assumed that the performance is not re-tested on altitude test stands but merely by recalculation. Random checks seem essential.

I urgently request that the necessary amendment instructions be issued and the required form changes to be made at the *Gruppen* by industrial teams. Withdrawal of aircraft to industrial plants or to air bases situated rearward is unacceptable for military reasons.

Signed Kesselring
Generalfeldmarschall

JOHANNES WIESE

Right: ON THE BUTT. Harmonising the guns of Major Adolf Galland's Bf 109E of III./JG 26, which he commanded, at Caffiers, 1940. The rudder 'scoreboard' indicates a tally of 67 victories to date./*A Weise*

Below: Hauptmann Jürgen Harder, 'Gruppenkommandeur' of I./JG 53, stationed in Sicily in the summer of 1943, talking to the armourers replacing the underwing 20-mm cannon of his Bf 109G-6 with Wfr Gr 21. The wing's undermarkings are BS+NA./*Bundesarchiv*

Through the Kommandeur's Eyes

Major Johannes Wiese *Kommandeur* I./JG 52, later Kommodore JG 52; 133 confirmed victories, 75 unconfirmed:

The mission is over and, one sinks into an old armchair in the *Gefechtsstand* (command post) – a pretentious title, perhaps, for a cramped earthen bunker equipped with a few tables, maps, telephones, a stove (if one is lucky). The mission debriefing is over, a cigar has been lit, and slowly the inner tension and excitement is ebbing away. One begins to ask and answer questions about the *Gruppe* and its support, about comrades who are still fighting. And then the *Spiess* (senior non-commissioned officer) is standing to attention at one's elbow, reporting and introducing a new arrival, Leutnant X, who has been transferred to the staff of the *Gruppe*. The Leutnant, tall, in flying kit with the prominent mark of the *Jagdflieger* (fighter pilot) a yellow silken scarf. He stands at attention and reports himself. A handshake and he is brought into the circle of men in the *Gruppenstab*. Where has he come from? How long has he been flying? Has he brought along a new 109? How was the weather? Who flew with him? Has he seen his new quarters? – just some of the questions put to the newcomer. Have you ever been afraid? is the *Kommandeur's* question. Immediately – how could it be otherwise? – the answer is, 'No, Herr Major'.

'Well, that's it for the moment. I welcome you. Take your time getting used to things. Meet the adjutant, Leutnant Plücker, and the signals officer, Oberleutnant X. You'll have to get acquainted with the others yourself. Then we'll see each other again. You can ask me any questions that might arise . . . and think about that one of being afraid!'

Yes . . . if he only knew how often fear jumps at one's throat during combat, when the tracers flash by, overhead, underneath, and at the sides. When the rudder starts fluttering in a tight turn, so tight that the good old 109 can hardly take it without stalling; when the grey flocks of the AA suddenly start to explode all round as if they wanted to transform you – you and nobody else – into a ball of fire, to make the shreds fly around. *Luchhund* (Lying dog) the north-Germans call anyone who keeps saying he isn't frightened. Of course one could have flown on quietly on a steady course, always stolid and upright. But what does one do?

Stick forward, kick the rudder, maximum rpm. Next second one clobbers one's head against the plexiglass canopy as once again the straps aren't tight enough. One pulls out of the too-fast dive without realising properly how one does it. Pull in one's head as far as possible to the left, because there was a fleeting shadow off the left wing. Pull one's machine into a reciprocal course and imagine having just missed the nose of a Red aircraft. One wants only one thing, to make any defensive movement – then, suddenly, everything has meaning and purpose again and – who knows where he came from? – an enemy glides in front of one's gunsight, as if he'd never heard that such a thing could be dangerous. It can only be fractions of a second in which one reacts, sets one's luck, thinks, then uses it. Red nose, red star, big engine, LAGG – at it! 'Tabak 2?' (Tobacco 2 – call-sign). My *Rottenflieger* – forgotten for a second – no, not forgotten – linked by command obedience, drill, expertise, knowing one's machine. Less than 50 metres separate the LAGG in front of me from the hail of gun and cannon fire that now forcibly thunders into the body of the enemy aircraft. Only the time it takes to blink is left to dive underneath it and climb in a steep turn in front of it; just in time to see the machine explode into a thousand pieces. Fear is gone; elation is already over, because the next shadow is sitting beside me.

Change direction again, looking around, then come the words of relief, 'Tabak 1 from Tabak 2. Confirm shooting down. Am behind you.' Only now does one get a 'lift'; only now does one relax a little. We look into each others

Above: Werner Mölders, 'Kommodore' JG 51, at a Russian airfield during summer of 1941. He was the first 'General der Jagdflieger' (General of the Fighter Pilots), but was killed on 22 November, 1941, travelling as a passenger in a Heinkel He 111, on his way to attend Ernst Udet's funeral in Germany./ *W Schäfer*

Below and bottom: Johannes Wiese, 'Kommandeur' of I./JG 52, giving 'fatherly' advice to some junior members . . . !/*J Wiese*

eyes; we wink at each other; see the torch beneath us that lights up on the vast plain – not me, not you, but him. I will ask the new *Leutnant* again how he feels about fear. Before he comes with me on a real combat mission he'll get this question many times. Only when he *knows* fear, *and* knows what to do about it will he go with me – he has to become a fighter pilot on my staff after all – to give us both a chance. It would soon be lost if one could not count upon him being 'with it'; that he has learned how to conquer fear.

We meet again in the evening. 'Seen everything yet? Everything as expected? Talked to the other pilots yet? You might as well have a haircut, then your flying helmet fits better and you sweat less. And you can leave your yellow scarf in your suitcase; we don't fly over the sea here. Is your machine ready? Concern yourself about it; watch closely how it is serviced, it won't do you any harm. And you must become well acquainted with your *Wart* (mechanic). We may have a tour around tomorrow, though not to the Front, to see what you can do.'

'Everything all right?' is the only question I ask next day. I didn't want or need to ask more. I know our mechanics and their conscientious work, but I also know my other pilots who will have told the newcomer more about myself than is perhaps good. I hold a short briefing, pointing out which area we'll be flying in, where the front line is, where they can find the more important recognition points even after an aerial combat, and then; 'Shall we go then'.? We go to our aircraft, strap ourselves in, put on our headsets, put on gloves, give the signal to start the engine, let the inertia starter come to full rpm, pull the starter knob, let the propeller blades get underway and, after checking the magnetos, give more throttle to roll towards the take-off spot. By then I talk to him on the radio, not really in a fatherly way, but at least soothing and encouraging.

Now then, lightly on the brakes – more throttle – a bit more – more – all right – now, up and away. We leave the airfield and are already in the circuit. I position myself in front of him, he beside me, uncertain.

'Well, how are things? Everything all right?'

'Viktor, Viktor'

'Do come a bit closer – still more – more – that's it – all right – easy on the throttle – not so violent with the rudder – relax.'

And so we fly, climbing, getting away from the front line. The sun is already in the west.

'Tabak 2 from Tabak 1 asks Viktor?'

'Tabak 1 from Tabak 2, Viktor'.

When we reach our altitude I let the formation open out, and point out an airstrip below us from where we set course for our own, eastwards.

And then we start to corkscrew about just as

Left, top to bottom: The 44th victory of Oberleutnant 'Tutti' Müller of JG 53 is painted onto his aircraft rudder. He crashed to his death on 29 May, 1944 while landing at Salzwedel airfield./*Bundesarchiv*

Feldmarschall Hermann Göring, Chief of the Luftwaffe, visiting JG 2, 'Richthofen' in November 1940. At his left elbow is Major Helmuth Wick, appointed to command of the 'Geschwader' on 20 November, but killed eight days later. The pilot in the peaked cap is Werner Machold, who had just been promoted from 'Oberfeldwebel' to 'Leutnant'; and who was forced to belly-land at Swanage, Dorset in southern England on 6 June, 1941 and became a prisoner.

JG 52's accommodation at this Rumanian airfield bordered on the primitive . . ./*G Rall*

Pilots of 8./JG 52 breakfast in the open on a Rumanian airfield in August 1941./*G Rall*

Above right: Feldwebel Stefan Litjens of 4./JG 53, greeted by his friends as he vacates the cockpit of his Bf 109E-4 after a mission./*S Litjens*

Right: MAN'S BEST FRIEND. 'Troll', the pet of Feldwebel Stefan Litjens sitting on his master's Bf 109E-3. Litjens lost his right eye on 11 September, 1941 during combat, but continued to fly operations. On 23 March, 1944, however, his left eye was injured while attacking Allied bombers, thus ending his flying career./*S Litjens*

Below: Leutnant Leykauf of 8./JG 54 (centre) posing with his ground crew in front of his Bf 109E-4, 'Black Three'. The elaborate walking stick here was a fad very much in vogue at the time./*A Weise*

we do over the front line, four, five, six times daily – as one has to do in order to survive. Not elaborately as yet, but in such a way that I soon realise they have sent me a fellow who is already at home in a 109, who can do things with it. I begin risking a bit more, the turns become steeper and steeper while I direct him very cautiously – I don't want to scare him – he still follows. I announce a bunt, which he should copy, clearly hear his 'Viktor' and then roll my 109 on its back. Speed increases rapidly, the 109 starts to whistle, I decrease the throttle a little, see my *Katzcmarek* coming along behind me. 'Well done', I shout, 'Well done, pull the stick slowly, careful, draw in your head, push against the arteries', then in a distorted voice, 'Over quickly, pull out, but follow now'. Seeing black, with blood streaming away from the head into ton-heavy legs, we shoot upwards again. 'Well, had enough? Was it difficult?', I ask Tabak 2.

'Fine,' Tabak 2 replies.

'Very well done', I answer.

I let him take over, position myself on his left wing, don't give him much space to manoeuvre, order him to fly back home. He finds the airfield, lands – him first, after routine instructions – we finish the landing run, stop engines, he comes to me and reports himself as returned.

I ask, 'Well, were you frightened?'.

'No, Major', is his reply.

'Well done, well done as a start. Tomorrow we'll do it again, a little bit harder. And always – *Holzauge sei wachsam!* (Keep looking around).'

In this way we often fly around behind the front line, and I demand more from him in flying skill. He continues to tell me he isn't frightened; he knows my question by now but remains adamant – well, that's his business. Several times he has flown missions but without any contact with the enemy. We have flown across the lines on the deck, looking for enemy aircraft, but nothing has happened. To-day, we have taken off to some *Freie Jagd* – free hunting – and show ourselves low over the lines. With 500 on the clock we roar over the heads of our panzermen, infantry and artillery, then head deep into enemy territory. There they are! Six black dots detach themselves from the easterly horizon and come directly towards the German lines. Probably *Hanni* 500 (Hanni – height). '*Pauke, Pauke!* Attack! I'll cover you'. This will be the first break for the new boy. 'Calm now, calm. Take the first one from below – not yet – a bit to the right – not yet – like that – NOW!' Nothing happens, we pass by. The IL-2's have spotted us. The bombs tumble from their bays into the Russian lines – we've reached them at the right moment. They're already forming a defensive circle, no fighter escort to be seen. 'Tabak 2'

Top: The 'Liegeplatz' (accommodation) of Stab/JG 26 at Caffiers, 1940. Note the impressed Citroen car./A Weise

Above: Pilots of III./JG 26 at Vendeville, France in September 1943, in typical Luftwaffe operational fighter pilot garb./A Weise

follows my instructions for a new attack. I direct and correct his approach – now in the enemy circle. Again he gets behind an IL-2, then banks away without firing his guns. I then shoot down the first one, and soon get behind a second, so near that I close my eyes. He explodes in mid-air.

'Careful, Tabak 2. Attack again'. I'm above the defensive circle and again manoeuvre my *Rottenflieger* into an attacking position. He is not at all clumsy. He gets within firing range – now, at last his first one should go down, but again he banks away with no visible result. Immediately, I get lower and come between two enemy machines, dive a little, fire into the radiator, get away underneath it and out in a right turn, find a fourth in front of me and send a volley into the middle of its fuselage. She noses over and breaks apart, spewing flames. The two remaining have opened their throttles and dive away east. I can still see the rear gunner of the fifth one getting larger and larger. His tracers fly close to my nose. But will it help you? You or me, to the death. A hare in his form cannot press any closer to earth than me in my crate. Even today I duck my head, decades after this combat, and sweat maybe more now when writing this account than in my 109 then! Hard hit, the Stormovik crashes into the ground. I came so close to him that my machine bucked and

vibrated. If I remain below, arrive underneath it, then . . . A few touches with the rudder and I'm there, and wham-wham . . . nothing else. By God, I've used all my ammo! And my young friend? He floats beside me but I'll not order him to attack. The sixth Russian flies east, trailing black smoke but we can't chase it. With full throttle we roar towards our own lines. 'Down', I yell in the microphone, 'Down'. My *Rottenflieger* hears the warning and goes much lower than me.

Fliers' luck sees to it that we aren't hit by those small, small bullets from the infantry. It was lucky that we had flown over the German lines before and shown ourselves. At least no fire from our own lines greet us. After a few anxious minutes we climb. To the east we can see five dark mushrooms, five victories, each in front of our own lines . . . When we get back I waggle my wings and do a few rolls so that those below know what has happened. After landing we stop engines and walk towards each other. I hear the *Leutnant* report, 'Back from flight against the enemy.' I step past him towards his machine, step up onto the wing, grip the gun switch, and find it is not switched on. '*Mensch* . . .' is all I can say.

After a moment I call him to me and ask, 'Well? . . .'

Unwaveringly the answer comes, 'Yes, Major, I was afraid.'

272

Right: Oberleutnant Horten explains a point about the harmonisation pattern board to a colleague./A Weise

Below: Belly-landing by 'White Seven' of 7./JG 26 at Caffiers, 1940; illustrating graphically the normal rupture point for a Bf 109's fuselage if it crashed or landed too heavily./A Weise

In Latin Hands

Above: The defence of Rome was assigned to the 3°Stormo of the Regia Aeronautica, and one unit of that formation was the 7ª Squadriglia. Seen here at Cerveteri, Italy in July 1943 are Bf 109G-6s of this squadron, though other types used by 7ª included Macchi MC 202s, Macchi MC 205s and even a few Ambrosini SAI 207s./*G Ghergo*

Far left: A Bf 109G of the 3° Gruppo Caccia at Comiso, Italy, 10 July 1943. Just discernible above the exhaust pipes is the devil's head insigne; badge of 6° Stormo, to which 3° Gruppo belonged./*G Ghergo*

Left: Italian ground crews grouped in front of a Bf 109G-6 of the 7ª Squadriglia, Cerveteri, Italy, July 1943./ *G Ghergo*

Below left: Bf 109G-6 of 364 Squadriglia (150° Gruppo).

Just Routine Testing

The man who has flown the highest number of different Bf 109s must surely be Flugkapitän Wendelin Trenkle. He cannot remember precisely how many, but it must have been several thousands. After leaving high school, he started learning to fly at the DVS (Deutsche Verkehrsfliegerschule) in 1931, and soon obtained various flying licences, including seaplanes, and then flew as a co-pilot with Lufthansa. In 1933 he was one of the German pilots who, in secret, were given a fighter course of instruction in Italy; after which he was appointed as an instructor with the DVS at Schleissheim. Later, while still a civilian, he instructed at various Luftwaffe airfields. Finally he went to work for Messerschmitt, as chief pilot and head of the flying department of the new Messerschmitt plant at Regensburg, which was officially inaugurated on 20 March, 1937. On average he had some 20 pilots working under him, whose job was to test-fly every aircraft produced at Regensburg before it was

Left: Flugkapitän Wendelin Trenkle who tested several thousand Bf 109s./*K Schnittke*

Below: During take-off, the engine of CD+WV tore itself loose . . ./*K Schnittke*

turned over to the Luftwaffe. For a Bf 109 such a test-flight normally lasted about half an hour. Other duties included ferry flights and test flights at auxiliary airfields. From his total of about 15,000 flying hours; roughly 9,000 were flown in the service of Messerschmitt, of which 5,000 were flown in testing new Bf 109s of every possible version. An idea of the scale of this routine test flying is the fact that during the month of August 1944 alone no less than 750 Bf 109s were tested by the Regensburg team.

One of those test pilots was Heinz Frensdorff. Eighteen years old when he first learned to fly at the Reichssportfliegerschule (German Sport-flying School) at Rangsdorf, near Berlin, he soon became an auxiliary flying instructor; then joined the Flettner Aircraft Company at Berlin-Johannistall. In 1943 he joined the team at Regensburg – and lived through some hair-raising moments. He took up a Bf 109G for the first time but had to divert to the much larger airfield at Niedertraubling after the aircraft flaps refused to lower. Trenkle sent him to the Wiener Neustadt airfield for a month's practice on Bf 109s. Back again at Regensburg, his second flight also almost ended in disaster. Test flying BE+WP at about 5,000 metres, one of the engine connecting rods broke, and within seconds the windshield and canopy were covered in oil. Frensdorff tried to bale out but found the canopy was stuck tight. Again, by radio, he was diverted to Niedertraubling where he succeeded in making a wheels-up

landing. For some months than all went well – until he took up CD+WV. During the take-off at full revs, the engine tore itself loose and the spinning propeller made it cartwheel across the airfield before it finally came to rest in a field a kilometre away. The Bf 109 fuselage promptly ground-looped, but again Frensdorff was unhurt, although very shaken. As every flying accident was duly photographed, this 'incident' was no exception. Frensdorff was able to get negatives of some of the classified photographs through the help of a young Hungarian girl who worked in the Messerschmitt photo laboratory, and took the negatives to a camera shop in Regensburg for development. When he went to collect them, however, it took an awful lot of explaining to avoid being brought to trial! The Gestapo, suspecting espionage, were waiting for him...!

Below and bottom: The canopy was stuck, so Frensdorff belly-landed BE+WP at Niedertraubling; his windshield and canopy covered with oil./ *K Schnittke (both)*

Defending the Reich

Return from a mission, with the traditional low beat-up, accompanied by a wing-waggle if any victories were achieved./*G Rall*

Feldwebel Richard Heemsoth wrote the following account, which was published in *SIGNAL*, August 1944. Only a few weeks later, on 11 September, Heemsoth crashed to his death six km north-east of Burghofen/ Eschwege:

'That night I had already shot down two enemies and was in great form when I spotted the third one. He was right in my gunsight. I pushed the button . . . wham . . . wham . . . wham it went, then it became silent. My cannon had ceased to fire. I continued firing with the machine guns, but surely with these alone I would not be able to send down this four-engined bomber. The rear gunner of the

bomber must have been killed instantly because his machine guns were silent. I came a little closer, fired again until the last of my ammunition had gone. What now? I was 20 metres behind the bomber which made the craziest turns and tried to get away in the dark. The only thing I could still do was to ram him. Slowly I came closer. It was difficult to keep the aircraft steady in his slipstream but I succeeded. My propeller crashed into the Englishman's rudder. It was a real buzz-saw. It cut through the rudder and tore it to shreds. The Englishman zoomed downwards; my own machine went out of control and I was thrown out. While floating down with my parachute I lost the bomber in the darkness. Then

Supply Drops by Bf 109s

Date	Aircraft	Cargo
16 March, 1945	16 x 109s	Dropped 2.4 tons ammunition
20 March, 1945	14 x 109s	Dropped 2.1 tons ammunition
22 March, 1945	6 x 109s	Dropped 0.9 tons ammunition
23 March, 1945	8 x 109s	Dropped 1.2 tons ammunition
4 April, 1945	21 x 109s	Dropped 3.55 tons ammunition
10 April, 1945	12 x 109s	Dropped 1.85 tons ammunition
12 April, 1945	16 x 109s	Dropped 3 light field howitzers, & one infantry gun.
13 April, 1945	11 x 109s	Dropped 1.44 tons ammunition
14 April, 1945	16 x 109s	Dropped 3.38 tons ammunition
15 April, 1945	18 x 109s	Dropped 3.18 tons ammunition
16 April, 1945	16 x 109s	Dropped 2.66 tons ammunition
21 April, 1945	7 x 109s	Dropped 1.05 tons ammunition
22 April, 1945	10 x 109s	Dropped 1.50 tons ammunition
26 April, 1945	9 x 109s	Dropped 1.35 tons ammunition

suddenly I saw a great fire-glow down below. It had spattered with its bombs in a meadow. I came down not far away, and a quarter of an hour later I stood near the widely-scattered pieces of wreckage, near a large crater in the ground . . . somewhat further away some cows stood lowing . . .'

Oberfeldwebel Arnold Döring, originally a bomber pilot with III./KG 55, took a conversion course to fighters at Altenburg/ Thuringia after completing 348 bomber missions. He then joined JG 300, and his first night mission came on 9 September, 1943: 'There is a new moon, pitch-dark, but glorious weather. Our advance warning system has detected indications of a mission by the Tommies; all nightfighting units are in the highest state of readiness. Ready and all dressed up, we wait in the bus to be driven to the machines standing ready in the take-off area. Into the machines, strap-up, instruments checked with a darkened torchlight. The first 'Wart' helps us. Canopy shut, eyes closed to get acclimatised to the darkness. There, two green Very lights from the *Gefechtsstand* – order to take-off. The 'Wart' who has been sitting on the wing is already cranking away like mad, because it is his pride that his pilot will be the first to take off. '*Frei*' (Free), the 'black man' shouts. I pull the starter, open up the throttle and the engine catches with a crackle. Canopy open, the *Wart* places the starting handle behind in the luggage locker, canopy closed, locked, throttle slowly fully opened, test brakes. Yes, everything's OK. Throttle closed, wheel chocks away, position lights on so that nobody is dragged along. A shadow scurries by and exhaust flames and scattering sparks tell me that a machine has just taken off diagonally. That can only be wild Schäfer who is often up to such pranks. Then I am ready for take-off. I align the bird, open the throttle fully and am soon swallowed by darkness. Undercarriage and flaps up, position lights off . . .

'I adjust my radio and the voice of the ground controller comes through clearly, "Wilde Saue to the Leuchtfeuer Ludwig.* Four-engined enemy bombers over the mouth of the River Scheldt, Hanni 6,000, course towards the east." I fly on course and slowly gain height. I have time and reach the beacon Ludwig before the Tommy. What city will he attack tonight? Will he turn towards the Ruhr area? Will he attack Bremen, Hanover, Berlin? "From Gefechtsstand Heuberg. This is the situation in the air. Dicke Autos in map reference XY, Hanni still 6,000, course towards the east. Out" – The quiet voice of the

Major Günther Rall, recovering after his left thumb had been shot away by an 8th Air Force Thunderbolt over Germany. In all, Rall was shot down five times, but survived the war with 275 accredited victories./G Rall

speaker from the divisional command post which has now taken over control comes through loudly. I compare my position with that of the Tommies; I should meet the tip of the enemy formation over beacon Ludwig.

"Four-engined heavy bombers now at map reference XX, stretched out, height 4,500 to 6,500, course eastwards. Out. Out."

'The Tommy comes near the Reich's border, the night fighter units from Holland, Belgium and northern France have probably broken up the stream. But still he keeps to the same course, approximately towards Hanover-Berlin. A light flashes intermittently in front of me; . – . . , . – . . ; the Ludwig light beacon. A large searchlight also moves around.

"All Wilde Saue to Bremen, all Wilde Saue to Bremen."

'What's this? The situation isn't clear. I have a funny feeling that something isn't right, so I stay in the vicinity of Ludwig, and soon the order comes through to set course for Berlin. I wasn't wrong after all.

'Searchlights flare up in front, flashes of light make me presume AA fire, it must be Hanover. I fly along the southern border of this AA area, and a few times I have to grab my Very pistol because some AA bursts are dangerously close. Down below my signals are recognised and the firing stops. Even so something must be the matter in this area. I turn towards the north, and fly around Hanover, but not a target is to be seen in the searchlight cones. A new situation report signals the enemy formation near Hanover, also to the north and south of it. Nevertheless, the order still stands to set course towards Berlin. One last turn and I fly east towards the Reich's capital. There, in front of me, red ground markers! For the first time I see this fire-marvel, the "Christmas Tree" lights which the Tommy uses for destruction of German cities, cascading down so slowly. They look beautiful . . . horribly beautiful. Searchlights flash up, flak fires, cascade after cascade, in between illumination, bombs and phosphorous. It must be Brunswick, and immediately I report my observations to Heuberg. They acknowledge, but then over Hanover the real magic starts behind me. Brunswick was only a diversion! Full throttle back to Hanover. Blood-red fires in front of me, then light red, pink to yellow. Hanover is burning. Innumerable phosphorous (incendiary) containers will already have been dropped on the unfortunate city. All around I see aerial combats, the tracers darting back and forth. I see fires starting and quickly becoming larger, then a four-engined bomber falls towards the earth like a torch and ends in a violent explosion as it impacts. I almost ram one of these black monsters when we fly straight at each other. Suddenly his shadow looms ahead; incredi-

---

*Ludwig: code name for a radio beacon situated near Lake Dümmer.

bly quickly it becomes larger and I can barely haul back on the stick and zoom over it, a hair's breadth away. Where there's one, there must be more.

'By watching the fragmentation bombs detonating below I can figure out the direction of the attack, and position myself across the approach path, constantly curving about. I watch an aerial combat below me ending in a victory. At last I spot an enemy to the right, in front of me, but before I can reach him he is ablaze – one of my colleagues was quicker than me. The same thing happens again, several times. Once I was about to open fire when I spot another 109 quietly destroying my bomber. Go to blazes then, I'm angry now. Another one is attacked by a comrade flying behind me. His bursts swish by right above my canopy and I only just manage to dive away. Way below it has got lighter, an enormous fire-cloud hangs over the burning city. Above it there is an uninterrupted barrage of AA fire, and higher still is the hunting ground of the Wild Boars and the heavy night fighters. Suddenly I see a large shadow above me, I open the throttle wide and the engine roars. I climb and position myself behind the Lancaster. This one *must* be mine – nobody is going to steal it from me! Nerves are taut. He should have seen me long before as I'm silhouetted against a light background. So, higher, exactly behind him, waiting until the twisting Tommy flies steady for a moment. Unfortunately I cannot get him before he drops his bombs, but to do this he has to fly straight and steady, and at the exact moment his eggs leave their racks, I let him have it. The rear gunner must be hit – not a shot comes from there. At 50 metres I continue firing and see my tracers bite into the fuselage and wings; see how finally the wing catches fire between the engines, and then how my victim dives steeply. The fire spreads, the wing tears away, the fate of the Lancaster is sealed. Lit up by three searchlights, it spins down and crashes on the southern edge of Hanover with a huge explosion. I yell "Horrido", and receive confirmations from several comrades, but then am startled when I see the red light blinking. This brings me back to reality – I only have fuel for 20 minutes left.

'I give up the hunt, throttle back, and call until finally a beacon answers and gives me a course and duration of flight to the nearest airfield. It's not easy – 30 other "Wild Boars" also need to land quickly and want directions to the nearest field. My fuel will be just enough to get me there. At last, after a few frightening minutes when the fuel gauges begin registering zero, a row of lamps appear in front; Rotenburg airfield, east of Bremen. The field is brightly lit. I lower the undercarriage, nip in

front of a Ju 88, quickly put on my spot-light and land, closely followed by the Ju 88. The engine coughs – the earth has me back again. Just before I could reach the refuelling point the engine stops. I feel rather upset. It is uncomfortable to realise that my engine could have stopped at any minute while on finals. At least there would have been no explosion when I crashed! I have been lucky again. I get out, peel off my flying suit and stroll towards the airfield control where many crews are already gathered. Among them are some familiar faces; nearly all report victories. My *Staffel-kapitän* has got three, our adjutant one, and I report mine. Congratulations from all sides. By telephone I report my success to our own

Top, left and right: Instead of graceful gliders, Wolf Hirth's factory at Nabern/Teck made wooden tailplanes for Bf 109s./ *Wolf Hirth* (both)

Above: A Bf 109G-6 of III./JG 26, flown by the 'Gruppen' adjutant, in September 1943 when the unit was part of the German defence network in France and other occupied countries. JG 26 was disbanded in March 1945./ *A Weise*

Dusk . . . and a Bf 109E-1 of
I./JG 20 (later VII./JG 51). /W Schäfer

command post at Hangelar, then we are invited to a substantial meal at the Casino.

'The Fatherland cares touchingly for the welfare of us "Wild Boars", the youngest branch of the German night fighters. We are called *Herrmannflieger* (Herrmann's pilots – after Major Hajo Herrmann, originator of the *Wilde Saue* tactics), suicide pilots – even death pilots. Indeed many comrades have crashed already as we have only one engine, and many more will crash. But we do have some advantages. We offer a smaller target for the enemy; have more speed and manoeuvrability; which makes a difference. Nevertheless, this kind of flying is not easy; the drawbacks are obvious – the undercarriage is weak; endurance and range too small; only one engine; no radar; no crew, like a wireless operator or navigator. Every mission causes many wrecks to be scattered on the airfields – there are dead and wounded. Still, the list of our successes grows with every mission.'

Arnold Döring survived the war, rising to *Leutnant* and being credited with 23 victories.

Because of the acute shortage of aircraft, the "Wild Boar" night-fighter pilots often had to use fighters normally used by day-fighter units. The units using these *Wilde Saue* tactics – JG 300, JG 301 and JG 302 – suffered such high losses that at the end of 1943 they were reconverted to day fighter units. Oberfeldwebel Stefan Litjens, who finally accumulated a score of 38 victories, lost his left eye on 11 September, 1941 while attacking a Russian bomber. His injury did not prevent him becoming a successful Reich defender.

'On 23 March, 1944 we were stationed at Eschborn, near Frankfurt, as part of the defence of the Reich, We took off at 0907 hours to tackle approaching American four-engined bombers on their way to Berlin. At a height of about 8,000 metres we reached the enemy formation which consisted of several groups of more than 100 bombers. An attack on such a compact formation was a risky undertaking when you consider that in order to ensure hitting them you have to close to 100 metres. During this attack I received several hits from the defending gunners. My intact eye was injured, and I had to break off my attack as I was almost blind.'

During the last months of the war the word *Reichsverteidigung* (Defence of the Reich) acquired a peculiar meaning for certain Bf 109 pilots. In some cases the Bf 109 was used . . . as a transport aircraft! From 15 February, 1945, Breslau, capital of Silesia (now Wroclaw, Poland) had been surrounded by the Red Army. While the siege lasted – until 6 May – the task of supplying the town with arms and ammunition was given to the Luftwaffe. In the main Junkers 52/3ms and Heinkel He 111s were used, plus some Gotha Go 242 and DFS

Above: In Burbank, California, some of the Bf 109's deadliest opponents, the Lockheed P-38 Lightnings were being mass-produced in the open . . . / *Lockheed Company*

Right: . . . and at San Diego, Consolidated B-24 Liberators, soon to be droning over the Reich, were rolling off the never-ceasing production line./ *Consolidated Coy.*

230 gliders; but Bf 109s were also used to drop supplies in. The War Diary of Luftflotte 6 mentions the drops by Bf 109s given in the table on page 119.

After Berlin had been surrounded by Russian forces it became necessary to supply that city by air too. At first light on 26 April a large formation of Bf 109s dropped jettisonable supply containers over the devastated city centre, but only about one-fifth of these could be retrieved among the ruins. It was during this same period that the doubtful distinction of being the first Luftwaffe pilot to be retrieved by a Luftwaffe helicopter fell to a Bf 109 pilot. In the morning of 6 March, 1945, a Bf 109 pilot of 1, NAG. 4 had lost his way in a snowstorm, and made an emergency landing near the Danzig-Praust airfield. A Focke-Achgelis Fa 223E-0, GW+PA (*WN* 22300051), piloted by Leutnant Gerstenhauer, had been ordered by Hilter to fly to Danzig (now Gdansk, Poland), and it took off to search for the missing pilot. The helicopter finally found him near Goschin, where the injured man was taken aboard and flown to the airfield.

At the E' Stellen

The first prototype Bf 109 spent its first New Year halfway between Berlin and Rostock. There amidst the north-German plains of the former Gau Mecklenburg lies Lake Müritz, and beside the lake, an airfield – Rechlin. During World War 1 this airfield had been used for testing aircraft, and from 1925 military aircraft were secretly tested there; despite the strict ban imposed by the Versailles Treaty. To camouflage the activities at Rechlin the base was titled somewhat ponderously Erprobungsstelle Rechlin des Reichsverbandes der deutschen Luftfahrtindustrie – literally, Rechlin Testing Site of the Reich Organisation of the German Aircraft Industry. The German navy had its own testing facility from 1928, when the former Caspar Flugzeugwerke works was bought and converted into the Seeflugzeug-Erprobungsstelle Travemünde; which was later titled – for security reasons – Erprobungsstelle Travemünde des Reichsvebandes der Deutschen Luftfahrtindustrie – Travemünde being near Lübeck, on the Baltic Sea. When in 1933 aviation in Germany was reorganised, both testing stations were taken over by the RLM and each became an Erprobungsstelle der Luftwaffe; generally referred to as E'Stelle Rechlin and E'Stelle Travemünde. At the end of 1936 a special section of the Travemünde centre developed into a separate testing establishment for all kinds of armament used by the Luftwaffe, and became titled E'Stelle Tarnewitz – Tarnewitz being near Wismar, 40km east of Travemünde.

Before this however another E'Stelle had been planned in a rather desolate region near the small fishing village of Peenemünde, which had been discovered by Professor Wernher von Braun about Christmas 1935. Eventually two testing centres were built here; one for the Luftwaffe, Peenemünde-West, which bordered on Peenemünde-Nord, used by the German Army. During the war more E'Stellen were established at Gotenhafen, Werneuchen and Udetfeld, an airfield in Silesia named after Ernst Udet, the Luftwaffe's GL (*Generalluftzeugmeister*: Chief of Aircraft Procurement and Supply). For some time Erprobungs-Kommandos (testing detachments) were even set up outside of Germany, like at Cazaux, France, Foggia, Italy; and Bengasi, Libya. Thousands of tests and trials were performed at the E'Stellen, and each was the subject of a secret report with a limited circulation. Representative tests involving the Bf 109 included, Erprobung Nummer 2574 at E'Stelle Rechlin; a test whereby the improvement in performance of a Bf 109E was measured when GM-1 Stoff (carried in liquid form under pressure in a cylindrical container behind the cockpit) was injected into the engine's supercharger by compressed air. GM-1 Stoff was the ultimate code-name for N20 – nitrous oxide; – previously coded as HA-HA, but often referred to as *Göring-Mischung* (Göring blend). The report was dated 2 December, 1940. Flying with 2,400 rpm but with varying propeller pitch settings the use of GM-1 Stoff gave an increase in true air speed of between 60 and 105km/hr at heights ranging from 8,000 to 11,000 metres; while between 8,000 and 10,000 metres the climbing speed was improved by two to three metres per second. During the initial flights a periodical improvement and decrease in performance was noted, due to impurities in the gas used. These impurities partly blocked the nozzle until blown away, and was dealt with by improving the manufacture of the gas, and by use of filters while tanking and in the piping system.

Another Bf 109 experiment was fitting a fixed ski undercarriage to a Bf 109E-8. To ensure availability of snow, the Gardemoen airfield, 30km north of Oslo, was chosen for the tests. Dipl Ing Kloppe was appointed as supervisor for the experiment, while the test-pilot from Rechlin was Hans Fay during the 1940-41 winter. Fay had been inducted in the Luftwaffe on 23 July, 1939 and given a flying instructor's course. When war started he served with JG 53 'Pik As' until May 1940, and was then transferred to Rechlin as a test pilot and engineer. There his main job was to evaluate captured aircraft, mainly fighters, of British, French, Russian and American origin. Later in the war Fay became an acceptance test pilot at the Antwerp Erla Repair Depot; while on 30 March, 1945 he flew a Messerschmitt Me 262 intact to the Rhein/Main

airfield. It was established that the fixed ski-undercarriage reduced a Bf 109's performance by about 10 per cent. When all the tests required to establish changes in performance and handling qualities had been completed, a number of flights – so-called *Dauererprobung* (endurance tests) – were made to see how many take-offs and landings could be made before any technical fault developed. On the particular day 37 take-offs had already been made, with an outside ground temperature of −24°C. Thirty five years later Fay still remembered what happened on the 38th flight:

'I was coming in for a landing and was on finals. The sun, at my back, suddenly cast a shadow of the ski-equipped 109 onto the white runway. I noticed suddenly that the shadow cast by the left ski was much longer than that of the right ski. One of the two attachments must have broken or become loose and the ski was hanging vertically! At the same time I saw some mechanics fire a red Very light. It had been decided beforehand that if any serious trouble developed in flight I was to bale out rather than attempt a landing. I climbed back up to 3,500 metres where I baled out. Below me were nothing but woods, and in these the abandoned 109 was later found, totally wrecked. We only learned later that it crashed near a very large ammunition depot!' After this crash the ski-experiment was abandoned.

The E'Stellen also had the responsibility for drawing up the *Kennblatt* (Technical Notes), giving exact description, measure-

WL-IGKS, a Bf 109E-1, being tested in the wind tunnel at the DFL (Deutsche Forschungsanstalt für Luftfahrt) at Braunschweig-Völkenrode, 1941.

ments, armament, equipment, performance, operational limits etc for each Luftwaffe aircraft variant. An example is the report for *Auftrag* (Work Order) E2-48/7, compiled by E'Stelle Travemunde on 23 December, 1941 – the *Kennblatt* for the Bf 109 T-2. The T-2 variant was a development of the T-1, and essentially a Bf 109E-1 adapted for use on the German Navy aircraft carriers *Graf Zeppelin* and *Peter Strasser* that were being built at that time. In the event, the T-2, minus arrester hook or catapult points, saw some service in Norway. The report – *Geheime Kommandosache* 556/41 – consisted of eight pages of text, one page of photographs, and one page with a three-view GA drawing; only 37 copies were printed.

Auftrag E6 19201/42 IIF, which resulted in Report No. 112/41 by the E'Stelle Tarnewitz of 2 September, 1942, dealt with the installation of a pair of MG 151/20 cannon in under wing gondolas on a Bf 109-F4. The aircraft had been modified by the Messerschmitt Augsburg works and equipped with the necessary field conversion kits, but due to bad weather conditions the aircraft could not be flown to Tarnewitz. The prototype conversion kit was sent by rail to Tarnewitz where it was installed in *WN* 7449. First firings showed so many jams and stoppages that the cannon were removed and tested in a firing jig to cure the causes of the stoppages. When, on 24 March, 1942, the first air firing test was made, further stoppages occurred; and only

Left and above: Test Number 2574 at Rechlin; injecting GM-1 Stoff into the engine's intake. First photo shows the flexible tubing that brought gas to the intake; then, the gas container is put on a weighing scale; and an alternate – slightly awkward – method of filling the cylindrical container behind the cockpit.

Above: Test pilot Fay climbing out of the ski-equipped Bf 109E-8. The wartime German censor carefully cropped the photo to avoid showing the actual ski-undercarriage here.
H Fay

Right: The Bf 109E-8 with ski-undercarriage at Gardemoen airfield, Norway, in the winter 1940-41.

after 60 flights and certain modifications did the gondola-cannon installation prove satisfactory. Further trials were carried out with *WN* 13149, while between 11 and 16 May, 1942, four Bf 109Gs were equipped with the MG 151/20 conversion kit and sent to the front for operational evaluation. Not all pilots liked the gondolas. In 1974 Gunther Rall, who survived the war as a major with 275 accredited victories, remembered:

'We had those gondolas but when turning with a high G-factor the metallic cartridge links often gave way and the cannon jammed. They also caused additional drag, so I said "Get them off".'

A lesser-known activity of the Messerschmitt works was the development of variable propeller pitch mechanisms for engines of different horse-power. The series ran from Me P1 to Me P7; the last named being much used before the war in the Bf 108. It could run for 200 hours without servicing, and was one of the lightest and simplest mechanisms of its kind. It was manufactured by Messerschmitt but took wooden propeller blades supplied by Propellerwerk Gustav Schwarz GmbH of Berlin-Waidmannslust. Intended for much higher power was the Me P6. One of these was modified so that negative pitch could be used to obtain reverse thrust. It was installed in Bf 109-F4, *WN* 70003 and flown for 30 hours at Rechlin, during which about 100 braked landings were made. The trials ran under Erprobungs Nr 2601, and on 12 October, 1942 the final report was issued. It was intended to develop the Me P6 so that ultimately it could be used for braking purposes after touchdown by multi-engined aircraft, and as an air brake for dive bombers. The first trials were made with a 'feeler' extending below the fuselage. As soon as this feeler contacted the ground, negative pitch was automatically selected. However, too many malfunctions were experienced, and the feeler idea was discarded. Tests showed a markedly reduced roll-out after touchdown. If negative pitch was selected at the moment of touching down, roll-out distances of 135 to 150 metres were obtained. If however negative pitch was selected before touchdown, at a height of approximately 0.5metres, then the distance was only 110-130metres. Later on six Bf 109Gs were equipped with the special Me P6 at Wiener-Neustadt and tested by Erprobungskommando Lärz. Ultimately, the Me P6 'braking propeller' was used in variants of the Bf 109 such as G-2/U1, G-4/U1 and G-6/U1; as witnessed by Rechlin Erprobungsbericht Nr 136/43 gKdos – which in fact was the *Kennblatt* of the Bf 109G-1 with DB605A engine – issued on 8 March, 1943.

In early 1938 trials with 65-mm rockets had been initiated at Tarnewitz using a Bf 110. Report E6/1362/43 geh, issued by E'Stelle Tarnewitz on 19 May, 1943, constituted the manual for the Bf 109 F2 equipped with eight EG RZ65 underwing rocket launchers. Besides practice ammunition, two types of rocket could be used. AZ65 had an explosive charge of 130g which exploded on impact, but could only be used against ground targets. ZZ 1577 exploded on impact, or approximately four seconds after leaving the launcher tube, so could be used against ground or air targets, and had an explosive charge of 190g. The manual pointed out that due to the longer flight duration of the rocket compared to gun or cannon shells, and due to greater variations between flight trajectories caused by rocket propulsion, the aiming results were worse than with normal armament. The slightest inaccuracy in flying – slipping or skidding – produced even poorer results. The EG RZ65 was especially effective against enemy bomber formations. The manual specified two types of attack against such targets; both from a range of 1,000 metres. The first was from behind. Because the rocket lost five metres of height for every 100 metres flown, releasing the rockets had to be done while the Bf 109 was flying at a positive angle of attack of about 1.2 degrees. Aim had to be taken at the formation centre, not at individual bombers. This also applied to the second form of attack recommended – frontally. Using the EG RZ65 against small targets, or while shooting with large deflection, was not recommended.

During 1942 the Rheinmetall-Borsig firm developed a new type of 30-mm cannon, the MK 108, which was tested at Tarnewitz in 1943. The first 30 Bf 109G6-U4s to be equipped with two wing-mounted MK 108s were also tested at Tarnewitz. The aircraft were delivered there without cannon, and Report E6/1777/43 geh, dated 21 July, 1943 covered the trials. The cannon were supplied by DWM at Posen where series production was just beginning; while necessary parts were supplied by the Rheinmetall-Borsig firm of Berlin-Tegel. At the end of May nine cannons had been delivered but, when tested in a ground rig, showed so many defects that it was pointless mounting them in the 109s. The cannons were sent back to the manufacturer who, in mid-June, sent a new batch of 24. This second batch was considerably better and could be installed in the aircraft. Never-

In the summer of 1943 a wooden wing for the Bf 109 was experimentally built by Wolf Hirth GmbH. Here it can be seen aboard a lorry in August 1943 prior to delivery to the Luftwaffe.

theless, several misfirings still occurred, and cannon often had to be dismounted and rectified on the ground. When the report was compiled only 10 Bf 109s were at Tarnewitz; the other 20 were still at Schwerin and Lärz. The most common faults were listed as;

* Failure to fire due to firing pin striking cap off-centre
* Shells failing to eject due to too-tight fit
* Faults in shell feed due to manufacturer's errors
* Cracks in cannon mantle. Cured by welding on strengthening; but after firing 200 rounds, ten cannon showed cracks of such magnitude that weapons became useless.
* Fracture of small items.

At the end of 1943 Haupt-Ing Volak of the RLM and Dipl Ing Schneider of the E'Stelle Rechlin visited JG1 in Holland to investigate the problem of icing on the inside of the cockpit of Bf 109G-5s and G-6s, and Focke-Wulf Fw 190s. Their report was compiled at Rechlin on 20 December, 1943. While climbing or flying horizontally at height, the G-5s and G-6s cockpits often started icing up, starting at the rear and eventually covering the whole canopy interior – except the front armoured window – with ice. The reason was found to be a lack of air circulation inside the insulated cabin. This was often caused by pilots not pressurising the cabin – either because they did not like the noise made by

Top: The right tailplane of a factory-fresh Bf 109G-6, Wk Nr 165689, showing how the total wooden covering had become unglued.

Above: Bf 109, Wk Nr 166261, the elevator of which came loose from the hinge-carrying spar.

the compressor; or simply because no pressure was developed anyway, due to insulation leakage.

As the war progressed the scarcity of aluminium forced the German aircraft industry to revert to the use of wood. Several variants of Bf 109G had wooden tailplanes, but these caused many complaints. On 22 August, 1944, I./JG3 sent a complaint to Rechlin concerning Bf 109 wooden tailplanes and immediately five of the unit's fighters were examined by Hauptmann Lichtenecker from Rechlin. The resulting report, dated 22 September, 1944, also covered deficiencies in wood items and assemblies in the Bf 110, Junkers Ju 352, and Kalkert Ka 430. Three G-6s were found to be defective; *WN* 166261 had been standing in the open since 21 July, 1944 and flown a total of 23 hours 30 minutes. The right elevator showed three cracks of 15 millimetres length, cracks in the front spar, and a poor protective layer on the hinge-carrying spar; *WN* 165485, with a total flying time of three hours, and no exposure to the elements, showed cracks near the right elevator hinge; while *WN* 165689, fresh from the factory, showed a 60mm long crack in its right elevator, and ungluing of the rear spar of the right tailplane. This tailplane was taken off and sent to Rechlin for closer examination. The report stated that use of this tailplane would have caused an accident. It went on to state that neither the gluing, nor the protection of the wood, nor the craftsmanship was done in an expert manner. 'In view of such faulty manufacture the further use of wooden tailplanes must be questioned; the safety of the Bf 109 is highly endangered.' The reason for such poor manufacturing was the fact that the small woodworking firms that supplied the tailplanes to Messerschmitt simply did not have labour or staff with adequate experience in wood-working. Quite often foreign workers had to be employed. Some came to work in Germany voluntarily, but many had been forced to do so – sabotage was a tempting way of 'getting even.'

One of the many independent – unconnected with any university – aviation research facilities in Germany, in which some research on the Bf 109 was done, was the 'Ernst Udet' German Gliding Research Facility, temporarily situated at Ainring airfield, near Bad Reichenhall. This was also the nearest airfield to the Salzberg, Hitler's favourite haunt, and as such widely used by courier aircraft. Its history goes back to November 1924, when the Rhön-Rossitten-Gesellschaft e. V was founded to further gliding flight. It was named after the two main German gliding centres, and in 1925 its research institute took up its activities, mainly at the Wasserkuppe and Darmstadt. With the Nazi reorganisation

of aviation in Germany in 1933, the institute was renamed as the German Research Institute for Gliding, and placed under the jurisdiction of the German Air Sports Association. Soon after, however, it was transferred to the RLM, like all other independent aviation research facilities, and from then on was known as the Deutsche Forschungsanstalt für Segelflug (DFS) and located at the Darmstadt-Griesheim airfield. As soon as war broke out it was transferred to Brunswick and had to take on a wide range of research, some of which had no relation to gliding whatsoever. In the summer of 1940 it was transferred yet again, this time to Ainring airfield; and after the death of Ernst Udet on 17 November, 1941, the head of DFS, Prof Dr phil Dr Ing E.h. Walter Georgii, obtained permission to add Udet's name to that of DFS, in recognition of Udet's many services to the facility.

Among the trials and tests performed by the DFS were those investigating the possibilities of various *Mistel-Anordnungen* – pick-a-back combinations – some involving Bf 109s. A report dated 17 June, 1943, for example, gave its findings on a Junkers Ju 88A-4 and Bf 109F duo. In this example the Ju 88 was used as an unmanned bomber and the combination steered by the Bf 109 pilot only. In this manner it was possible to fly $3\frac{1}{2}$ tons of explosive over a range of 1,500km. The DFS had by then already tried a combination of a Me 328 with a Dornier Do 217, in which the Do 217 was used to fly the Me 328 glider-fighter above an enemy bomber formation. This proposal was dropped when it was decided to fit the Me 328 with two Argus As 014 pulse-jet engines. However, high hopes were placed in the Bf 109-Ju 88 combination, which acquired the name *Mistel* – Mistletoe – especially when the Ju 88 was equipped with a hollow charge warhead in its nose. Some *Mistels* were used against the Allied invasion fleet, and later against bridges over the River Oder captured by the Red Army, but no spectacular effect was ever achieved. Another pick-a-back combination – sometimes known as *Vater und Sohn* (Father and Son) – was a Bf 109E mounted on a DFS 230 transport glider, about which a report was compiled on 9 January, 1944. Formerly DFS 230s had been towed by a Klemm Kl 35 in this manner, also by a Focke-Wulf Fw 56. A new undercarriage had to be designed for the DFS 230, able to stand the stresses imposed by the weight of the Bf 109, especially when landing. DFS 230, D-14-884 was duly equipped with an undercarriage transmitting the weight of the Bf 109 directly to the wheels of the glider, which had been cannibalised from a Junkers W34.

The Bf 109 was fitted with supporting pads just forward of the wheels, and also near the

Left: PICK-A-BACK. D 14-884, a DFS 230, being 'towed' in pick-a-back fashion by a Bf 109E, June 1943. After release the glider – initially – tended to strike the Bf 109s under-fuselage.

Below left: Trajectories of the shells and bullets from the Bf 109's fuselage M-17; the engine MG 151/20; and the gondola MG 151/20 for comparison.

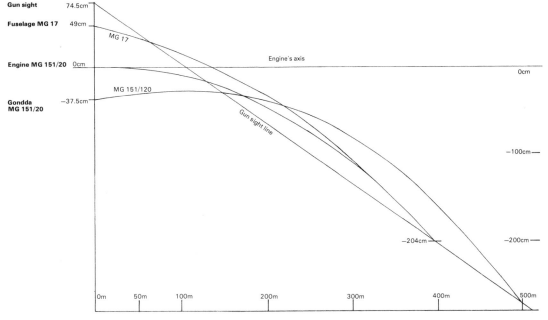

main spar-fuselage anchorage point. The DFS 230 was fitted with the necessary supporting struts. At first it was thought that Ainring airfield would not be big enough to carry out the tests safely, and it was decided to transfer them to Hörsching, near Linz. There the first tests were made on 21 June, 1943 which immediately made it clear that Ainring would be adequate, and the whole trial was re-transferred back to Ainring. It proved necessary to alter the support struts of the glider, as the latter usually struck the underside of the Bf 109 after release. A new system was installed on DFS 230, D-IEXX and on 16 July the trials were resumed. Again, the glider pitched upwards on release and hit the Bf 109. A special dive brake was therefore fitted on the

glider, and the tests were finally completed to the satisfaction of the pilots involved – Flugkapitän Ing Zitter, Flugzeugführer Opitz, and Flugzeugführer Schieferstein. The DFS 230/Bf 109E combination resulted in perfect handling characteristics both in flight and on take-off and landing. It was controllable when using either the DFS 230s or the Bf 109s controls. When the controls of both were used in unison, overall control was extremely effective. It was possible to separate in flight, or to land while still coupled. The report ended by stating that further tests were being prepared whereby the control movements of the Bf 109 would be transferred to those of the DFS 230, and that no difficulties were expected.

An Emil called Mike

Early in 1941 a Japanese military mission made arrangements with Messerschmitt to build the Bf 109 under licence in Japan. After Messerschmitt's test pilot Willy Stör had demonstrated a Bf 109 and Bf 110 before the commission at Regensburg, he was asked to go to Japan to help supervise the assembly, do the test flying, and then help to train Japanese pilots. Stör left Germany on 4 May, 1941 and, travelling through Russia with his mechanic Herbert Kaden, he reached Tokio, where he was greeted by Wolfgang von Gronau – famous for his long distance flights with Dornier-Wal – and Heinkel's chief test pilot, Gerhard Nitschke. Stör took up residence at Gifa, where the Kawasaki Kokuki Kogyo KK works were situated, and where in the meantime three Bf 109E-3s and a Fieseler Storch had arrived. In October 1941 Stör's mission was completed but von Gronau kept him in Japan as adviser, and he often went to the Japanese testing centre at Tatshikawa to fly and give his opinion on various aircraft. By then the plan to licence-build Bf 109s in Japan had been dropped because of difficulties arising from the Allied blockade.

AN EMIL CALLED MIKE
Willy Stör with a
Japanese test pilot in front
of a Bf 109E, at Kawasaki
Kokuki Kogyo airfield, Gifu.

Stör was anxious to return to Germany, and on 18 April, 1942 was aboard a blockade-runner in the port of Yokohama when the ship was fired on by one of Jimmy Doolittle's 16 NA Mitchell B-25s which had taken off from *USS Hornet*. Another surprise came in the form of a telegram, ordering him to stay in Japan to direct the planned licence-construction of the Me 410 in Japan. A blockade-runner succeeded in bringing a Me 210 to Kobe, where it was assembled, though with difficulty because a second ship bringing the necessary blueprints had been sunk. The construction was planned at Kobe, but nothing came of it in the event. Due to the circumstances of the war Stör remained in Japan until February 1947, when an American troop carrier finally brought him back to Germany. Allied aircrews flying in the Pacific repeatedly reported sighting German aircraft types, and therefore it was – erroneously – believed that Japan was licence-building these and operating them. Though only three Bf 109Es were actually tested in Japan, the type was often reported, and given the code name Mike . . . it was an Emil called Mike.

Flying the Bf109

A captured Bf 109E in Paris,
21 November, 1939, in the
Place de la Concorde.

The war was only weeks old when, on 22 November, 1939, no less than three Bf 109s fell into the hands of the French; two of them wholly intact. One made a wheels-up landing near Puttelange, 15km south-east of Luxemburg city, alongside the cross-roads between Route-Nationale 56 and the road to Remering-les-Puttelange. Its pilot, a *Leutnant* of I./JG 76 (which unit became II./JG 54 in 1940), was captured and taken to the headquarters of the 41e Regiment de Mitrailleurs d'Infantrie Coloniale which guarded that section of the Maginot Line. The aircraft, Bf 109E, *WN* 1251, was exhibited in January 1940 on the Avenue des Champs Elysées; the proceeds of the display going to 'Pour ceux de l'escadrille' – a charity organisation of the French Air Force. A second Bf 109 made a normal landing at the Strasbourg-Neuhof aerodrome, south of Strasbourg. Its pilot, Vienna-born Oberfeldwebel Herfried Kloimüller of II./JG 51, was made prisoner, and the French air force decided to evaluate the machine. Capitaine Rozanoff of GC II/4, the experienced test pilot who had already flown a Bf 109 in Spain in February 1938, was detailed to fly the aircraft to the Centre d'Essais du Materiel Aerien (CEMA) at Orleans-Bricy aerodrome. He took off from Strasbourg on 28 November, escorted by Lieutenant Vinçotte and Adjutant Baptizet, also of II/4 and each flying a Curtiss 75. Flying very low in close formation at high speed, they reached Toul airfield where Rozanoff wanted to show the Messerschmitt to the pilots of GC II/5. Vinçotte broke away left, Baptizet to the right, but then Rozanoff decided to do a roll ... Baptizet remembered, 'I gave full throttle and climbed. It was then that a grey mass loomed up in front of me; the 109, flying inverted!' Rozanoff was later to record,' Baptizet, flying very close, literally chewed away my tail with his propeller. I had to leave the stricken aircraft and jump by parachute.'

Luckily, the French had a second intact Bf 109. It was *WN* 1304, landed by a *Feldwebel* of I./JG 76, a veteran of the Legion Condor, at Woerth, Bas-Rhin, 40km north of Strasbourg. This 109E arrived at Orléans-Bricy on 6 December and due to bad weather made only seven flights, totalling five hours, before the end of the month. CEMA distributed 40 copies of its evaluation report, Rapport d'essai 403/S/SD. This preliminary report confirmed the performances claimed by the Germans, amongst other things a maximum speed of approximately 570km/hr at 5,000metres, but stated that while it was perfectly possible to aim correctly while diving, accurate firing was difficult while climbing. As the engine's torque was poorly compensated for, it was difficult for the Bf 109 to turn right while climbing. The report ended by advising pilots attacked by a Bf 109, or wanting to get away after an attack, to make a climbing turn to starboard. The final report by CEMA was issued on 30 March, 1940, numbered 291 S/SD. In the meantime, in his letter of 23 January, 1940, General Vuillemin, commander of the French air force, had asked for the Bf 109 to be tested against the Dewoitine D 520; while General d'Harcourt, Inspector-General of Fighters, in a letter dated March 25th, requested a comparison test with the Bloch 152 as well. The CEMA drew up a programme of such tests, not only with those two fighters but also with the Bloch 174 and Potez 63-11 reconnaissance and observation aircraft. At the end of March the Bf 109 was delivered to CEMA and a 35-mm Debrie cine camera gun was installed. As bad weather hindered the evaluation tests, the aircraft was taken from Orléans-Bricy to Marignane, near Marseille, where the tests were flown between 1 April and 21 April, 1940. On 27 April the CEMA issued its report, which stated that though the Bf 109 had a superior performance to the two French fighters, this did not give it complete superiority in aerial combat, and the that French fighters could oppose a Bf 109 with confidence. The Bloch 174 and Potez 63-11 also stood a good chance against the Messerschmitt; the Bloch through its speed, almost equal to that of the Bf 109; the Potez through its good manoeuvrability. The French, having extracted everything they wanted to know about the type, then handed over the aircraft to the RAF.

The Bf 109 was flown to RAF Boscombe Down on 4 May, 1940, where it was appraised by the Aircraft and Armament Experimental Establishment (A & AEE); then later flown to the Royal Aircraft Establishment (RAE) at Farnborough for handling trials, and allocated the serial number AE479. The results of the RAE's evaluation were discussed on Thursday, 9 March, 1944 at a meeting of the Royal Aeronautical Society in London, at which M B Morgan and R Smelt of the RAE lectured on 'The aerodynamic features of German aircraft.' About the Bf 109E they had this to say: *Take-off:* This is best done with the flaps at 20 degrees. The throttle can be opened very quickly without fear of choking the engine. Acceleration is good, and there is little tendency to swing or bucket. The stick must be held hard forward to get the tail up. It is advisable to let the aeroplane fly itself off since, if pulled off too soon, the left wing will not lift, and on applying aileron the wing lifts and falls again, with the ailerons snatching a little. If no attempt is made to pull the aeroplane off quickly, the take-off is quite straightforward. Take-off run is short, and initial climb good.

Approach: Stalling speeds on the glide are 75mph flaps up, and 61mph flaps down. Lowering the flaps makes the ailerons feel heavier and slightly less effective, and causes a marked nose-down pitching moment, readily corrected owing to the juxtaposition of trim and flap operating wheels. If the engine is opened up to simulate a baulked landing with flaps and undercarriage down, the aeroplane becomes tail-heavy but can easily be held with one hand while trim is adjusted. Normal approach speed is 90mph. At speeds above 100mph the pilot has the impression of diving, and below 80mph one of sinking. At 90mph the glide path is reasonably steep and the view fairly good. Longitudinally the aeroplane is markedly stable, and the elevator heavier and more responsive than is usual in single-seater fighters. These features add considerably to the ease of approach. Aileron effectiveness is adequate; the rudder is sluggish for small movements.

Landing: This is more difficult than on the Hurricane 1 or Spitfire 1. Owing to the high ground attitude, the aeroplane must be rotated through a large angle before touchdown, and this requires a fair amount of skill. If a wheel landing is done the left wing tends to drop just before touchdown, and if the ailerons are used to lift it, they snatch, causing over-correction. The brakes can be applied immediately after touchdown without fear of lifting the tail. The ground run is short, with no tendency to swing. View during hold-off and ground run is very poor, and landing at night would not be easy.

Taxying: The aircraft can be taxied fast without danger of bucketing, but it is difficult to turn quickly; an unusually large amount of throttle is needed, in conjunction with harsh braking, when manoeuvring in a confined space. The brakes are foot-operated, and pilots expressed a strong preference for the hand operation system to which htey are more accustomed.

Lateral trim: There is no pronounced change of lateral trim with speed or throttle setting provided that care is taken to fly with no sideslip.

Directional trim: Absence of rudder trimmer is a bad feature, although at low speeds the practical consequences are not so alarming as the curves might suggest, since the rudder is fairly light on the climb. At high speeds, however, the pilot is seriously inconvenienced, as above 300mph about $2\frac{1}{2}°$ of port rudder are needed for flight with no sideslip and a very heavy foot load is needed to keep this on. In consequence the pilot's left foot becomes tired, and this affects his ability to put on left rudder in order to assist a turn to port. Hence at high speeds the Me 109E turns far more readily to the right than to the left.

Longitudinal trim: Five three-quarter turns of a 11.7in diameter wheel on the pilot's left are needed to move the adjustable tailplane through its full 12-degrees range. The wheel rotation is in the natural sense. Tailplane and elevator angles to trim were neasured at various speeds in various conditions; the elevator angles were corrected to constant tail setting. The aeroplane is statically stable both stick fixed and stick free.

'One control' tests, flat turns, sideslips: The aeroplane was trimmed to fly straight and level at 230mph at 10,000 feet. In this condition the aeroplane is not in trim directionally and a slight pressure is needed on the left rudder pedal to prevent sideslip. This influences the results of the following tests:

a *Ailerons fixed central.* On suddenly applying half-rudder the nose swings through about eight degrees and the aeroplane banks about five degrees with the nose pitching down a little. On releasing the rudder it returns to central, and the aeroplane does a slowly damped oscillation in yaw and roll. The right wing then slowly falls. Good banked turns can be done in either direction on rudder alone, with little sideslip if the rudder is used gently. Release of the rudder in a steady 30-degree banked turn in either direction results in the left wing slowly rising.

Bf 109E (Wk Nr 1304) of I./JG 76 undergoing evaluation by the French CEMA at Orléans-Bricy, and marked with French roundels over its German insignia. Note cine-camera (French) under wing. Along the leading edge of the wing was the inscription, 'Ne pas pousser ici' – Don't push here.

b *Rudder fixed central.* Abrupt displacement of the ailerons gives bank with no appreciable opposite yaw. On releasing the stick it returns smartly to central with no oscillation. If the ailerons are released in a 30-degree banked turn, it is impossible to assess the spiral stability, since whether the wing slowly comes up or goes down depends critically on the precise position of the rudder. Excellent banked turns can be done in either direction on ailerons alone. There is very little sideslip on entry or recovery, even if the ailerons are used very harshly. In the turn there is no appreciable sideslip.

c *Steady flat turn.* Only half-rudder was used during this test. Full rudder can be applied with a very heavy foot load, but the nose-down pitching movement due to sideslip requires a quite excessive pull on the stick to keep the nose up. When flat turning steadily with half-rudder, wings level, about half opposite aileron is needed. The speed falls from 230mph to 175mph, rate of flat turn is about 110.

d *Steady sideslip when gliding.* Gliding at 100mph with flaps and undercarriage up the maximum angle of bank in a straight sideslip is about five degrees. About 1/4 opposite aileron is needed in conjunction with full rudder. The aeroplane is fairly nose-heavy, vibrates and is a little unsteady. On release of all three controls the wing comes up quickly and the aeroplane glides steadily at the trimmed speed. With flaps and undercarriage down, gliding at 90mph, the maximum angle of bank is again five degrees 1/5 opposite aileron being needed with full rudder. The nose-down pitching movement is not so pronounced as before, and vibration is still present. Behaviour on releasing the control is similar to that with flaps up.

Stalling test. The aeroplane was equipped with a 60 foot trailing static head and a swivelling pitot head. Although, as may be imagined, operation of a trailing static from a single-seater with a rather cramped cockpit is a difficult job, the pilot brought back the following results:

Lowering the ailerons and flaps thus increases C_L max by 0.5. This is roughly the value which would be expected from the installation. *Behaviour at the stall.* The aeroplane was put through the full official tests. The results may be summarised by saying that the stalling behaviour, flaps up and down, is excellent. Both rudder and ailerons are effective right down to the stall, which is very gentle, the wing only falling about 10 degrees and the nose falling with it. There is no tendency to spin. With flaps up the ailerons snatch while the slots are opening, and there is a buffeting on the ailerons as the stall is approached. With flaps down there is no aileron snatch as the slots open, and no pre-stall aileron buffeting. There is thus no warning of the stall, flaps down. From the safety viewpoint this is the sole adverse stalling feature; it is largely offset by the innocuous behaviour at the stall and by the very high degree of fore and aft stability on the approach glide.

Safety in the dive. During a dive at 400mph all three controls were in turn displaced slightly and released. No vibration, flutter or snaking developed. If the elevator is trimmed for level flight at full throttle, a large push is

needed to hold in the dive, and there is a temptation to trim in. If, in fact, the aeroplane is trimmed into the dive, recovery is difficult unless the trimmer is wound back owing to the excessive heaviness of the elevator.

Ailerons. At low speeds the aileron control is very good, there being a definite resistance to stick movement, while response is brisk. As speed is increased the ailerons become heavier, but response remains excellent. They are at their best between 150mph and 200mph, one pilot describing then as an 'ideal control' over

300

this range. Above 200mph they start becoming unpleasantly heavy, and between 300mph and 400mph are termed 'solid' by the test pilots. A pilot exerting all his strength cannot apply more than one-fifth aileron at 400mph. Measurements of stick-top force when the pilot applied about one-fifth aileron in half a second and then held the ailerons steady, together with the corresponding time to 45 degrees bank, were made at various speeds. The results at 400mph are given below:

Max sideways force a pilot can apply conveniently to the Me 109 stick 40lb.
Corresponding stick displacement 1/5th
Time to 45-degree bank 4 seconds
Deduced balance factor Kb2 —0.145

Several points of interest emerge from these tests:

a Owing to the cramped Me 109 cockpit, a pilot can only apply about 40lb sideway force on the stick, as against 60lb or more possible if he had more room.
b The designer has also penalised himself

ness has disappeared. Between 200mph and 300mph the rudder is the lightest of the three controls for small movements, but at 300mph and above, absence of a rudder trimmer is severely felt, the force to prevent sideslip at 400mph being excessive.
Harmony: The controls are well harmonised between 150mph and 250mph. At lower speeds harmony is spoiled by the sluggishness of the rudder. At higher speeds elevator and ailerons are so heavy that the word 'harmony' is inappropriate.
Aerobatics: These are not easy. Loops must be started from about 280mph when the elevator is unduly heavy; there is a tendency for the slots to open at the top of the loop, resulting in aileron snatching and loss of direction. At speeds below 250mph the aeroplane can be rolled quite quickly, but in the final stages of the roll there is a strong tendency for the nose to fall, and the stick must be moved well back to keep the nose up. Upward rolls are difficult. Owing to elevator heaviness only a gentle pull-out from the dive is possible,

Left: The moment of tension before a take-off. Uffz Schubert of 3./JG 1 at De Kooy, Holland, strapped in and ready to go./*W Schäfer*

Centre left: START! The exhilaration of a formation take-off, depicted by a 'schwarm' of Bf 109Es of JG 53, 'Pik As'./*S Litjens*

Bottom left: 'ROTTEN-FLIEGER'. A Bf 109E-3 of 4./JG 53 tucks in close to his leader as they roar low across the plains./*S Litjens*

Above: The 'rachetic' undercarriage. A Bf 109E-4 of III./ZG 1 in 1941 which came to grief. At right is a 'Heuschrecke' – literally, locust – a hydraulic lifting jack. / *W Schäfer*

by the unusually small stick-top travel of four inches, giving a poor mechanical advantage between pilot and aileron.
c The time to 45-degrees bank of four seconds at 400mph, which is quite excessive for a fighter, classes the aeroplane immediately as very unmanoeuvrable in roll at high speeds.

Elevator. This is an exceptionally good control at low air speeds, being fairly heavy and not over-sensitive. Above 250mph, however, it becomes too heavy, so that manoeuvrability is seriously restricted. When diving at 400mph a pilot, pulling very hard, cannot put on enough 'g' to black himself out; stick force-'g' probably exceeds 20 lb/g in the dive.
Rudder. The rudder is light, but rather sluggish at low speeds. At 200mph the sluggish-

and considerable speed is lost before the upward roll can be started.
Fighting qualities: A series of mock dogfights with our own fighters brought out forcibly the good and bad points of the aeroplane. These may be summarised as follows:

a Good points;
  *High top speed and excellent rate of climb
  *Engine does not cut immediately under negative 'g'.
  *Good control at low speeds
  *Gentle stall, even under 'g'.
b Bad points;
  *Ailerons and elevator far too heavy at high speeds
  *Owing to high wing loading the aeroplane stalls readily under 'g' and has a relatively poor turning circle

*Absence of a rudder trimmer, curtailing ability to bank left in the dive
*Cockpit too cramped for comfort.

A few of these points may be enlarged upon. At full throttle at 12,000 feet the minimum radius of steady turn without height loss is about 890 feet in the case of the Me 109E, with its wing loading of 32lb/sq ft. The corresponding figure for a comparable fighter with a wing loading of 25lb/sq ft, such as our Spitfire 1 or Hurricane 1, is about 690 feet. Although the more heavily loaded fighter is thus at a considerable disadvantage, it is important to bear in mind that these minimum radii of turn are obtained by going as near to the stall as possible. In this respect the Me 109E scores by its excellent control near the stall and innocuous behaviour at the stall, giving the pilot confidence to get the last ounce out of his aeroplane's turning performance.

The extremely bad manoeuvrability of the Me 109E at high air speeds quickly became known to our pilots. On several occasions a Me 109E was coaxed to self-destruction when on the tail of a Hurricane or Spitfire at moderate altitude. Our pilot would do a half-roll and a quick pull-out from the subsequent steep dive. In the excitement of the moment the Me 109E pilot would follow, only to find that he had insufficient height for recovery owing to his heavy elevator, and would go straight into the ground without a shot being fired.

Pilots' verbatim impressions of some features are of interest. For example, the DB 601 engine came in for much favourable comment from the viewpoint of response to throttle and insusceptability to sudden negative 'g'; while the throttle arrangements were described as 'marvellously simple, there being just one lever with no gate or over-ride to worry about.' Surprisingly though, the manual

Below: 'AUFSTEIGEN' – take-off; a Bf 109G-2 at the point of getting airborne. Probably a training machine from one of the 'Jagd-fliegerschulen (Fighter Pilots' Schools)./Bundesarchive

Bottom: This Bf 109E-4/Trop of I./JG 27 crashed and partly burned at Graz airfield (now in Austria), 6 April, 1941. Original photo taken by the Bildstelle Fliegerhorst Graz (Graz airfield Photo Section.)

operation of flaps and tail setting were also liked; 'they are easy to operate, and being manual are not likely to go wrong'; juxtaposition of the flap and tail actuating wheels is an excellent feature.'

Performance by 1940 standards was good. When put into a full throttle climb at low air speeds, the aeroplane climbed at a very steep angle, and our fighters used to have difficulty in keeping their sights on the enemy even when at such a height that their rates of climb were comparable. This steep climb at low air speed was one of the standard evasion manoeuvres used by the German pilots. Another was to push the stick forward abruptly and bunt into a dive with considerable negative 'g'. The importance of arranging that the engine should not cut under these circumstances cannot be over-stressed. Speed is picked up quickly in a dive, and if being attacked by an aeroplane of slightly inferior level performance, this feature can be used with advantage to get out of range. There is no doubt that in the autumn of 1940 the Me 109E in spite of its faults, was a doughty opponent to set against our own equipment.'

Selected comments from the men who flew and fought in the Bf 109E make interesting footnotes to the foregoing 'enemy' opinions: *Hauptmann Günther Schack, 174 victories;* 'In March 1941, as a Gefreiter, I joined

Jagdgeschwader Mölders, JG 51, stationed at
St Omer, France. By then I had only taken off
with the 109 straight into wind, and never from
a concrete runway. On 4 April, during a
cross-wind take-off on the concrete runway,
the 109 swung so much to the left that I feared
it would crash into some other machines
parked along the edge of the field. I closed the
throttle and my first crash began. The machine
swung left even more, the left undercarriage-
leg broke, and the 109 dropped on its left wing.
This happed to me twice – second time on 10
April – and my future as a fighter pilot seemed
sealed . . . In all, I was shot down 15 times . . .
on one occasion I saw the right wing of my 109
flying right alongside me! During an attack on
a bomber formation I was hit by an enemy
fighter, right in one of the main spar attachment lugs. Luckily, I was over 2,000 metres
high, but even then I only succeeded in getting
out of the crazily-spinning machine close to
the ground. I crashed against the tailplane,
and for the next two weeks I could only walk
bent in two . . .'

Major Günther Rall, 275 victories:
'The 109? That was a dream, the non plus
ultra. Just like the F-14 today. Of course,
everyone wanted to fly it as soon as possible.
I was very proud when I converted to it.'

*Generalleutnant Werner Junck, Inspector of
Fighters, 1939:*
'The 109 had a big drawback, which I didn't
like from the start. It was that rackety – I
always said rackety – undercarriage; that
negative, against-the-rules-of-statics undercarriage that allowed the machine to swing
away.'

Top and above: About to
over-shoot into the trees
beyond, this Bf 109E-1 pilot
chose to do a violent
ground-loop. It resulted in
the right undercarriage leg
being torn off completely./
W Schäfer

Below : FROM RUSSIA WITH
HATE. A happy pilot of
III./JG 54 viewing the
damage in the tail section
of his Bf 109F-2 after a
near-miss from Soviet
anti-aircraft guns./
Bundesarchiv

Top: Ground collision between two Bf 109G-2s of III./JG 54./*A Weise*

Above: Despite the already cramped cockpit, two-seat versions of the fighter were evolved. Two Bf 109G-12 versions at Pau, France in 1944. The nearest is 'Yellow 27' – formerly BJ+DZ – of 2./JG 101./*A Weise*

Left: Refuelling 'Yellow 27'. The Bf 109G-12 two-seat variant was delivered to several 'Jagdfliegerschulen' as conversion trainers in late 1943; and in the following year also used by most training 'Geschwadern'./*A Weise*

Above: A 'Bf 109' which
never flew – a decoy
wood-and-canvas 'fighter' to
fool marauding Allied
fighters./*Bundesarchiv*

Right: Closing in . . .

Facing page: The Bf 109's
nose . . . /
Bundesarchiv (all four)

Bf 109B-1   Bf 109E-1

Bf 109F-0   Bf 109G-4.

Appraisal

RUDOLF SINNER

'As long as the war between fighter and fighter assumed priority for us during the 1939 – 41/42 period, the 109 proved itself to be an excellent and more or less universal fighter, superior to any Allied fighter of the time, except perhaps the Spitfire. It was also useful for fighting the small and poorly defended bomber formations that appeared sporadically at the period. However, it rapidly lost its high status as a standard fighter when more and more compact, heavily-defended and protected enemy bomber units came to be used. Due to its vulnerability to enemy fire, and its weak armament for such targets, it proved to be poorly suited for an attack under fire from the defensive armament of close-flying bomber formations. Trying to improve the Bf 109Gs armament by so-called gondola cannon resulted in poorer handling qualities, and therefore the aircraft became inferior in combat with enemy fighters. To my mind – without that additional armament – the 109 remained superior to the Russian YAK 9 until the end of the war; more or less useful in battle with the Mustang; but inferior in certain important aspects to the Spitfire and Tempest.

'The devastating losses suffered by the 109 during the last years of the war should not be attributed so much to superiority of enemy fighters, as is generally assumed. They were caused by a combination of various circumstances. First, German fighters then always faced an overwhelming number of enemy fighters. Their assigned task required a consistent concentration against enemy bombers, which usually kept them from any offensive operations against enemy fighters. Concentrating on the bombers forced them to use a number of technical and tactical measures which made it easier for enemy fighters to shoot them down with less risk to themselves. Formating, climbing, approach and attack in close formation, often with aircraft hindered and slowed by cannon gondolas or rockets; flying back after attacking the bombers, little fuel and no ammunition, often alone, damaged, possibly wounded; then having to find a bombed airfield, under enemy fighter assault; all this, and the storm attacks under massive fire from the bomber gaggles, caused heavy

losses – which could not be made good because scarcity of fuel allowed no further training of operationally fit replacements. In short, until 1941-42, the 109 gave us superiority in combat with enemy fighters universally. In fighting heavily defended targets in the air or on the ground, it rapidly proved less suited than other types of fighter which Germany was by then producing. A timely strengthening of the day-fighter arm with units equipped with other types (of fighter) and a simultaneous specialisation (of roles) would have been possible and expedient. For fighting against enemy fighters and fighter-bombers, the 109 remained useful until the end of the war, but was in no case a superior weapon. From 1942-43 there were types (of fighter) better suited for further development, and which were ready for use.'

Above left: TAKE-OFF. Bf 109Es of 7./JG 53 'Pik As' at Caffiers, 1940./*A Weise*

Far left: 'ALARMSTART'! Mechanics jump into action as the alert signal sounds . . . November 1939 scene.

Left: Helping the pilot into his parachute. The Hakenkreuz (swastika) on this Bf 109E overlapped the rudder; a practice officially discontinued in March 1940 though some aircraft still displayed the out-dated marking months later.

Below: BROTHERS IN DEATH. A Bf 109E-4 and a Hawker Hurricane lie together on a deserted beach; both victims of an aerial combat./*G Rall*

Left: Above the clouds, a 109E-4 patrolling./*M Villing*

Top right: The undercarriage . . . always, that undercarriage! A Bf 109E-3 with a bent left leg, after a Bumslandung (bumpy landing).

Centre right: UNDER THE ROMAN SUN. Ground crews relax in Italian sunshine near their 'charge', an oddly camouflaged Bf 109G-6/R3 belonging to the 'Gruppen' adjutant of JG 77, 1944./*Bundesarchiv*

Bottom right: Undercarriage problems for the ground crew of this Bf 109E-1 of JG 331 (later JG 77) at Frankfurt-Oedheim airfield, 1939. The personal insigne on the nose of the aircraft is a cartoon boot./*W Schäfer*

Under New Management

Bf 109G-2 (Wk Nr 10639),
captured in Sicily, and in
1944 with No 1426 Flight,
RAF as RN 228./
Imperial War Museum

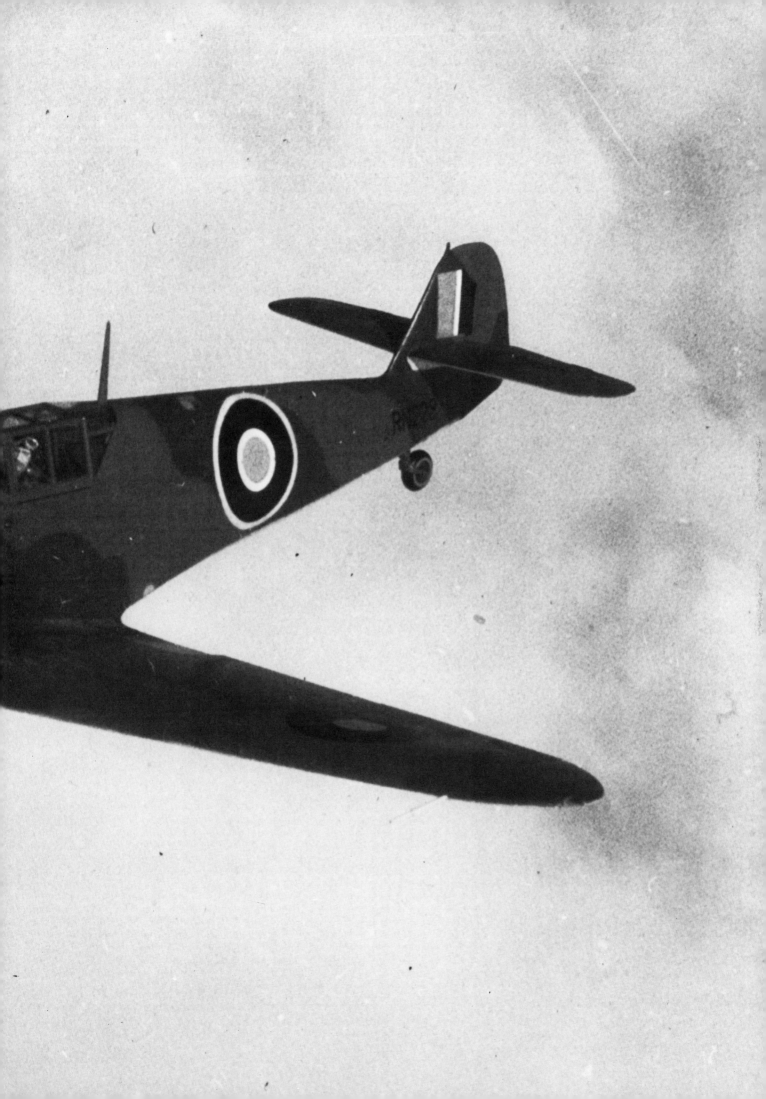

Above: The Bf 109F-1, flown by Rolf Pingel, 'Kommandeur' of I./JG 26, which was brought down virtually intact on 10 June, 1941 during a combat over St Margaret's Bay, near Dover, Kent. The 22 victory symbols were marked in scarlet on the bright yellow rudder. This aircraft was repaired and then test-flown as ES 906. Pingel had flown about 550 missions by that date, including sorties in Spain, where he had claimed an additional four victories./*Imperial War Museum*

Far left: Intact Bf 109G-6/R6 of II./JG 53, 'Pik As' on a Sicilian airfield, complete with underwing gondola cannons; alongside a Spitfire IX of the Desert Air Force./*Imperial War Museum*

Left: This Bf 109G-14/AS was captured at Stendahl, 50 km north of Magdeburg, by American troops. They also discovered a number of operational Me 262 jets of 3./JG 7, 'Nowotny'./*USAF*

Below left: Two American fighter pilots of the 9th Tactical Air Command get to 'close range' with a Bf 109G-10, abandoned on a French airfield, and look over its DB 605AS engine installation. Left is 1st Lt Charles Katzenmeyer of Vicksburg, Miss, and right, 1st Lt Zell Smith of Monroe, La., USA./*USAF*

Aftermath

Wilhelm Kellermeier, retired Treasurer of Duingen, a small village some 40km south of Hanover, did not know where his father lay buried. His mother had simply told him that her husband had fallen in June 1915, in the Vosges hills. Where he was buried was, apparently, unknown – until his son took a holiday trip through France in 1970 and finally located his father's grave. Fifty five years had passed, but the grave had been cared for by the Volksbund Deutsche Kriegs-gräberfürsorge – the German association which looked after the graves of every German fallen in battle.

This discovery served to intensify Kellermeier's long efforts to establish the identity of the fighter pilot who had crashed at Duingen during World War 2, but whose body had never been recovered. His son-in-law had personally seen how, on 20 February, 1944, a Bf 109G had been attacked by a P-47 Thunderbolt, and how the Bf 109 had dived straight into the ground after a short burst from the American fighter. The German pilot did not leave his aircraft, which crashed in a brook. At the spot where the aircraft had come down little was to be found; a dark pool in the brook, covered with oil, and some wreckage from the wings. A few days later, a Wehrmacht recovery/salvage party arrived, diverted the brook, and started to search – in the wrong spot, not believing what local inhabitants had told them. Finding nothing, the search was soon discontinued, and parts of the aircraft wing and tail were taken away.

Nothing more was done until 1964, when Wilhelm Kellermeier first heard about it and started his efforts to raise the wreck so that the pilot's identity could be established. This proved easier said than done as little help was forthcoming. At last, on 13 November, 1973, the wreck was salvaged, and the pilot's skeleton found. A few days later the pilot's identity was established as Feldwebel Gerhard Raimann; and on 19 November his remains were buried with full military honours at the Salzderhelden Soldiers' Cemetery. Raimann had belonged to 7./JG 54, and when his former *Staffelkapitän*, was located in Switzerland, the full story became clear. On the day

318

that Raimann crashed, 'Big Week' had started – a series of bombing attacks upon the German aircraft industry – and that day the American 8th Air Force despatched 16 combat Wings to attack 12 targets in Germany. One of these was against the Erla works near Leipzig, where the Bf 109 was being licence-built in large numbers.

One of the German fighter units to attack the American armada was 7./JG 54, based at Ludwigslust, in Schwerin, about halfway between Hamburg and Berlin. The *Staffelkapitän* was Hauptmann Rudolf Klemm, 42 victories, and now living in Basle, Switzerland. On 3 March, 1944 he wrote to Raimann's parents to tell them that their son was missing in action, ' . . . the Gruppe took off to attack a US bomber unit, protected by numerous fighters, intending to bomb targets in central Germany. About 1300 hours we contacted the head of the enemy formation. Your son was flying next to me when I shot down an enemy bomber out of a mass formation of 60 aircraft. Your son also took part in two subsequent attacks needed to shoot down the enemy bomber. During the last attack your son was bounced by an enemy fighter. He probably didn't hear the warning I gave through the

radio, and I myself was at that moment in a disadvantageous situation so that I could not intervene in time. Your son's aircraft went into a vertical dive after a short burst from behind, and was trailing smoke as it disappeared in to the cloud cover below. Our hope that your son might have jumped by parachute and, being wounded, had been taken to a hospital, is unfortunately no longer possible. Regrettably, we must now presume that he died during the aerial combat from wounds. The actual position of the aircraft is unknown; a precise location could not be made because of the cloud, and because the combat took place at 6,000 metres. I understand the Osnabrück-Hanover area seems indicated. Searching continues in this area . . .'

A few days after Raimann's burial, it was discovered that his mother was still living in the German Democratic Republic, aged 77. She was invited to stay for some time in Duingen, and arrived there on 16 February, 1974. A short while later she stood by her son's grave, clutching a yellowing, tear-stained piece of paper – the letter written by her son's *Staffelkapitän*, Klemm, 30 years before. Until that moment it had been the last she had ever heard of her son . . .

Top left: It was necessary to dig to a depth of five metres.

Left: Feldwebel Gerhard Raimann, pictured here as an Unteroffizier (Uffz) – who was 'missing' for nearly 30 years.

Above left: Wilhelm Kellermeier (rt) at the spot where the remains of Raimann's Bf 109G were found; two bent propeller blades and a Rheinmetall-Borsig MG 131.

Top: The pilot's watch, after 29 years, still indicating the time of the crash – five minutes before two o'clock . . .

Above: TO THE FALLEN . . . the tombstone at the head of Gerhard Raimann's grave at the Soldiers' Cemetery, inscribed with the wrong date of death. Since this photo was taken, this date has been corrected to 20 February, 1944.

Acknowledgements

The author wishes to extend his grateful thanks for the help received while researching this book. Especially to the ladies: E. Gemählich, T. Grether, C. Hirth, M. Knoetzsch, G. Lusser and F. Schacker and the following Gentlemen: F. Bartsch, W. Batz, K. Beeken, H. Birkholz, C. Cain, G. Debrödy, A. de Heppes, J. Dillen, A. Döring, J. Ellingworth, W. Eisenlohr, W. Falck, H. Fay, A. Fischer, F. Fuchs, A. Galland, G. Ghergo, W. Gollwitzer, J. Goodwin, H. Greiner, G. Handrick, F. Haubner, H. Herb, D. Holeczy, H. Horber, W. Hörning, F. Jaenisch, W. Junck (+), W. Kellermeier, F. Kirch, A. Köhler, F. Kovacs, H. Kroschinski, E. Leykauf, S. Litjens, A. Maes, H. Meier, F. Morzik, E. Neumann, E. Obermaier, T. Olausson, R. Olejnik, K. Pfeifer, G. Rall, A. Remondino, W. Rethel, K. Riess, B. Robertson, R. Rombaut, R. Rothenfelder, O. Rumler, H. Sander, G. Schack, W. Schäfer, H. Schliephake, H. Schlötzer, K. Schnittke, H. Scholl, R. Sinner. W. Schroer, J. Thévoz, H. Thurnheer, G. Thyben, H. Trautloft, W. Unger, G. van Acker, M. Villing, W. Voigt, H. von Bülow, P. von Schalscha-Ehrenfeld, A. Weise, J. Wiese, B. Widfeldt, D. Wollmann, E. Wren and H. Wurster. Also the following institutions: Abteilung der Militärflugplätze, Dübendorf Air Force Museum, Ohio Air Historical Branch (RAF) London Bundesarchiv, Koblenz and Freiburg Deutsche Dienststelle (WASt) Berlin Deutsches Museum, Munich Gemeinschaft der Jagdflieger e.V., Lütjenburg Imperial War Museum, London Lufthansa, Cologne Messerschmitt, Bölkow, Blohm GmbH, Ottobrunn Musée de l'Air, Paris Public Records Office, London R.A.F. Museum, Hendon Service Historique de l'Armée de l'Air, Vincennes Staats- und Stadtbibliothek, Augsburg Stadtarchiv, Augsburg Stadtarchiv, Regensburg Stadtbibliothek, Regensburg Z.L.D.I., Munich I also want to thank Mr Chris Wren for permission to reproduce some of his "Oddentifications", the Ministry of Defence, London for permission to use the wartime "Cummings" cartoons which are Crown Copyright, Coward, McCann and Geoghegan, Inc, New York for permission to quote from "Airpower" by A. Williams and Harcourt, Brace, Jovanovich, Inc, New York for permission to quote from the "Wartime Journals of Charles A. Lindbergh".